*W*ildlife
Travelling Companion
EAST AFRICA

*W*ildlife
Travelling Companion
EAST AFRICA

Paul Sterry

The Crowood Press

First published in 1992 by
The Crowood Press Ltd
Ramsbury, Marlborough
Wiltshire SN8 2HR

British Library Cataloguing in
Publication Data
A catalogue record for this book is available from the British Library.

ISBN 1 85223 585 3

Acknowledgements

I would like to thank everyone at Bushbuck Adventures for their safari assistance, in particular Gail and Edwin Sadd, Bernard Musila and Simon Muoka. I also thank my mother for looking after everything during my absence.

Field Guide plates on pages 174–197 by **Michael Benington** and those on pages 198–213 by **Chris D Orr**.
Maps by **Kathy Merrick**.

Title page photograph: a vast flock of Greater Flamingos on Lake Bogoria, Kenya. Photograph this page: Wildebeest in Amboseli National Park, Kenya.

Edited and designed by:
D & N Publishing
DTP & Editorial Services
5 The Green
Baydon
Wiltshire SN8 2JW

Printed and bound by Times Publishing Group, Singapore

CONTENTS

SECTION I:
COUNTRY GUIDE

INTRODUCTION TO THE BOOK

For most people, a safari trip to East Africa is the holiday of a lifetime. Thanks to extensive television coverage of African wildlife, many of us are familiar with the day-to-day lives and struggles of animals, such as Cheetahs, Lions and African Elephants; most of the great wildlife spectacles, such as Cheetahs killing their prey or the migration of Wildebeest in the Serengeti and Masai Mara, have been documented. Although it might be supposed that television would have devalued the experience of actually seeing these creatures for yourself, this is not the case. Few people can remain unmoved by the sight of their first wild Lion or African Elephant.

The word 'safari' comes from the Swahili word for a journey. Today, these are easy to arrange and are big business in East Africa. Indeed, tourism, much of which is wildlife oriented, is the largest earner of foreign revenue in Kenya. Unlike our predecessors who explored the continent in the last century, today's travellers can do so in style and comfort. Exactly what degree of luxury depends on the price you pay; the most expensive trips provide standards as good as those found anywhere in the world. However, most people opt for a happy medium where they can experience a taste of wilderness Africa with enough comforts to make it a holiday and not a test of endurance!

Opposite: *Defassa Waterbuck (Kobus defassa) are easily seen at Lake Nakuru.*

The aim of this book is to describe the best sites for wildlife observation in the most popular East African safari countries, Kenya and Tanzania. Rwanda and Zaire also deserve a mention, mainly because they offer Gorilla-watching treks which many visitors combine with a safari in Kenya or Tanzania.

Most but not all of the sites covered in the book have some degree of recognition and protection as areas rich in wildlife. Some are national parks while others are game reserves or national reserves. The text should help visitors decide in advance the areas they would most like to visit and, if on a 'do-it-yourself' safari, should help to locate the site and find the best areas within it.

A further aim of the book is to describe the most interesting species that are likely to be encountered. This is a rather subjective choice and I have concentrated on birds and mammals. Overall it is hoped that this book will inspire potential visitors with the wonders that East Africa still has to offer. Not only is the wildlife magnificent and varied, but the scenery is among the most stunning anywhere on Earth. It is hoped that the photographs provide an additional flavour of the region.

Although the East African countries covered in this book straddle the equator and therefore do not have seasons in the northern hemisphere sense, this is not to say that there are not climatic variations throughout the year. In particular, the rains are distinctly seasonal and have a profound effect both on the ability to travel on dirt roads and also on the abundance and distribution of the wildlife. For sites where there are marked seasonal differences, the book provides rough guidelines on what to expect at different times of year.

Once you have planned your journey and booked your safari, you may feel that what you see depends largely on luck and persistent searching. However, there are ways of getting the most from a trip and, wherever appropriate, the book provides helpful advice for the would-be safari traveller.

LANDSCAPE, GEOGRAPHY AND GEOLOGY

The landscape of East Africa is nothing if not varied. From the white sandy beaches, palms trees and mangroves on the coast, the land rises inland and supports vast tracts of savannah grassland and acacia woodland. Elsewhere, there are remnant pockets of true tropical forest, while many highland areas harbour lush montane forests which give way to unusual Afro-alpine flora above the treeline. A chain of lakes, many of which are alkaline in nature, run through East Africa, while at the other extreme there are harsh and inhospitable semi-deserts regions.

Geological features also abound in East Africa. Here we can find the anachronism of a permanently snow-capped mountain on the equator and witness the effects of glaciation and volcanic activity. Most impressive of all the geological features, however, is the Great Rift Valley which runs the length of the region.

THE GREAT RIFT VALLEY
The Great Rift Valley is a geological scar clearly visible from space. Its progress through East Africa northwards to the Red Sea, and beyond into Asia, can be traced for more than 2500km and in places it is as much as 70km wide and up to 600m (1970 feet) deep. Along some stretches the boundaries of the Rift Valley become obscure but in certain parts of East Africa it is at its most dramatic. The most spectacular views can be had on the road from Nairobi to Lake Magadi, where the escarpment drops in a series of steps; along the old road to Lake Naivasha; and at Lake Bogoria, where the eastern wall of the Rift Valley forms a stunning backdrop for the lake and its flamingos.

The Great Rift Valley marks the boundary between two of the plates which make

Evidence of volcanic activity is clearly visible in many parts of East Africa, as it is here in Tsavo National Park in Kenya. The region's two highest peaks, Mt Kenya and Mt Kilimanjaro, are both volcanic in origin and more recent activity can be seen at Mt Sheitani near Tsavo which erupted roughly 200 years ago.

Visible from space, the Great Rift Valley runs like a scar down the length of East Africa. It was formed roughly 20 million years ago when a shift in relative position occurred between two of the plates that comprise the earth's crust. Alkaline soda lakes lie along its length and hot springs gush to the surface.

up the Earth's crust. A shift in their relative positions, roughly 20 million years ago, lead to the subsidence that formed the Rift Valley.

Not surprisingly, the fault line which the Great Rift Valley represents, is also a prime area for volcanic activity. Evidence of past and indeed present volcanic activity is everywhere to be seen. The volcanic cones of Mt Kenya and Mt Kilimanjaro are perhaps the most stunning features, while Ngorongoro Crater in Tanzania is one of the largest and best preserved calderas in the world; it has justifiably been called the 'eighth wonder of the world'. More recent activity can be seen at Mt Sheitani, which erupted approximately 200 years ago, and at the hot springs at Lake Bogoria which bear witness to the pent-up forces at work beneath the Earth's surface.

MOUNTAINS

Kenya and Tanzania harbour the two highest mountains in Africa. Mt Kilimanjaro lies in northern Tanzania, close to the Kenyan border and reaches 5895m (19,341 feet) at its summit. Mt Kenya (5199m; 17,057 feet) dominates central Kenya and straddles the equator. Both mountains are capped in permanent snow and ice fields, a fact that caused disbelief and dismissive scorn when they were first described in the mid-nineteenth century. It was considered quite impossible by as worthy a body as the Royal Geographic Society that snow could exist on the equator. The initial reports were soon verified of course, but the certain knowledge of the existence of these anomalies does not detract from the wonder of seeing them for yourself.

It comes as a surprise to many people how chilly it can be at night while on safari. Although you are close to the equator, much of inland Kenya and Tanzania lies at more than 1000m (3280 feet) above sea level. Nairobi itself lies at about 2000m (6560 feet) and it was because of its very altitude that the city grew as an escape from the heat and humidity of the coast.

FRESHWATER

Freshwater is at a premium in East Africa. The rains are seasonal with the result that many of the rivers either have severely reduced volumes during the dry season or cease

Often seen in pairs, Crowned Cranes (Balearica regulorum) are amongst the most elegant and unmistakable of East Africa's birds. Although they are nowhere especially numerous, Crowned Cranes are widely distributed throughout the region. They can be seen in most national parks and reserves, frequenting marshy and swampy areas.

flowing above ground at all. Some great rivers such as the Tana and Galana (called the Athi River near its source and the Sabaki River at the sea) flow throughout the year. Even small rivers can be significant if they have a constant flow, their importance being roughly proportional to the aridity of the surrounding land. Thus the Uaso Ngiro River in Samburu National Reserve acts as a focus for the wildlife of the region, the waters of the Mara River in the Masai Mara Game Reserve attract migrating Wildebeest in their hundreds of thousands and Mzima Springs in Tsavo National Park, fed by underground streams from the meltwaters of Mt Kilimanjaro, harbour Hippopotamuses and Crocodiles.

Many of the Rift Valley lakes are soda lakes and extremely alkaline. Although the chemistry of the water does not suit all forms of life, birds such as flamingos, Black-winged Stilt, Avocet and other waders seem to thrive. However, on the western borders of Tanzania and Kenya lies Lake Victoria. It is the largest freshwater lake in the world and one of the sources of the River Nile.

Mida Creek Marine National Park on the Kenyan coast. Although much of the Kenyan coastline has been given over to tourism, this large area receives protection and is a haven for marine wildlife and naturalists alike. Habitats within the park include sandy beaches and dunes, mudflats, mangroves and coral reefs.

COASTS

The coasts of Kenya and Tanzania stretch 1400km from the border with Somalia in the north to that with Mozambique in the south. With white, sandy beaches and warm, blue waters they are a playground for foreign tourists. Although many parts of the Kenyan coast have developed rapidly to accommodate the needs of visitors, the Tanzanian coast remains largely unspoilt. Along the entire length, coral reefs occur offshore while the miles of beach are interrupted in places by estuaries, mudflats and coastal lagoons, and in some places mangrove swamps.

THE PEOPLE

The culture and way of life of the East African people is almost as rich and varied as the wildlife and scenery that surrounds them. The influences that have modified and tempered the culture originate from settlers from all over Africa and from areas farther afield, such as Europe and Asia. However, by contrast, all of us, no matter where in the world we come from, can trace our origins back to this continent.

ORIGINS

It was in the Great Rift Valley in Kenya and Tanzania that the human race's distant ancestors first took to walking on two feet and fashioning tools from wood and stone. Several million years ago East Africa was indeed the 'cradle of mankind'.

Both Kenya and Tanzania are rich in archaeological sites and the depth of knowledge that has emerged over the last few decades is mainly due to the efforts of one family. The late Dr Louis Leakey and his wife Mary pioneered these excavations and their interpretations of the finds were not without controversy. Their son Richard continued in the family tradition for some time and is now Director of Kenya's Wildlife Service.

Although some archaeological sites, such as that studied by Richard Leakey on the eastern shores of Lake Turkana, are difficult to reach, others are more accessible. Olorgesaillie National Park is a good example with axe heads and tools made by our early ancestors laid out just as they were first discovered. Perhaps most famous of all, however, is Olduvai Gorge in Tanzania, the site where the Leakeys found the skull of 'Nutcracker Man'.

The Samburu represent one of forty-two tribes in Kenya alone. The richness of their culture and way of life complement the diversity of wildlife and the grandeur of the scenery in which they live. Exercise caution and consideration when photographing the people: many consider this to be an infringement of their rights.

The earliest members of *Homo sapiens*, modern man, survived as hunter-gatherers, leading a nomadic lifestyle. Fire, used in a controlled manner, would have been an integral part of their lives. It has even been speculated that systematic and regular burning may have helped create the open, grassy savannah so characteristic of much of Kenya and Tanzania, the trees and bushes not having a chance to regenerate.

AGRICULTURE
Over the centuries, the hunter-gatherer way of life became modified by the influences of peoples from other parts of Africa; some cultivated crops and tended livestock while others were strict hunters. In those tribes that still live in a traditional manner, these practices persist with their livestock not only representing a means of survival but serving as a sign of wealth and position.

Over the last century, human influence on the wildlife and natural habitats of East Africa has accelerated dramatically, with much of the responsibility for losses falling on the shoulders of European settlers. They saw the transition from natural vegetation to tea or coffee plantation as an entirely necessary progression and indeed it must be said that these two crops remain as significant earners of foreign revenue to this day. However, with the loss in habitat went much of the wildlife associated with it and there was even a positive effort to eradicate certain species.

Driving through some parts of the Kenyan Highlands, visitors from England in particular will be struck by the similarity of the landscape to parts of southern England; rolling fields of wheat and other cereals dominate the scene. Although it may not have been the prime intention to kill wildlife, by removing the natural habitat, these cereal fields, together with the huge tracts of coffee and tea plantations, effectively eliminate all but the most adaptable species just as surely as if they had been shot.

PEOPLE AND WILDLIFE:
HARMONY OR CONFLICT?
While many of Kenya's forty-two tribes, including many Masai and Samburu, continue steadfastly to live the pastoral existence of their forbears, modern Nairobi could not be more different. This bustling city has all the trappings of the twentieth century and many of the key positions are held by members of the Kikuyu tribe.

Kenya has the largest population growth of any country in the world, more than 4% per year, a factor which may cause increasing conflict with wildlife in years to come in the search for new land. However, there is a growing awareness, both in Kenya and Tanzania, of the richness of their resources and the need to conserve them for future generations. In tangible terms, these resources manifest themselves in the form of foreign revenue, safari tourism being amongst the most important sources of this vital commodity. It is obvious to all concerned that the tourists would not come in the same numbers that they do today if there were no Elephants, Lions or Giraffes to see.

The achievements of the East African authorities in creating the superb national parks, national reserves and game reserves and associated infrastructure is clear for all to see. There can be few countries, developed or developing, that can boast of having conserved so much land and so many species; in Tanzania, a staggering 25% of the land is national park or reserve.

All is not harmony, however. The efforts of a comparatively small number of ruthless poachers could, quite conceivably, eliminate

African Elephants (Loxodonta africana): spectacular but under threat from ivory poaching.

fate for the creature and what a sad indictment of the human condition.

For those who actually poach the rhinos and Elephants, the tusks and horns represent nothing more nor less than money. To combat this powerful inducement, the Kenyan authorities, under the supervision of Richard Leakey, now operate a skilled anti-poaching team who hunt the poachers in the same ruthless manner that the poachers hunt their quarry. This has had a dramatic impact on poaching statistics in the short term but it remains to be seen what the future holds for these creatures. Perhaps the only long-term hope is to educate purchasers of ivory and horn as to their irresponsible actions which are nothing short of biological vandalism.

FLORA AND FAUNA

From the wildlife point of view, East Africa is a region of superlatives. With the exception of pristine areas of South American and South-east Asian rainforests and the Antarctic, there can be few regions on earth that can boast such rich biological diversity and abundance of large animals. For many people, the range of large game mammals cannot be equalled anywhere.

It is not only the sheer numbers of species that occur in the region that is staggering (more than 100 species of larger mammals, more than 1000 birds and upwards of 10,000 plant species), but the number that visitors are likely to see for themselves. It would not be unusual, for example, for more than fifty species of mammal to be seen during a two-week comprehensive safari in Kenya. The numbers of birds seen depends on the perseverance of the observer and the time of year, but on a trip in August, that included a visit to the coast, a keen birdwatcher could

two of the most dramatic East African species, the Black Rhinoceros and African Elephant, from the region within the next decade if left unchecked. East Africa has lost more than 60% of its Elephants and more than 90% of its rhinos over the last twenty years.

Elephants are hunted for their ivory tusks and rhinos are killed for their horns. The ivory is used mainly for ornate carvings: dagger handles in Arab countries and official seals in Japan being two of the uses to which it is put. Rhino horn, on the other hand, is considered to have aphrodisiac and medicinal properties in the Orient. Even if this were true, one cannot help thinking on seeing a dead, hornless rhino, what a pathetic

expect to see over 350 species. Add another 100 species for the same trip in December.

I know a group of people who, on a three-week, non-stop birding trip to Kenya in December, saw 580 species of birds. However, it should be said that this single-minded approach was at the expense of mammal watching and they did not see a single Lion during the visit. Most people are more than content to enjoy whatever they see, whether it be mammal, bird, reptile or plant.

The other striking thing about bird and mammal watching in East Africa is just how well you see things. In most of the parks and reserves, mammals have become accustomed to vehicles and show little fear of them. This confidence seems almost infectious and the birds also provide stunning views; even migrant visitors from Europe and Asia seem to adopt this attitude during their stay in Africa. European Rollers and Isabelline Shrikes, for example, which are not birds generally noted for their tolerance of man, often sit within

Herds of Zebras (Equus burchelli) and Wildebeest (Connochaetes taurinus) are a feature of Amboseli National Park in Kenya.

a few metres of vehicles showing complete indifference to their presence.

MAMMALS

One of the most amazing aspects of the mammalian fauna of East Africa is the extraordinary speciation found among the antelopes. They range in size from the massive Eland to the diminutive Suni and Dikdik and each one is adapted to a slightly different niche in the environment. Different species are found in almost every East African habitat from semi-desert to swampy marsh, and open savannah to high-altitude moorland.

Antelopes are the African equivalent of deer, there being no true deer on the continent. Most species have horns, at least in the males, and in some they are present in both sexes. Some, like the Dikdik, live in pairs while others, such as Thomson's Gazelle, may form sizeable herds. Most antelopes graze ground vegetation or low bushes with one notable exception. The Gerenuk, sometimes known as the Giraffe-necked Antelope, invariably stands on its hind legs to feed, its long legs and neck enabling it to browse tender leaves and shoots out of reach to all other antelopes.

The other interesting aspect of the mammalian fauna of East Africa, and a major attraction to tourists, is the large mammals. Giraffes are the tallest mammals in the world while Elephants are the heaviest land mammals, with Hippos and rhinos not far behind. Big cats are also well represented with Lions, Leopards and Cheetahs all being widespread throughout the region.

There is an increasing trend, particularly noticeable among the large mammals and predatory species, for their ranges to become confined to the boundaries of national parks and reserves. Whether by intent or accident, man has caused the decline of many species so that they are either endangered or extremely local. Lions and Cheetahs, although not classed as rare, are nevertheless seldom seen outside wildlife areas in parts of East Africa where man lives in any numbers. Cheetahs and Leopards suffered in the past from hunting for their skins and now it is the turn of Elephants and rhinos to face the threat of poaching for ivory and horn respectively.

BIRDS

On the whole, East Africa's birds have fared rather better. Although larger species, such as Ostrich and Kori Bustard, have suffered from hunting, many other species are of little interest to man; habitat loss is their major threat.

As an added bonus for the birdwatcher, during the months of October to March, East Africa receives hundreds of thousands of visiting migrants from Europe and Asia. These birds have flown south to escape the rigours of winter in the northern hemisphere and commonly encountered species include Bee-eater, Roller, shrikes, Swallow, Yellow Wagtail, terns and a wide variety of waders.

HABITAT TYPES

The East African region possesses an extraordinary range of habitat and vegetation types, a fact not unconnected with the diversity and richness of its flora and fauna. Within the region covered by this book, there are no true rainforests, except perhaps for small pockets in the Usumbara Mountain in Tanzania. Those forest types most allied to rainforest are found at Kakamega Forest in

Isabelline (Red-tailed) Shrikes (Lanius isabellinus) are widespread visitors to the region in winter.

western Kenya, Arabuku-Sokoke Forest in coastal Kenya and Nyungwe Forest in Rwanda; these are perhaps better described as lowland, west African-type tropical forest, coastal tropical forest and highland tropical forest respectively. There are also no vast deserts of shifting sands. However, almost every other habitat that Africa has to offer can be found in the region, from savannah to Afro-alpine vegetation.

Numerous distinct habitats have been described, altitude and rainfall being significant factors in determining the distribution of each one. The following are the most widespread and frequently encountered of these.

MONTANE FOREST

Between altitudes of about 2000m (6560 feet) and 3300m (10,830 feet), the forests can be considered as montane. As might be expected, areas which have high rainfall have lusher forest than regions with less precipitation. On the lower slopes of Mt Kenya and Mt Elgon in Kenya, and Mt Kilimanjaro and Mt Meru in Tanzania can be found magnificent stands of forests comprising species such as African Olive, Camphor and Podocarp.

The trees are festooned with epiphytic plants (plants which grow on other plants for support), including orchids, mosses and lichens, while the ground layer is covered with a dense carpet of ferns and nettles. Drier highland forest would have once cloaked many of the hills around Nairobi. There is a small, remnant pocket in the Nairobi City Park and farther afield there are more extensive areas in the Chyulu Hills. However, many areas of montane forest have long since been cleared for timber and firewood.

Forest bird life is varied but not always easy to see. Species such as Cinnamon-chested Bee-eater and Silvery-cheeked Hornbill are conspicuous while Narina's Trogon and Hartlaub's Turaco are considerably more elusive.

With the exception of species such as Vervet Monkey and Syke's Monkey, there are few mammals left in areas of dry tropical forest where man also roams. In remote areas and the four forested mountain slopes mentioned above, however, animals as large as Elephants and Buffaloes still persist. Duikers, Bushbucks and Black-and-white Colobus Monkeys are also present, although difficult to see.

In common with the lower slopes of many of the region's mountains, those of Mt Kenya are cloaked in lush montane forest. Protected by its status as a forest reserve, the forest comprises species such as Camphor and Podocarp. It offers a refuge to large numbers of birds and mammals.

Mutual grooming is common between Black-faced Vervet Monkeys (Cercopithecus aethiops).

TROPICAL FOREST

Although strictly speaking, there are no true rainforests in East Africa, areas of tropical forest still remain and harbour a rich diversity of life. Some of the most outstanding remnants can be found in the Arabuku-Sokoke Forest Reserve and Shimba Hills National Reserve in coastal Kenya, Kakamega Forest National Reserve in western Kenya and Nyungwe Forest in Rwanda.

Tropical forests are characterized by dense stands of majestic hardwood trees which form a dense tree canopy. They are also noted for their diversity: upwards of 100 species of tree may be found in a few acres of habitat.

Because of the comparatively low light levels that reach the forest floor, relatively few plants prosper. Instead, there are many epiphytes and climbers that reach the light with assistance. However, in clearings caused by fallen trees or along ravines and gorges, plants such as ferns proliferate, taking advantage of the availability of light.

Mammals are few and far between in East African tropical forests, although how much of this paucity is a reflection of their natural abundance and how much due to man's hunting activities is difficult to assess. Elephants would no doubt have been resident throughout the coastal tropical forests in the days when these stretched all along the coast; they still persist in Arabuku-Sokoke Forest. Elephant Shrews and Duikers still occur but are difficult to see.

Insect life is abundant and there are numerous other invertebrates to be found on the forest floor and in the tree canopy. Not surprisingly, bird life is also prolific, although the low light levels and dappled foliage often make observation difficult. Various species of turacos, woodpeckers, sunbirds and weavers abound and several of the remnant forests are the non-breeding haunt of African Pittas.

OPEN WOODLAND AND SAVANNAH

When most people imagine East Africa, they think of endless stretches of grassy plains, dotted with flat-topped acacia trees. Indeed, this habitat is widespread in many parts of the region and is a dominant habitat in several national parks and reserves.

In reality, the term savannah covers a whole spectrum of habitats, each with differing proportions of grassland, thornbush or woodland. *Acacia* and *Combetrum* species are the dominant trees in open savannah country while *Brachystegia* prevails in the *miombo* woodland that is characteristic of parts of northern Tanzania. Altitude and climate,

In February and March, Samburu National Reserve's acacia trees burst into flower.

especially rainfall and temperature, are influential factors in determining the exact nature of the habitat.

In all their forms, these habitats are without doubt the most productive for game mammals and certainly provide the best opportunities for observing them. Wildebeest, Giraffes, Impalas, African Buffaloes, Zebras, gazelles, together with predatory species such as Lions, Cheetahs and hyenas are among the most common residents. Sites such as Masai Mara Game Reserve, Samburu National Reserve and Nairobi National Park in Kenya, and Serengeti National Park in Tanzania are among the best known in the region and contain much savannah habitat.

Bird life is not only abundant in this habitat but also relatively easy to see. Birds like bustards, Secretary Bird, Yellow-necked Spurfowl and guineafowls are common with others such as rollers, bee-eaters and birds of prey using isolated bushes and trees as lookout posts.

SEMI-DESERT

An African desert conjours up images of the seas of shifting sands associated with the Sahara. Although there are areas of inland sand dunes and barren stretches of volcanic desert, these are by no means typical of the

Chestnut-bellied Sandgrouse (Pterocles exustus) are adapted to life in arid, semi-desert habitats.

arid regions of East Africa. In any case, these plantless habitats are comparatively lacking in wildlife. More familiar are the tracts of semi-desert, characterized by low-growing, sparse vegetation which often appears entirely leafless. This habitat, so typical of the Northern Territories of Kenya (north of Marsabit and across to Lake Turkana) is home to many specialized and fascinating creatures.

Four groups of birds in particular seem especially suited to this arid environment: larks, coursers, sandgrouse and bustards all have several representative species in the region. Some can obtain all the water they need from their diet, but sandgrouse often regularly fly long distances to waterholes to drink and bathe.

FRESHWATER

Not surprisingly, freshwater is extremely important to the wildlife of East Africa, its importance being made more acute by the seasonal nature of the rainfall and localized distribution of the water. Freshwater is found in many situations in the region: lakes, rivers, springs and waterholes. Many of the rivers and waterholes dry up at certain times of the year, and some of the lakes, seemingly appealing in appearance, are alkaline soda lakes and therefore not attractive to all mammals and birds. Permanent rivers include the Mara River, Tana River, Uaso Ngiro River and Athi River in Kenya and the Pangani River and Great Ruaha River in Tanzania. Freshwater lakes include Lake Naivasha and Lake Baringo in Kenya, and Lake Victoria on the western borders of both Kenya and Tanzania. The best-known freshwater springs are Mzima Springs in Tsavo, much frequented by Hippos.

Both freshwater lakes and rivers often support good numbers of both Nile Crocodiles and Hippos. The former need a supply of fish and the latter require good grazing on the surrounding land. Almost all the game mammals come to drink or bathe in freshwater, some on a more regular basis than others, and large numbers of birds congregate at the margins. Herons, egrets, ibises, wildfowl and waders are particularly well represented.

SODA LAKES

Soda lakes are an interesting feature of the Great Rift Valley in East Africa, although not all the water bodies in this region share their salt-rich, alkaline chemistry. Only a limited

Both Lesser and Greater Flamingos find ideal feeding conditions in many of the Great Rift Valley's alkaline soda lakes. If their food is particularly abundant, hundreds of thousands of birds can be present. Flamingos are fickle creatures, however, and will soon move elsewhere if conditions change. These Lesser Flamingos (Phoenicopterus minor) are feeding on Kenya's Lake Nakuru.

19

and specialized flora and fauna can survive in these rather hostile conditions. The birds and mammals that frequent the lakes are consequently somewhat restricted in terms of species, but not necessarily in numbers.

The best-known soda lakes are Lake Nakuru, Lake Bogoria and Lake Magadi in Kenya, and Lake Natron in Tanzania. The birds most associated with the soda lakes are the flamingos. If the feeding conditions are right (flamingos are notoriously sensitive to changes in the water chemistry and hence the availability of their food) both Greater and Lesser Flamingos can be present in their hundreds of thousands. On occasions, an estimated 2 million birds have been present at Lake Nakuru while at other times the numbers may drop to a few thousand. Lake Natron is the most regular breeding site for the flamingos which are as fussy about where they breed as they are about where they feed.

The flamingos' diet comprises blue-green algae and small crustaceans that can be abundant in these alkaline waters. The freshwater animals also serve as food for Avocets and Black-winged Stilts as well as a variety of other waders. If there are fish in the lake, then birds such as egrets, herons and cormorants are generally present.

THE COAST

The East African coast is many holiday-makers' idea of the perfect environment. The climate is pleasant, although sometimes it becomes a little too warm and humid, the seas are warm and clean and the white, sandy beaches are a delight to sunbathe on. Not surprisingly, the landward side has been much affected by man over the centuries and much of the natural vegetation has disappeared; the Kenyan coast has suffered more than Tanzania. However, the coastal habitats themselves, mudflats, estuaries,

mangroves and coral reefs, have fared rather better and there are still some superb examples to be seen.

Compared to sandy beaches, mudflats and estuaries support a far greater wealth of wildlife. Consequently, they provide far better feeding grounds for birds and areas, such as the mouth of the Sabaki River near Malindi and Mida Creek at Watamu, are fabulous for birdwatchers. In addition to resident species, for example egrets, herons and gulls, there are seasonal visitors from farther afield. Thousands of waders from Europe and Asia are present from September until March along with Crab Plovers which disperse from their Red Sea nesting grounds.

Offshore, the coast is fringed with extensive coral reefs which harbour a fantastic array of marine life. In addition to the many colourful species of corals themselves, there are sea anemones, starfish, spiny lobsters, Moray Eels and reef fish in abundance. Fortunately for the visitor, many of the reefs are easily accessible and provide wonderful snorkelling.

THE AFRO-ALPINE ZONE

In many ways, the Afro-alpine zone is the most unusual and interesting of the East African habitats. At high altitudes, extraordinary plants have evolved to cope with a harsh environment. Many of them are endemic to the particular mountain on which they are found.

Above the treeline, about 3300m (10,830 feet) on Mt Kenya, the landscape is dominated by high altitude moorland comprising mainly tussock grass and with increasing altitude, giant species of lobelias, groundsels and spurges appear. These are adapted to a life of extremes: within a single 24-hour period they may experience fierce sun and intense ultraviolet radiation during the day, and sometimes temperatures below freezing at night. Dense rosettes of leaves and flower spikes and hairy leaf surfaces are adaptations to this environment.

Perhaps surprisingly, these high altitude regions harbour large game mammals: Eland, Buffalo and Elephant often venture quite high. Bird life is comparatively limited but specialities include Mountain Chat and Scarlet-chested Malachite Sunbird. The best examples of Afro-alpine vegetation can be found on Mt Kenya, Mt Elgon and the Aberdares in Kenya, and on Mt Kilimanjaro in Tanzania.

CLIMATE

The East African region covered in this book straddles the equator: the equatorial line cuts through the southern half of Kenya with Tanzania and Rwanda lying in the southern hemisphere. In contrast to what might be expected, the climate is considerably more temperate and pleasant than areas at similar latitudes elsewhere in the world.

The coast of East Africa does suffer from heat and humidity but even here the extremes are tempered by the south-east and north-east monsoon winds that prevail at different times of the year. Away from the coast, the climate becomes steadily more temperate, the main influence being altitude.

A large part of East Africa lies well above sea level: much of Tanzania is a plateau above 1000m (3280 feet) and the central highlands of Kenya lie at approximately 2000m (6560 feet) above sea level. As a consequence, although daytime temperatures may be hot, the nights can be chilly and many people are surprised to find that they often need a thick jumper after dark on safari. There are exceptions to this climatic generalization: the Northern Frontier region around Lake Turkana can be blisteringly hot, as can some of the low-lying Rift Valley lakes farther south, such as Lake Magadi.

Lying on the equator, the East African region does not experience the same seasonal effects seen at higher latitudes in both hemispheres: spring, summer, autumn and winter cannot be defined and the enormous changes in day length are not experienced. Nevertheless, there are changes throughout the

Rainfall in East Africa is distinctly seasonal with most falling in April and May. At other times of the year, permanent rivers and water bodies become focal points for much of the region's wildlife. Doum Palms (Hyphaene coriacea) mark a river's course in Samburu National Reserve, Kenya, and serve as a useful indicator from a considerable distance.

year. There is up to forty minutes difference during the year in sunrise and sunset times, and there are distinct rainy and dry seasons. Most of the rain falls between November and May, the so-called short rains being concentrated in November and December and the long rains falling in April and May. There is usually dry weather and clear skies in January and February, and July to September are generally dry months.

Although some of the region's mammals are effectively independent of water, gaining much of the water they need from their diet, most are strongly influenced by the seasonal rains. For many, this simply means reliance on permanent water bodies, such as waterholes and rivers, at the drier time of the year with the consequent concentration of game. With others, it may mean more dramatic migrations, those of the Serengeti's Wildebeest and Zebra being the most famous. In this particular area, the herds move northwards to the permanent water of the Masai Mara when the dry season affects grazing in the Serengeti.

East Africa's wildlife is not the only thing to be influenced by the rainy seasons. In many of the more remote areas or regions

of particularly high rainfall, dirt tracks may become impassable. If you are hiring a self-drive vehicle, check with the hire company about the state of the roads on your proposed route.

CONSERVATION AND TOURISM

Conservation, in one form or another, has a long history in East Africa, the first national park, Akagera in Rwanda, being established in 1934. The first in Tanzania was Serengeti in 1940, while Nairobi National Park, established in 1946, was Kenya's first. On the whole, the wildlife protection areas work well but the recent fate of Akagera, which has effectively become a battle zone, shows just how fragile their statuses are.

In the East African region, there are several different categories of area where wildlife and vegetation are protected. National Parks are administered by a governmental department and wildlife protection is generally their prime directive; human activities, other than controlled tourism, are strictly prohibited. Marine National Parks,

Safari tourism is an important source of foreign revenue to East African countries. From a visitor's point of view, it is important to select a safari operator carefully. Study the itinerary to make sure they visit the best areas and assess the degree of luxury on offer.

as their name suggests, protect areas of the coast from development and exploitation. National Reserves are administered by county councils and the activities of native peoples, such as pastoral farming, are permitted with wildlife conservation sharing equal importance. Forest Reserves are areas of forest which are generally managed to ensure they remain intact.

The status and land area of these designated sites is by no means fixed in perpetuity. Sites have had their designation changed or have been declassified and have been reduced in size for a variety of reasons, including the need to make better use of limited resources in a smaller and better defined area.

If anything is going to encourage conservation and the retention and policing of national parks and reserves in the region, it is tourism, or rather the prospect of the foreign revenue it brings and will continue to bring while there is still wildlife to see. However, as in many other areas of the world, the impact of tourism alters, invariably adversely, the very thing that attracted the visitors in the first place.

Amboseli National Park is a classic example. Until recently, vehicles freely drove off-road with the result that there was widespread soil erosion in the park on a massive scale. Large numbers of tourists visit the park and most have a strong desire to see Lions and Cheetahs. Understandably, there was a strong financial incentive for drivers to find the cats to please their clients. The result was often a family of Cheetahs surrounded by fifteen or more vehicles; not surprisingly, the hunting behaviour and social life of the cats became noticeably altered. Nowadays, the authorities have taken the problem in hand and off-road driving is strictly prohibited. The cats are more difficult to see, generally keeping away from well-used roads, but the park is beginning to recover from its eroded state.

Poaching of Elephants and rhinos for ivory and horn respectively pose two major threats to conservation in East Africa. The worldwide ban on trade in ivory and horn products has undoubtedly had a significant effect in reducing the slaughter but would have more effect if it were truly worldwide. Sadly, however, while a market, albeit illegal, still exists there will always be some trade in these products, given the price they command, and hence the slaughter will continue.

There can be few sadder sights for the safari visitor than that of a dead Rhinoceros (Diceros bicornis) with its horn cut off. Without anti-poaching units, the fate of these amazing creatures would be certain extinction in the wild; even so their future still looks bleak. It goes without saying that visitor's should never buy animal products in any form.

Anti-poaching units have a daunting task but have had a major impact on poaching. In smaller, more manageable parks the job is considerably easier than in the vast tracts of sites like Tsavo National Park in Kenya. All in all, prospects for these two magnificent animals seem gloomy outside guarded areas.

NOTES FOR PHOTOGRAPHERS

For anyone with an interest in photography, an East African safari is a wonderful experience. For much of the day the light is strong, the scenery is dramatic and colourful, and many of the mammals and birds are indifferent to safari vehicles and thus make excellent subjects. What more could any budding photographer ask for?

LIGHTING
On a game-watching safari, there is usually enough light for photography for most of the twelve-hour day. However, the light does not always make for good photographic results despite the fact that a fast shutter speed and good depth of field may be achieved.

Because East Africa lies on the equator, the sun passes directly overhead at midday. From about 10.30am until 2.30pm the sun casts intense shadows from above with the result that the upper half of an animal may appear 'burnt out' in the resulting photograph while the underside is almost black. Landscape photographs also suffer at this time of day, skies appearing 'bleached' even with the aid of a haze filter, and intense contrast is a feature of landscape itself. You can try using a polarizing filter to combat this, but overall, pictures taken during the middle of the day will be very disappointing.

The optimum times for photography on safari in East Africa are undoubtedly the first two or three hours after dawn and the last two or three before sunset. The relatively low angle of the sun results in more pleasing lighting and less intrusive shadows. Even then, however, it is wise to consider the direction of the sun in relation to your subject; results are generally more effective with the sun directly behind you unless you choose to shoot directly into the sun for a backlit effect.

LIGHT METERING
Nowadays, most photographers use a 35mm SLR camera with automatic light metering and interchangeable lenses. The metering systems in most moderately priced cameras can usually cope with all types of lighting situations but under certain circumstances, even they can be fooled. If you are shooting under conditions of high contrast, it is a wise idea to bracket your exposures, taking a couple of shots deliberately under- and over-exposing the metered reading by half or one stop.

FILMS
Ultimately, the choice of film is a matter of personal preference. Under most circumstances, a film speed of 64 ASA is more than adequate and Kodachrome 64 transparency film is an excellent choice. Many people opt for faster films, 100 to 400 ASA films being popular. These have the advantage of allowing a combination of greater depth of field and faster shutter speed to be employed, the latter resulting in the reduced likelihood of camera shake. However, it should be borne in mind that with an increase in film speed comes a decrease in quality and contrast. Weigh these different factors up carefully before deciding which film speed to use.

Many visiting photographers seriously underestimate the amount of film they need to take since it is easy to get carried away and in any case the photographic opportunities are legion. As a rough guide, think of the maximum number of films you think you could possibly get through on a trip and double it!

LENSES

A wide range of lenses of different focal lengths are available for all makes of modern 35mm SLR cameras. For a safari, it is useful to have a range of lenses for different purposes: a standard lens or wide-angle for scenic shots, a medium telephoto lens (135mm to 150mm) for composing portraits and a longer telephoto (300mm to 400mm) for more distant animals. Some people prefer to use a zoom lens.

An immature Bateleur Eagle (Terathopius ecaudatus). In flight the short tail is distinctive.

Telephoto lenses are extremely useful since they allow you to get a good image size without having to be right on top of your subject. However, they should be used with a degree of caution since there is a potential problem associated with their use. The longer the lens, the greater its ability to magnify any camera movement and hence suffer from camera shake; it is a good idea to use a bean bag to rest the camera on, or a window support whenever possible. As a general guide, try to use a shutter speed which is roughly similar to, or greater than, the focal length of the lens in use, even when a support is being used. Therefore, for a 300mm lens, you should aim for a shutter speed of $1/250$ second or faster.

PROTECTING YOUR CAMERA EQUIPMENT

An East African safari can be an extremely punishing test of the durability of camera equipment. Roads and tracks within the boundaries of national parks and reserves are invariably rough. Although you may get used to being thrown around and bumped inside your vehicle, your photographic equipment may be less tolerant. If possible, keep your camera and lenses in an easily accessible padded bag or, failing that, protect them in transit by wrapping them in clothes.

The constant rattling and banging has a nasty habit of encouraging dials and switches to move. Regular checking of your settings should avoid the disappointment of finding that you have just taken a stunning sequence with the ASA rating double what it should have been or with your metering system set on manual.

Another problem associated with East African safaris is the dust. In places, such as Amboseli National Park, it is incredibly fine and is seemingly capable of getting into every part of your camera. Regularly clean lenses and camera bodies with a soft cloth and protect them from the worst effects of dust by keeping them in capacious plastic bags.

BEING PREPARED

However relaxed an approach to photography you adopt on safari, you should still be able to take some good photographs, or at least to have some wonderful opportunities. By giving some thought to potential opportunities and being prepared for all eventualities, you can increase your chances of success dramatically. Just simple things like keeping your longest lens on the camera while driving around can help. Scenic shots, requiring a short lens, will wait while you change lenses, mammals and birds may not be so patient. Anticipate which side of the vehicle is going to provide the best photographic opportunities, bearing in mind the direction of the sun, and seat yourself appropriately. Lastly, all the best opportunities seem to arise just as you reach frame thirty-three on your film. If you are approaching something potentially exciting, a Lion kill for example, waste a couple of shots and change

films *before* you arrive on the scene. It is amazing what you can miss during the time it takes to rewind and load.

PHOTOGRAPHING PEOPLE

As a general rule, unless you have express permission to do so, do not photograph local people in East Africa. Many take vigorous and often violent exception to what they see as an infringement of their rights. More than this, some believe that a photograph removes part of their soul. In many areas, especially around Amboseli National Park, the Masai have a pragmatic approach to this loss: the going rate for a photograph is about 100 ksh!

TRAVEL TIPS

CHOOSING THE RIGHT SAFARI

Safari tourism is such an important source of foreign revenue that there is, not surprisingly, a huge range of alternatives from which to choose. Some cater for visitors who are prepared to 'rough it' while, at the other extreme, others offer an extraordinary level of comfort and luxury.

Camping in the bush is undoubtedly the best way to get a real 'taste' of Africa. Meals cooked over an open, wood fire acquire a unique flavour and the sounds of the African night provide a lasting memory for the visitor. This safari camp in the Loita Hills, Kenya, was part of a Bushbuck Adventures safari.

Needless to say, these safaris also vary greatly in cost. Obviously, you will want to choose something to fit your price range but bear in mind that paying a higher price does not necessarily mean you will get more of the African experience. It may simply mean that you get champagne instead of beer with your meals, sleep in luxury tents and have twice as many people looking after your needs.

This is not to say that luxury safaris and the 'African experience' are mutually exclusive; of course they are not. However, there is a tendency among expensive tours to assume that clients put comfort before wildlife watching. It should also be borne in mind that, unless you have organized a private safari, you will be travelling with a group of people you have never met before who can make or break a trip.

Ultimately it is up to you to choose the sort of safari that suits you. Study the itineraries of the companies and try to pick one that visits exciting areas, on the whole avoids lodges and whose ethos is the spirit of adventure. It is wise to contemplate the sort of clients that each type of safari company is aiming to attract and consider whether they would be compatible with what you hope to get from the experience. For moderately priced, organized safaris which offer a real taste of Africa I can recommend Bushbuck Adventures, PO Box 67449, Nairobi, Kenya, Tel: 212975/6.

Some visitors prefer to go it alone and hire a car or four-wheel-drive vehicle themselves. This has advantages and disadvantages. If you have plenty of time and a spirit of adventure then there is no reason why you should not do so in Kenya at least. In Tanzania, it is not usually possible to hire a vehicle without a driver and hire cars cannot normally be driven across the border from Kenya. Car hire is not cheap, however, and

the logistical problems of buying food, obtaining water and fuel, repairing punctures and navigating all add to the journey times.

A prior knowledge of the routes and road surfaces is also important. There are many routes, which may look good on a map, that are quite impossible for ordinary vehicles. During the rainy season, some roads are impassable to all vehicles. Even tarmacked East African roads should be treated with a degree of caution and respect since large potholes are common, even on the best surfaced roads, and animals frequently cross or stand on the road, especially after dark.

If you have only a limited amount of time available but still want a personal experience of Africa, then possibly the best way is to hire a landrover, driver and cook with a small group of like-minded friends. In this respect, I can also recommend Bushbuck Adventures. This not only means that you reach your destinations and travel around the parks and reserves with the minimum of hassle and time-wasting but, having a cook, also means that a camp can be established and left during the daytime.

FIRST AID AND MEDICAL PRECAUTIONS

Before embarking on a trip to East Africa consult your doctor about necessary medical precautions. Advice may vary from year to year and you will get different contemporary advice from different doctors when it comes to the efficacy of certain inoculations and the need to have them.

Malaria is most people's main concern when visiting the region and it is certainly prevalent in many areas; two types of malarial prophylactic are currently prescribed. However, these do not *guarantee* against contracting the disease and the drugs themselves have unacceptable side-effects if taken for a long time. Mosquitoes and other biting insects are a nuisance, particularly at dusk; take insect repellant and anti-histamine cream.

WHEN TO TRAVEL

Different times of year have different things to offer the safari visitor to East Africa. The rainy seasons from November to December and April to May can make travel and wildlife observation difficult. However, you will see the vegetation greener than at other times of year. Overall the best times of year for a safari are in January and February and from July to September.

ACCOMMODATION AND REGULATIONS

Safaris in Kenya usually start from Nairobi while those in Tanzania often start from Arusha. Both have hotels of varying standards and prices. There are usually lodges, situated in or near most national parks and reserves in the region, and public campsites, details of which will be available at park entrances. Toilets and water are present in some of the campsites but their availability should not be relied upon and you should plan accordingly.

In most parks and reserves, there are strict rules about driving. Sometimes the permitted period is dawn to dusk but there is often no driving allowed before 6.00am and after 6.30pm. This means you must anticipate how long it will take to return to camp as sunset approaches. In almost all areas, off-road driving is not permitted and visitors are not allowed out of vehicles except in designated spots. If you break down, stay inside your vehicle until rescued.

Sunset at Amboseli, Kenya.

SECTION II:
SITE GUIDE

In the pages that follow, fifty of the best sites to see wildlife in East Africa are described. The sites have been divided into four convenient regions, and the main sites begin with a map showing the principal towns, roads, rivers, and positions of the various lodges and campsites. The map on page 32 shows the whole of East Africa with the positions of all the sites, numbered from one to fifty, marked on it.

Every site begins with a summary box which gives the location and main features of the site at a glance. The sub-headings in the summary boxes are fairly self-explanatory but mean the following:

Location: the general position of the site relative to the capital or nearest tourist centre;

Access: how easy or difficult the site is to reach and travel around, with comments on any restrictions to access;

Terrain: the habitat and general topography;

Specialities: unusual, rare or exciting species for which the site is renowned which should enthuse the traveller to visit the site;

Accommodation: details of where to stay. Lodges and compsites are referred to where appropriate.

The main text for each site describes how to get there, what to expect at the site in terms of scenery and habitat, and what particular species to look out for. The types of local accommodation available are also elaborated upon.

Throughout the section, species of particular interest in the region are highlighted in *Special Species Boxes*. The measurements given in these boxes relate to length (L) or height (H) and are given in centimetres.

On pages 214–217 is a checklist covering the species most likely to be encountered on safari. Space has been left to write in any additional species seen on your trip.

Opposite: *the Yellow-billed Stork (Ibis ibis) is widespread and common around lake shores, marshes and on the coast.*
Right: *the Superb Starling (Spreo superbus) is one of many highly coloured starlings which can be seen in the region.*

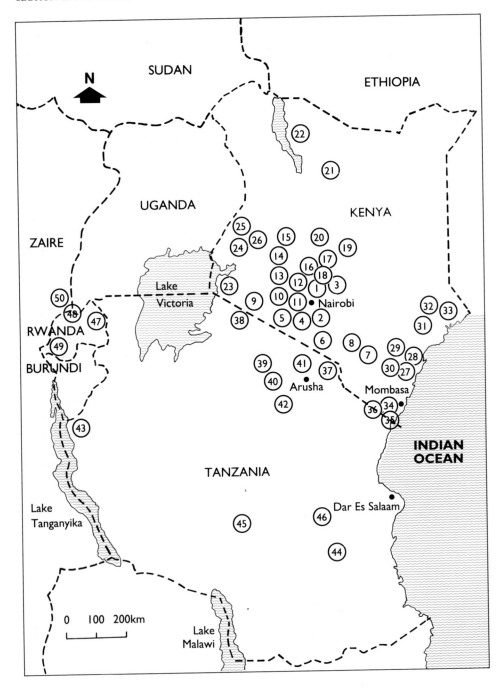

1. INLAND KENYA

INTRODUCTION

Kenya is very definitely on the tourist map and receives thousands of visitors each year. Although in some parts of the country the number of visitors devalues the feeling of wilderness Africa, Kenya is still *the* country to visit for anyone contemplating a safari. The national parks and reserves offer so much variety and abundance of wildlife that the prospect of meeting a few other tour vehicles hardly seems to matter.

Most of Kenya's safari interest is concentrated inland, the coastal stretch having little to offer in the way of game watching. There are numerous parks and reserves away from the coast and many of these are within a day's drive of the capital, Nairobi. By visiting two or three of the better locations, visitors on a ten-day safari could expect to see Elephants, Lions, Buffaloes, Hippopotamuses, Cheetahs, Wildebeest, Zebras, Giraffes and gazelles. Black Rhinoceroses and Leopards would be a bonus but more than 150 bird species would not be unusual.

As a country, Kenya is far from uniform. Nairobi and much of central Kenya are in the highlands, a great deal of which would have been cloaked in forest at one time. Away from the hills, the land drops considerably in altitude and many reserves and parks are dominated by savannah and acacia woodland. In the Northern Territories, the land becomes steadily more arid and there are vast regions of desert and semi-desert.

One of the best-known geographical features of Kenya, and indeed of East Africa as a

Opposite: map of East Africa showing the positions of the fifty numbered sites described in the following section.

whole, is the Great Rift Valley. Alkaline lakes form a broken chain along its length and are home to vast numbers of flamingos and other waterbirds. By contrast, Mt Kenya, the Aberdares and Mt Elgon offer high-altitude exploration for those who want a more physically demanding trip.

Kenya's tourist infrastructure and the friendliness of its people are important factors in making a safari in the country one of the most rewarding in Africa. Road and air links are, in general, good and most parks and reserves have a wide range of types of accommodation. In short, it is a country where the maximum number of animals and plants can be seen with the minimum amount of hassle.

THE ENVIRONS OF NAIROBI	
Location:	S Kenya
Access:	Good roads; public transport, taxis and hire cars available
Terrain:	Parks, gardens and remnant areas of highland forest
Specialities:	Fiscal Shrike, Black Kite, Syke's Monkey
Accommodation:	Numerous hotels; one campsite

About the city
Nairobi is the capital of Kenya and a bustling city. The centre comprises towering modern buildings while in the suburbs around the outskirts are splendid former colonial residences as well as sprawling areas of rather squalid shanty towns. For the most part, Nairobi is a comparatively safe city although a degree of common sense should always be exercised when out and about. Visitors would be well advised to confine their explorations on foot to the hours of daylight.

Although Nairobi lies only 139km south of the equator, the climate is mild and pleasant. This is mainly due to the altitude, as the city lies at approximately 1830m (6000 feet) above sea level on the Athi Plains. Daytime temperatures are usually warm when the sun is not obscured by cloud but nights can be decidedly chilly. During the wet seasons of March to July and October to December, prolonged periods of heavy rain are not unusual and so clothing appropriate to the season should always be carried.

Nairobi's wildlife
One of the first wildlife sights to greet visitors to Nairobi are the Black Kites which are ubiquitous, scavenging refuse throughout the city. Visitors are usually first alerted to their presence by their mewing call which is uttered in flight. For European birdwatchers who have never visited Africa or Asia before, the sight of Black Kites flying along city roads and picking scraps of food from the pavements is an extraordinary one. Close views reveal that the East African race differs from its European and Asian counterparts in having the base of the bill yellow instead of black; the dark-billed race is, however, a winter visitor to the region.

Speckled Mousebirds (Colius striatus) are comical birds usually seen in small parties.

Many of the quieter suburbs have mature gardens which attract considerable numbers of birds. The grounds of many hotels, such as the Fairview, also harbour a wide variety of species. Fiscal Shrikes can be found in most gardens and recreational parks; they perch on exposed branches and fence posts, scanning the ground below for insects. Small flocks of Superb Starlings, surely one of Africa's most colourful birds, are also a common sight in and around Nairobi.

The Olive Thrush is a common garden resident in Nairobi and visitors often awake to the sound of its loud song or harsh, scolding call. Birdwatchers should also look for Speckled Mousebird, Common Bulbul and Paradise Flycatcher among the bushes and trees, and Augur Buzzards circling overhead.

Flower borders not only attract butterflies but also birds, such as Reichenow's Weaver and Amethyst Sunbird. Overgrown patches of vegetation should be searched for African Citril, Streaky Seedeater and White-eyed Slaty Flycatcher.

At Museum Hill near the University, there is a small patch of woodland beside the River Nairobi. Despite the rather scruffy appearance of the habitat visitors should find White-breasted Tit, Blue-eared Glossy Starling, African Firefinch, Bronze Manakin and Holub's Golden Weaver. In the past, fortunate observers have even seen Mountain Wagtail and Red-breasted Wryneck at this spot.

Nairobi City Park
For added variety, visit the Nairobi City Park which lies on Limuru Road near the Aga Khan Hospital; take a taxi from your hotel to the park entrance. The park comprises areas of formal flower gardens set amidst remnant patches of highland forest. Syke's Monkeys and Vervet Monkeys are accustomed to

In addition to these formal gardens with their Bougainvilleas, Nairobi City Park also harbours remnants of highland forest. Bird life, including species such as Silvery-cheeked Hornbill and Cinnamon-breasted Bee-eater, is rich and varied, and the Vervet Monkeys and Syke's Monkeys are accustomed to humans.

man's presence and will sometimes come to food around the open recreational areas.

Forest birds are common and include Cinnamon-chested Bee-eater, Narina's Trogon, Silvery-cheeked Hornbill, Grey-headed Kingfisher, Straight-crested Helmet- shrike, Hartlaub's Turaco and Sulphur-breasted Bush-shrike. A speciality is the Lemon Dove found on the forest floor.

Dawn and early morning are the best times of day for birdwatching in Nairobi City Park. Although the park is generally safe, visitors are advised not to travel alone and to leave valuables, other than binoculars, at their hotel.

Although not especially secretive, many of the forest birds will sit motionless in the undergrowth if alarmed. One way to see them is to find a likely looking spot and stand quietly for a few minutes watching everything that moves. Some of the smaller birds feed in mixed species flocks so be prepared for periods of intense birdwatching activity interspersed with spells where nothing at all is moving.

Swifts are commonly seen over the highlands of Kenya but often fly too high for certain identification. However, prior to electrical storms and heavy rains, parties of these aerobatic birds descend low over the tree tops around Nairobi City Park. Look for Mottled Swift, Little Swift and White-rumped Swift.

2 NAIROBI NATIONAL PARK	
Location:	8km S of Nairobi
Access:	Tracks lead from entrances on roads to Karen and to Mombasa
Terrain:	Open plains and areas of acacia woodland crossed by a network of roads; most are suitable for hire cars; nature trail beside the Athi River
Specialities:	Common game animals with the exception of Elephant; Ostrich, Giraffe, Zebra and Wildebeest are easy to see
Accommodation:	No camping is permitted in the park

Getting there
The main entrance to Nairobi National Park is on the road from Nairobi to Karen (Langata Road) at which there is a small

35

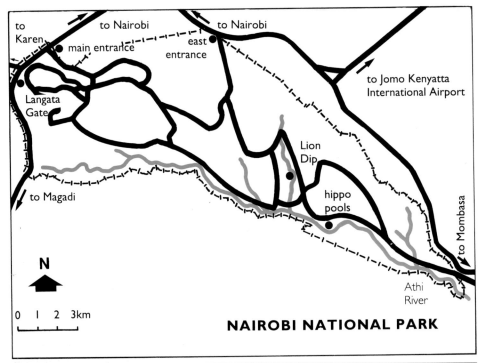

to Karen
to Nairobi
to Nairobi
main entrance
east entrance
to Jomo Kenyatta International Airport
Langata Gate
Lion Dip
hippo pools
to Magadi
to Mombasa
Athi River
N
0 1 2 3km
NAIROBI NATIONAL PARK

Ostrich *Struthio camelus*

Standing nearly 2.5m tall, the Ostrich is unmistakable. Its powerful legs allow it to run at speeds of up to 50kph to escape danger. The male bird has a black-and-white plumage while the females are greyish brown. The legs and neck are bare and pink. Female Ostriches lay the largest egg of any bird. Several females often lay together in the same nest and the eggs are guarded by one male. After hatching, the young gather together to form crèches for protection.

Although Ostriches are common in most of Kenya's national parks and in East Africa as a whole, they have disappeared from much of their African range. Their decline is due largely to persecution by man for meat and for the male's plumes which were once highly prized in the millinery trade.

Opposite above: *map of Nairobi National Park.*
Opposite below: *Kongoni or Coke's Hartebeest (Alcelaphus buselaphus) standing alert.*

Giraffes (Giraffa camelopardalis) use their height to browse vegetation out of reach to other mammals.

zoo/animal orphanage. There is another entrance, the Embakasi Gate, on the road from Nairobi to Mombasa and the airport and there are gates on the road south from the main entrance. During the dry seasons from January to March and August to September, the roads within the park are suitable for ordinary cars. At other times of year, many of the tracks may require four-wheel-drive vehicles. Organized safaris, either half-day or full-day, can be arranged at most hotels in Nairobi.

About the park

Lying so close to the heart of Nairobi, it is not surprising that this is one of the most visited of Kenya's national parks. Within half an hour of leaving the city centre, visitors can be watching herds of Wildebeest and Zebra grazing on grassy plains. Despite the number of people that visit the park and the undoubted disturbance this causes, the area still holds considerable wildlife interest. Although Elephants are absent, almost all the other common game mammals occur; Black Rhinoceroses were introduced and are now the subject of a breeding programme with some offspring being relocated to other national parks in Kenya.

The park boundary adjacent to Nairobi is fenced off to prevent animals straying into the city. However, to the south migrating game animals such as Wildebeest and Zebra are free to wander across the Athi Plains following game corridors to find the rains and resulting fresh growth of grass.

Game mammals

Soon after you enter the park boundary via the main entrance you will see your first game mammals. Small herds of Zebra, Wildebeest and Impala feed unobtrusively in the open woodland and on the open plains beyond. Kongoni, Eland, Thomson's Gazelles and Grant's Gazelles are also easy to see and there may be a temptation to linger at every new species you see. However, the best game watching is to be had farther into the park and so it is worth driving on for a mile or two beyond the gate.

Big cats

Not surprisingly, Lions and Cheetahs thrive thanks to the abundance of game mammals. Although they are well camouflaged among the grasses, visitors would be unlucky not to see them. More in evidence, however, are the remains of their kills which attract large numbers of vultures; look carefully and try to distinguish White-backed, White-headed, Ruppell's and Lappet-faced Vultures, all of which occur. The latter is the largest species and has a colourful, if rather grizzly looking, head. Marabou Storks, standing more than 1.2m tall, are also usually in attendance.

Parties of Yellow-necked Spurfowl (Francolinus leucoscepus) are a common sight in open country. Although comparatively large, they can be rather unobtrusive even amongst low vegetation. They are commonly preyed upon by birds of prey such as eagles.

Birds

Driving across the open plains, you will soon see common birds such as Crowned Plover, Rufous-naped Lark, Yellow-necked Spurfowl, Yellow-throated Longclaw, Helmeted Guineafowl and Ostrich. Isolated bushes serve as look-out posts for Fiscal Shrikes and birds of prey such as Augur Buzzard, Black-winged Kite and Tawny Eagles.

The nature trail

Fortunately, there is a nature trail beside the Athi River where it is safe for visitors to park their vehicles and walk on foot through the riverine forest of Yellow-barked acacia trees. The main wildlife attractions at this spot are the Hippos and Nile Crocodiles that bask in the murky water; these are easily viewed from the safety of the bank. Hippos emerge from the water at night to graze the surrounding grassland. During the day they spend most of the time in water, often with only their noses and eyes above the surface.

As you walk beside the river you will see terrapins basking on exposed logs in the water. Bird life is also abundant along the

Warthog *Phacochoerus aethiopicus*
L 105–150 (head and body)

Although Warthogs can by no stretch of the imagination be described as elegant, most visitors find them engaging creatures and are amused by their antics. They have a pig-like appearance with warts on the head and a pair of prominent tusks. The skin is covered in bristly hairs and the grey-brown colour is usually masked by mud as Warthogs love to wallow in mud.

When alarmed, Warthogs hold their tails stiffly upright; the sight of a sow followed by her litter of young, all running with their tails held high, is an amusing and memorable one. Their diet comprises mainly grasses, shoots and roots. When feeding on low-growing plants, they often rest on their front 'elbows' in order to reach the ground more easily. Warthogs rest in hollows in the ground, sometimes taking over and enlarging abandoned Aardvark holes. They are common and widespread in East Africa and often seen in Nairobi National Park.

arrive on the scene. Consider yourself lucky if you see one.

Hammerkops occasionally hunt for frogs and fish beside the water; a few pairs nest in Nairobi National Park, building huge twiggy constructions in acacia trees. These extra-ordinary looking birds have a head shaped like a hammer, hence the origin of their name. Water is a comparatively scarce commodity on the Kenyan plains and even the man-made Narogoman Dam attracts water birds; African Darters dry their wings on the banks and Goliath Herons are occasionally seen here.

Gorges and plains
Visitors are also allowed out of their cars at Observation Hill from where panoramic views over the plains can be had. The southern part of the park comprises rocky valleys and gorges. The slopes are home to Rock Hyraxes, mammals which, despite their appearance and small size, are most closely related to Elephants. They keep a wary eye open for predators which include Leopards and birds of prey such as Verreaux's Eagles which are occasionally seen here. These elegant raptors can be easily recognized by their distinctive flight silhouette. They have long wings which become noticeably narrower towards the body. They are often seen in pairs.

Safety in the national park
In common with Kenya's other national parks, visitors are not allowed out of their vehicles except at designated spots deemed to be safe. With a back-drop of city skyscrapers, it is easy to forget that the animals in Nairobi National Park are wild. However, there are very real dangers to anyone outside the safety of a car and this regulation is strictly enforced by the park rangers.

banks of the Athi River; look for the diminutive Malachite Kingfisher whose plumage is a dazzling array of blue and orange. Also present are Little Bee-eaters, Green Herons and Singing Cisticolas. This stretch of river is also one of the most reliable sites to see Peter's Finfoot. This rather secretive water-bird is best searched for early in the morning since it becomes more retiring as visitors

When to visit

Early mornings and late afternoons offer the best opportunities for wildlife observation in Nairobi National Park. These times coincide with peaks in activity of the birds and mammals and are also when the park is least crowded with tourists. Most organized tours tend to arrive mid-morning and depart mid-afternoon. As dusk approaches some of the park's more nocturnal residents emerge and become active. Photographers can get superb shots in the park at sunset with the African dust enhancing the orange glow of the dying rays of the sun. The park opens at 6.30am and shuts at 7.00pm, and the last entry is at 6.15pm.

3 OL DOINYO SAPUK NATIONAL PARK	
Location:	50km NE of Nairobi, near Thika
Access:	Roads leading to the summit of the mountain
Terrain:	Densely forested slopes restricting access off the main track
Specialities:	Buffalo, Bushbuck and birds of prey
Accommodation:	None within the park; hotels in Thika

Getting there

To reach Ol Doinyo Sapuk from Nairobi, take the A 2 north-east towards Thika and turn right towards Kithimani on the A 3. Shortly after leaving Thika, fork right and the road runs around the north and east side of Ol Doinyo Sapuk.

About the park

By Kenyan standards, Ol Doinyo Sapuk

National Park is tiny, comprising just over 18km². It is dominated by the domed granite mountain of the same name which rises to over 2000m (6560 feet) at the summit. The mountain is also known as Kilima Mbogo, which means 'Buffalo Mountain' in Swahili, and indeed these large animals occur here in some numbers.

The slopes of Ol Doinyo Sapuk are largely covered in montane forest. The dense vegetation means that the park's mammals, even species as large as the African Buffalo, can be difficult to locate especially when compared to open savannah country. Other game animals include Bushbuck, Impala, Duiker, Colobus Monkey and Leopard, the latter species proving particularly difficult to locate. The African Buffalo is a large cow-like mammal, standing over 1.5m at the shoulder and weighing up to nearly a tonne. It has a reputation for being among the most unpredictable and dangerous of Africa's animals, so never underestimate the threat that might be posed by coming across one in the undergrowth.

Birds

Birds are somewhat easier to locate in the park. Birds of prey such as Bateleur Eagle are sometimes seen overhead. This impressive bird is readily identifiable by its short-tailed flight silhouette. Harrier Hawks and Augur Buzzards perch on dead branches beside the road and several species of sunbirds and weavers can be found on the slopes of Ol Doinyo Sapuk.

When to visit

Ol Doinyo Sapuk is best visited early in the morning. Not only are visitors likely to get the best scenic views at this time of day but the park's birds and mammals will be at their most active and conspicuous.

4 OLORGESAILLIE PREHISTORIC SITE

Location:	65km SW of Nairobi
Access:	Good road from the capital; paths and a field museum at the site; contact the National Museum office in Nairobi prior to visiting
Terrain:	Flat terrain with archaeological remains
Specialities:	Fossil remains of man's early ancestors
Accommodation:	Campsite and bandas

Getting there

Olorgesaillie can be reached from Nairobi via the road to Lake Magadi. Indeed the two sites can be visited in a day trip from the capital. From Nairobi, take the Langata Road. Just beyond the main entrance to Nairobi National Park, fork left instead of continuing to Karen; this is the Magadi Road. The road passes through the township of Angata Rongai and climbs the Ngong Hills. The ground soon drops away steeply providing dramatic views towards Lake Magadi below. Olorgesaillie Prehistoric Site is clearly marked at the town of Oltepesi. The road from Nairobi to Magadi is tarmacked for its entire length to facilitate exploitation of Lake Magadi by the Magadi Soda Company.

About the site

The site was originally discovered in 1893 by John Gregory, the geologist who gave the Great Rift Valley its name. It was not until 1924, when Olorgesaillie was cleared and studied by Dr Louis Leakey, that its true significance to the origins of man became apparent.

The site was, and in places still is, covered with bones which mostly belong to a long-extinct species of giant baboon. The evidence that Leakey pieced together demonstrated that Olorgesaillie had been a dwelling place around 400,000 years ago for our ancestors and that they had fashioned stone weapons to kill their quarry. At that time, the site would have been on the shores of a lake whose source river was diverted when the Great Rift Valley formed.

Olorgesaillie's wildlife

Because it lies at a lower altitude than Nairobi, the Olorgesaillie area is considerably hotter and drier than the capital. A few dry-country birds can be seen around the site and beside the Magadi Road. These include Schalow's and Capped Wheatear, White-fronted Bee-eater, Laughing Dove and Lilac-breasted

Archaeological remains, including bones and tools, cover the ground at Olorgesaillie National Park.

Roller. A few Thomson's Gazelles can also be found but herds of Masai cattle predominate along the roadsides.

5 LAKE MAGADI	
Location:	I I0km SW of Nairobi,
Access:	Reached by tarmacked road from Nairobi; causeways and paths around the lake's margins
Terrain:	Vast soda lake whose soda ash is commercially exploited; hot springs; hat and sunglasses essential
Specialities:	Flamingoes, Chestnut-banded Sand Plover
Accommodation:	Camping permitted on request but no facilities

Getting there
To reach Lake Magadi the visitor has to drive south-west from Nairobi for 110km on the C 58 passing Olorgesaillie Prehistoric Site *en route.* Thanks to the Magadi Soda Company, the road is tarmacked for its entire length and the journey is easier than most in Kenya. From Nairobi, take the Magadi Road where it splits from Langata Road just beyond the main entrance to Nairobi National Park. Continue south, pausing to admire the stunning views as you descend in 'steps' down the side of the Great Rift Valley. At Magadi town on the east side of the lake you pass through a Magadi Soda Company security post where you must report your arrival.

About the lake
Lake Magadi is the southernmost of Kenya's rift valley lakes and lies at an altitude of approximately 610m (2000 feet) above sea level. The surrounding countryside is arid semi-desert. What little rain that falls, collects in the basin of the lake from which there is no outlet. Searing daytime temperatures, which may exceed 40°C, fuel the process of evaporation and cause the concentration of salts for which the lake is famous.

Lake Magadi is a vast alkaline waterbody covering an area of over 104km^2. When seen for the first time, the term 'lake' may appear a little misleading, since large areas of the surface are covered with an encrusting layer of white soda. Man-made evaporation pans accelerate the process of crystallization and elsewhere the red soda ash which lies beneath the surface is excavated and stains the white surroundings.

Soda production and export contributes significantly to Kenya's foreign exchange.

Lake Magadi is a working lake, producing large quantities of soda for export.

Lake Magadi is the world's second largest producer of trona after California's man-made Salton Sea, which lies below sea level in the Colorado Desert.

Birds

Birds are the main wildlife attraction of Lake Magadi and a wide variety of species can be seen from the eastern and southern shores. Although the encrusting lakeshore is not firm enough to support the weight of bird-watchers, thereby preventing too close an approach in most places, causeways provide an excellent means of observing the birds at close range. Areas of hot springs around the southern end of the lake also tend to concentrate the birds.

Given the searing temperatures and the alkalinity of the water, it is a wonder at first sight that anything survives here. However, a few species of algae are able to thrive under these conditions and provide the basis of a food web which supports a few species of invertebrates in abundance.

Lake Magadi's flamingos

Flamingos are the most conspicuous and colourful residents of Lake Magadi. Lesser Flamingos usually outnumber their Greater relatives; not only are they smaller but the bill is a deep carmine-red, compared with the Greater Flamingo's pale pink bill with a black tip, and the Lesser's plumage is flushed deep pink. Both species tend to concentrate around the southern end of the lake and can be seen feeding in the characteristic flamingo manner, filtering tiny plants and animals from the water with head immersed and bill upturned.

The number of flamingos at Lake Magadi is rather unpredictable and can vary greatly even from week to week. They have very precise requirements for optimum feeding and birds regularly commute between Magadi and neighbouring Lake Natron, which lies just across the border in Tanzania, if conditions do not suit them. If feeding is particularly good, however, they sometimes even breed at Lake Magadi.

Other waterbirds

Although the flamingos immediately catch the eye of visitors to Lake Magadi, bird-watching interest is not confined to them by

White pelicans (Pelecanus onocrotalus) are common on many of East Africa's lakes, including Lake Magadi. Their numbers are boosted during the northern hemisphere winter by migrants from Europe and Asia. White Pelicans catch fish in their pouches. Sometimes they fish co-operatively, groups of birds surrounding shoals of fish.

SECTION II: SITE GUIDE

any means. White Pelicans and Pink-backed
Pelicans cruise serenely across the water's
surface and Goliath Herons, Saddle-bill
Storks, African Spoonbills and Little Egrets
feed around the margins.

Among the wading birds, Black-winged
Stilts and Avocets are the species most commonly found around the shores. Stilts are
easily recognized by their black-and-white
plumage, long, thin bill and incredibly long
red legs. Avocets on the other hand have a
distinctive, upturned bill with which they
scythe through the water.

Several other species of wader occur on
passage but it is for the very rare Chestnut-
banded Sand Plover that Magadi is renowned in birdwatching circles: this is the
only place in Kenya where it can be found. It
occurs around the lake margins and can be
recognized by its typical plover-like appearance and the narrow and pale, yet distinct
chestnut band across the breast. It is roughly
the same size and shape as the more widespread Kittlitz's Plover.

When to visit

Most people visit Lake Magadi on a day trip
from Nairobi and consequently arrive during
the mid-morning as temperatures are beginning to soar. The earlier you can time your
arrival the better; not only will there be more
bird activity but conditions will be more
suitable for birdwatching.

The surrounding arid country is also good
for wildlife and much can be seen from the
road as you approach the lake. Mammals,
such as Impala, Fringe-eared Oryx, Gerenuk,
Giraffe and Grant's Gazelle, all occur and
baboons are sometimes seen crossing the
road. A variety of birds such as Kori Bustard,
White-bellied Go-away Bird, Spotted Stone
Curlew and Pale Chanting Goshawk can be
found in the scrub.

6 AMBOSELI NATIONAL PARK	
Location:	S of Nairobi; nearest towns Namanga and Oloitokitok
Access:	Dirt tracks; four-wheel-drive vehicle advisable
Terrain:	Open plains; acacia woodland; swamps
Specialities:	Elephant, Black Rhinoceros, Gerenuk, Kori Bustard, waterbirds, views of Mt Kilimanjaro
Accommodation:	Several lodges, campsite and bandas

Above: Amboseli is one of Kenya's most popular
national parks.
Opposite: map of Amboseli National Park.

44

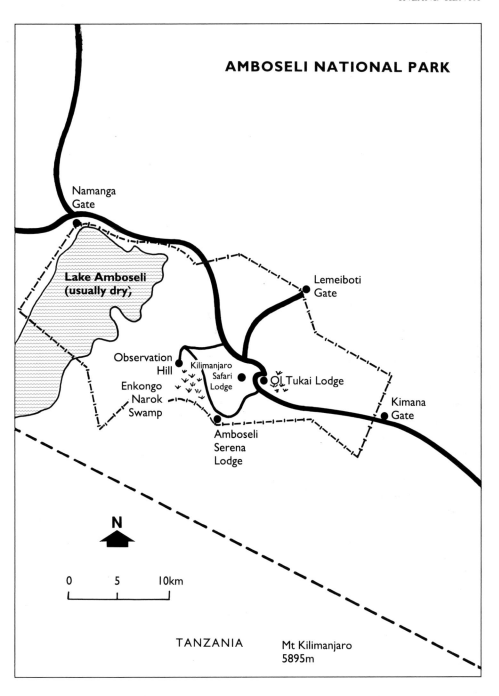

AMBOSELI NATIONAL PARK

Namanga
Gate

**Lake Amboseli
(usually dry)**

Lemeiboti
Gate

Observation
Hill

Kilimanjaro
Safari
Lodge

Ol Tukai Lodge

Enkongo
Narok
Swamp

Amboseli
Serena
Lodge

Kimana
Gate

N

0   5   10km

TANZANIA   Mt Kilimanjaro
5895m

45

Getting there

To reach Amboseli National Park involves a drive south from Nairobi of about 240km. There are two main routes and both involve leaving the city on the A 109 Mombasa road. The most popular route leaves the A 109 at the town of Athi River and heads south on the A 104 to Kajiado and Namanga; the road continues over the Tanzanian border to Arusha. At Namanga turn left onto the C 103, a rough but passable road which leads to the Namanga Gate entrance to the park and on to Amboseli Lodge, Ol Tukai Lodge and the swamps.

The alternative route to Amboseli involves leaving the A 109 Mombasa road at the town of Sultan Hamud and heading south on the C 102, also known as the Pipeline Road, towards Oloitokitok. Before the town turn right towards the park; you enter Amboseli by the Kimana Gate. This second route has advantages and disadvantages compared to the Namanga road. The road surface is rough and consequently the journey takes longer. However, there are generally more birds and mammals to be seen along the way. As a rough guide, if you are in a hurry take the Namanga route, but if you can afford to go slowly, take the Oloitokitok route.

About the park

Amboseli has enjoyed protected status in one form or another since 1948 although its fate has been somewhat chequered and not without controversy. In 1948, the area became the Amboseli Reserve with part of the area being set aside for wildlife and the rest being used by the Masai people; in 1961 it became a Masai Game Reserve.

Although the wildlife suffered little direct harm from the Masai, grazing pressure from the Masai herds eventually began to conflict with the interests of the game animals. In 1970 the Masai were excluded from land around the swamps. While this benefitted the wildlife in the short term, it caused considerable ill-feeling among the Masai who responded by taking direct action against Amboseli's rhino population. Fortunately the problems were resolved when bore holes were created for the Masai and 3199km² of the game reserve acquired national park status.

Amboseli National Park gets its name from Lake Amboseli, whose dry bed is an almost permanent feature of the west of the park. However, the most distinctive feature of the area lies outside the park boundaries and is not even in Kenya. Mt Kilimanjaro, across the border in Tanzania, towers above the surrounding land and dominates the landscape.

Kilimanjaro is Africa's highest mountain reaching 5895m (19,341 feet) above sea level. Seen from the park, the summit, Uhuru Peak, is on the right while the sharper peak, Mawenzi, is on the left and reaches 5149m (16,893 feet). The snow-capped peak can be rather elusive, however, and is often shrouded in mist and cloud. Early mornings or late afternoons generally provide the best opportunities for uninterrupted views.

The name 'Amboseli' derives from the Masai word for salt dust and indeed first impressions of this national park are of an arid dustbowl. However, spend more than a few hours here and the richness of its wildlife soon belies the bleak and inhospitable landscape; it is undoubtedly one of the best places in Kenya for viewing mammals and birds.

Mammals

The dry plains which comprise much of the terrain in Amboseli are surprisingly rich in game animals. Impala, Wildebeest and Zebra and Thomson's and Grant's Gazelles are all common. Naturally, predators also do well and both Lions and Cheetahs are regularly encountered. In the past, it was a sad indictment of the level of tourism in Amboseli that by far the easiest way to find the big cats was to watch for dust trails on the horizon as landrovers and trucks rapidly converged when a family group was sighted. Today, off-road driving is prohibited so erosion is less marked, but as a consequence the cats are more difficult to see.

Big cats usually hunt at dawn and dusk and it is still possible to watch this gripping spectacle in Amboseli although nowadays you are seldom able to watch them alone. If you feel that the animals are being disturbed, then please back away and watch from a distance. There is a regrettable, but understandable, tendency for vehicles to drive right up to a kill on the assumption that the cats do not mind.

Although largely nocturnal, Bat-eared Foxes are sometimes seen on the open plains of Amboseli. They live in burrows and dens but like to bask in sunshine at the entrance, especially in the early morning. Bat-eared Foxes usually live in small groups and so where you see one you may be lucky enough to see several.

Bird life in the park

Dry-country birds are also abundant in Amboseli National Park. Ostriches are not difficult to find and there are several species of bustards present for the birdwatching

Herds of Common Zebras, Wildebeest and Elephants concentrate around the swamps where grazing is good.

Top: *Spotted Stone Curlew* (Burhinus capensis).
Bottom: *Lilac-breasted Roller* (Corocias caudatus).

Kori Bustard *Ardeotis kori* H 120

Kori Bustards are huge birds which stand over 120cm tall and, apart from Ostriches, are the largest species of landbird encountered in East Africa. Unlike Ostriches, however, they are capable of flight and are the heaviest bird in the world still capable of doing so.

The powerful legs are yellow while the wings and back are brown; the pale neck is finely marked with vermiculations. In most places, and especially in Amboseli National Park, Kori Bustards are indifferent to tourist vehicles and can be watched at close range as they strut across the plains at a leisurely pace. Males have an extraordinary display involving inflating the throat to the shape of a balloon. Several other species of bustards occur in East Africa, often sharing the same habitat as the Kori Bustard. However, this species is easily recognized by its size alone.

enthusiast. The largest species is the Kori Bustard, the heaviest bird capable of flight. Lucky visitors may even see a male displaying: the neck is inflated like a balloon and the tail raised over the back. Other bustards found in Amboseli include White-bellied, Buff-crested and Black-bellied. Chestnut-bellied Sandgrouse, Spotted Stone Curlew, Temminck's and Two-banded Courser are other plains birds which may be seen.

Wildlife of the acacia scrub
Patches of acacia scrub provide an interesting alternative habitat to the open landscape. Gerenuks, long-necked antelopes that often feed standing on their hind legs, are often seen, and birds include several species of birds of prey such as the diminutive Pygmy Falcon, which breeds in the nests of White-headed Buffalo Weavers, and Tawny Eagles, Greater Kestrels and African Hawk Eagles. White-crowned Shrikes and Taita Fiscals can also be found and Taveta Golden Weaver, a bird almost unknown outside the boundaries

of Amboseli, is commonly seen. One of the most spectacular of Kenya's birds can also be found among the acacias by careful searching. Verreaux's Eagle Owl stands over 60cm tall, and roosts unobtrusively amongst the foliage by day. The best field character is its whitish face with a black border.

Amboseli's swamps

Although the open plains offer superb opportunities for watching wildlife, it is the marshes and swamps that are most rewarding. They not only harbour birds and mammals that are tied to water, but they also act as magnets for the wildlife of the surrounding arid countryside; sooner or later you will find almost all of Amboseli's species around the swamp's margins.

Mt Kilimanjaro not only provides a superb backdrop to Amboseli but it is also responsible for maintaining a constant supply of water to the swamps. Meltwaters from the snow-capped peak feed streams which trickle through the volcanic soil and in turn feed underground springs within the park boundaries. Amboseli Lodge and Ol Tukai Lodge lie at the focal point of wildlife interest in the park; to the west lies Enkongo Narok Swamp while to the east is Laginye Swamp. Main roads border the Laginye Swamp on two sides and Enkongo Narok is bordered by tracks only suitable for four-wheel-drive vehicles.

Elephants and Rhinoceroses

Elephants are frequent visitors to the swamps and marshes. They bathe and wallow in the margins, drink the water and graze the comparatively lush vegetation that the swamps support. Stands of Yellow-barked Acacia which border the swamps often show considerable damage from these immense animals. Elephants that have had a recent dip

will have a noticeable tideline below which the dusty Amboseli soil has been washed off.

Black Rhinoceroses also favour the swamps and are best looked for at dawn and dusk. Despite the fact that they are large and cumbersome-looking creatures, rhinos can be extremely hard to find at Amboseli, especially if they are resting among tall wetland grasses. You can stare for hours on end at a patch of vegetation where you have been assured a rhino is resting and still see nothing. The impatient may give up, convinced that they are being hoaxed, but the more persistent may be rewarded when the animal finally decides to move.

Wetland birds

The bird life of Amboseli's swamps is prolific. A morning drive lasting no more than a few hours should produce species such as White Pelican, Pink-backed Pelican, Little Grebe,

Long-toed Lapwings (Vanellus crassirostris) are common around Amboseli's swamps.

African Darter, Squacco Heron, Purple Heron, egrets, Egyptian Goose and Knob-billed Duck. Black-winged Stilts and Kittlitz's Plovers feed around the margins, and Long-toed Lapwings and African Jacanas trot across the surface vegetation. The swamps provide excellent opportunities for observing the tiny Black Crake. This bird, and many others too, keep a wary eye open for African Fish Eagles which do not confine their diet entirely to fish by any means; listen for their loud mewing call which is reminiscent of a Herring Gull.

Observation Hill
One the best views in Amboseli is to be had from Observation Hill. To reach it, cross Enkongo Narok Swamp by the causeway that bisects it half-way along its length. From the parking spot at the base of the hill, it is a short hike to the top and the observation hut from which panoramic views of the swamps and open plains can be had. Visitors are often able to see large groups of Elephants feeding and bathing below.

When to visit
To get the most from a visit to Amboseli, try to do a drive at dawn or soon after to see the peak of activity among the birds and game animals. At this time of day you are most likely to see Lions or Cheetahs kill or, more likely, find them after the fatal event when they are eating their quarry. The open plains are worth searching first of all before you move on to the edge of the swamp for Elephants and waterbirds.

The main disadvantage about a dawn drive in Amboseli is that, unfortunately, almost everyone else will have the same idea. In most places in Kenya, sensible visitors take a few hours off at midday since the temperatures are at their hottest, the mammals and

Gerenuk *Litocranius walleri*
L 140–160 (head and body)

The Gerenuk is one of the most unusual antelopes found in East Africa and is frequently seen in groups of two or three. Sometimes called Giraffe-necked Antelopes, they are characterized by their exceedingly long necks and correspondingly long legs; the eyes are noticeably large and males have long horns which curve backwards over the head.

Gerenuks live in arid bush country where there is little vegetation to graze at ground level. Instead of searching here, they feed by standing on their hind legs and stretching up to eat leaves and shoots out of reach of other species of antelope. Gerenuks are so well adapted to life in a dry environment that they appear not to need to drink water. They are commonly seen in Samburu National Park and sometimes on the approach roads to Amboseli from Kimana to the east and Namanga to the west.

birds are at their least active and the light is poor for photography (the midday equatorial sun produces harsh shadows and unsatis-factory photographic results). However, at Amboseli, midday can be the time when fewest vehicles and people are out and about and this may be compensation enough.

Tourism and wildlife conservation
The increase in tourism at Amboseli is sadly leading to its deterioration as a wildlife habi-tat. Many of the big cats have changed their feeding and behaviour patterns to minimize their contact with the tourists, and the sheer number of vehicles is eroding the fragile semi-desert vegetation and turning much of the land into a dustbowl. It is to be hoped that the Kenyan authorities can find a happy compromise which allows people to visit and enjoy Amboseli and also ensures the survival of the wildlife. Certainly, banning off-road driving has greatly improved matters.

Staying at Amboseli
Amboseli caters well for visitors and there is a good range of types of accommodation and prices to match. Cheapest of all is camping; there is a campsite which lies close to and just outside the southern boundary of the park near Observation Hill. The campsite office, within the borders of the park, is well sign-posted and must be visited when you arrive. The campsite is home to Taveta Golden Weavers and White-tailed Mongooses which sometimes visit camp fires at night. In the past, Elephants occasionally plodded be-tween the tents during the night, but an electric fence now surrounds the site. The eerie screams of Spotted Hyenas may still keep those of a nervous disposition awake!

Also outside the park boundaries are the Kimana Safari Lodge near Kimana to the south-east and Kilimanjaro Buffalo Lodge

reached via the Lemeiboti Gate. Within the park itself, there are four lodges: Amboseli Lodge; Kilimanjaro Safari Lodge; Amboseli Safari Lodge, overlooking the Enkongo Narok Swamp; and Ol Tukai Lodge. There are also cheap bandas at the latter lodge.

7 TSAVO NATIONAL PARK

Location:	SE of Nairobi; bisected by Mombasa Road
Access:	Dirt tracks; many only suitable for four-wheel-drive vehicles
Terrain:	Thorn scrub; semi-desert; freshwater springs
Specialities:	Baobab Tree, Elephant, Lesser Kudu
Accommodation:	Safari lodges and campsites

Getting there
To reach Tsavo National Park, drive south-east from Nairobi on the Mombasa Road, (A 109). There are numerous entrances to the park but the main gate for Tsavo West is at Mtito Andei which lies about 240km from the capital. The main road is good but there-after those in the park deteriorate in quality.

About the park
Tsavo National Park is the largest national park in Kenya, covering over 21,000km². The Nairobi to Mombasa Road cuts through the middle of the park and for administrative convenience this marks the boundary be-tween the two halves. To the south-west of the road is Tsavo West with park head-quarters at Mtito Andei and Kamboyo, while to the north-east of the road is Tsavo East with park headquarters at Voi.

For the purist, Tsavo National Park offers a taste of 'real' Africa. The vast herds and

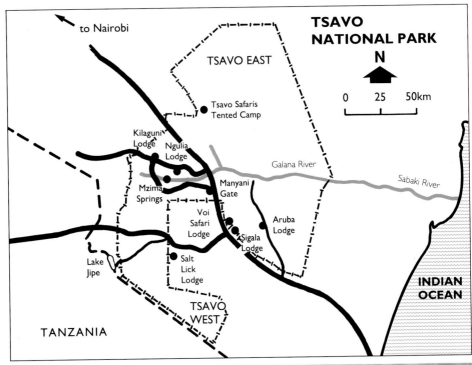

open landscape of Masai Mara and Amboseli are missing and are replaced for the most part by seemingly impenetrable thorn scrub. In Tsavo you have to work hard to see your animals; game mammals use the cover to best advantage and even Elephants, now sadly depleted in numbers due to ivory poaching, can be hard to locate. However, this is what Africa must have been like for the first settlers. The unspoilt, wild feeling that embraces Tsavo combined with the magnificent volcanic scenery and red soils make a trip here a memorable one.

Tsavo West

Tsavo West covers an area of over 9000km^2 and arid thorn scrub masking the characteristic red soils. Volcanic cones dot the horizon here and there making the landscape one of the most distinctive in Kenya. Just outside the boundary of the park there are solidified lava flows at Mt Sheitani, while within the park the famous Mzima Springs and the Tsavo River add to the variety.

There are several access points to Tsavo West. From the main Nairobi to Mombasa road there are gates at Mtito Andei, Tsavo and Manyani, while if you are approaching from Oloitokitok (coming from Amboseli) the Chyulu Gate affords access. If you are travelling from Arusha and Moshi in Tanzania, there is the Mbuyuni Gate just beyond Taveta and the Maktau Gate if you continue through the park on the A 23 towards Voi.

Wildlife from the road

Although Tsavo West holds almost all the mammals that visitors could expect to find in

Opposite above: *map of Tsavo National Park.* **Opposite below:** *these man-made waterholes in Tsavo National Park attract a wide variety of game mammals and birds.*

Mt Sheitani erupted roughly 200 years ago. The cone and lava flows can be explored.

Amboseli or Masai Mara, they occur in smaller numbers and are much harder to see. By their very size, Giraffes often stand head and shoulders above the scrubby vegetation, but the few remaining Elephants can be rather difficult to locate. If you are lucky enough to see a small herd you will immediately notice that their hides are stained red from mud and dust baths in the red soil.

Unlike their plains counterparts, the Zebras in Tsavo West can be hard to see, not so much because they are wary, but because their stripes serve as superb camouflage in this terrain. Likewise Impala, Gerenuk and Lesser Kudu, the latter a speciality of Tsavo, require persistent searching. If you have already been to one of the open savannah parks

53

Lion *Panthera leo* L 145–200 (head and body)

Lions are still present in Tsavo in good numbers but, as with other mammals, the terrain makes them difficult to see. They acquired notoriety for their consumption of workers building the Nairobi to Mombasa railway at the turn of the century as described in JH Paterson's book *The Man Eaters of Tsavo*. Although nowadays they confine their attentions to the game for the most part, they would present a very real danger to anyone foolish enough to dismount illegally from their vehicle at other than designated locations.

before visiting Tsavo, it may take a while to get adjusted to actually having to search for game mammals. If, on the other hand, Tsavo is your first stop it will seem like an exciting adventure; subsequent trips to Amboseli may seem rather tame by comparison.

The state of the park roads usually necessitates slow progress even in a four-wheel-drive vehicle. However, a slow speed is what is needed for optimum wildlife watching. Occasionally you will have to grind to a halt to allow a troop of Baboons to cross the road; they will leave you in no doubt as to who they think has right of way on Tsavo's roads!

Although Elephants still wander freely across Tsavo's vast landscape, albeit in greatly reduced numbers, the same cannot be said for the park's Black Rhinoceroses. Sadly, poaching for their horns has almost wiped them out and the only place you are likely to see one is in the sanctuary near Ngulia Safari Lodge.

Birds

Birdwatching from the car can often be more rewarding in terms of numbers of species seen than game watching. Namaqua Doves, usually seen in twos or threes, often feed beside the road along with Fawn-coloured Larks. In the scrub adjacent to the road look for Ostriches, Kori Bustards and Black-bellied Bustards; there is even a chance of seeing Ground Hornbills which often go around in pairs. These large birds are immediately recognized by their all-black plumage, immense bill, red wattles and plodding gait.

Because the vegetation is so dense in places, it is often only those birds that perch on exposed branches that can be seen well enough to be identified. Look for Taita Fiscal, Long-tailed Fiscal, Lilac-breasted Roller, Blue-naped Mousebird and Pygmy Falcon. Wherever you come across a flowering bush or tree it is worth stopping for a few minutes to see what comes to feed; lucky observers may find Hunter's Sunbird or Tsavo Purple-banded Sunbird. Some birds do not regularly use perches and spend much of the time in flight; look for the distinctive 'pinched-wing' silhouette of Verreaux's Eagles soaring in pairs near rocky outcrops.

Mzima Springs

Without doubt, the highlight of many people's trip to Tsavo West is a visit to Mzima Springs which lie about 10km from Kilaguni Lodge. As unexpected as they are welcome in

The Squacco Heron (Ardeola ralloides) is one of several species of herons and egrets to be found along the lake margins and swamps in East Africa. Like its relatives, the Squacco Heron relies on patience and stealth to catch its prey which includes fish and frogs. They often remain motionless for minutes at a time providing the wildlife photographer with excellent opportunities.

this arid terrain, the springs produce in excess of 50 millions gallons of water a day, 7 million of which are piped to the coast to quench the thirst of Mombasa's inhabitants. Their origins lie in the meltwaters of snow-capped Mt Kilimanjaro, although they are supplemented by underground streams in the Chyulu Hills. After percolating through the volcanic rocks the water reaches the surface at Mzima, cool, clear and pure.

Mzima Springs' large population of Hippopotamuses are the main attraction for visitors. These can be seen wallowing in the water from the banks of the springs but it is also possible to see them in their element. Mzima boasts a walk-in observation tank, built by a visiting film crew some time ago. The glass sides allow eye-to-eye contact with the Hippos along with Nile Crocodiles and a host of fish including barbel whose nibbling activities clean the Hippos' hides.

Early mornings are best for Hippopotamus watching since later in the day they move to find shade among the waterside vegetation. Another reason that the Hippos depart soon after visitors arrive is that inconsiderate people tap on the glass and drive them away. Visitors should exercise a degree of caution when entering the observation tank first thing in the morning, however, because on more than one occasion a cobra has been found that has taken up residence during the night!

Downstream from the observation tank the banks become overgrown with Papyrus, Date Palms and Raphia Palms. Keen birdwatchers may wish to try to identify the species of cisticolas (tiny warbler-like birds) that occur here or look for the secretive Peter's Finfoot which swims among the tangled water vegetation.

Wildlife around the lodges

Tsavo West is served by several lodges both within its borders and just outside. One of the most popular is the Kilaguni Lodge, which is conveniently situated for the Sheitani Lava Flows and Mzima Springs; it is surprisingly good for wildlife. Even if you are not booked in to stay there it is worth a visit. You can sit on the verandah sipping a cool drink while watching game animals and birds at close range.

On arrival at Kilaguni Lodge, the first

55

creatures to catch the attention of visitors are usually the Agama Lizards. Males, resplendent with orange heads and bright blue bodies, sit and sunbathe on prominent boulders and even in the flower borders. Inside the lodge itself, a verandah overlooks two man-made waterholes in a classic Tsavo setting with bright red soils and thorn scrub stretching as far as the eye can see.

Just beyond the verandah, food is put out for the birds and close views can be had of many colourful and unusual species. Red-billed Hornbills are particularly conspicuous but no less attractive are the colourful d'Arnaud's Barbets that also regularly appear. Also look for Superb Starling, Red-billed Buffalo Weaver and White-browed Sparrow Weaver.

Rock Hyraxes and Warthogs also venture close to the lodge buildings but most of the game animals come solely to the waterholes. Nevertheless, excellent views can be obtained of Wildebeest, Zebras and Giraffes often with Marabou Storks and Egyptian Vultures in attendance. If you stay until dark, other more nocturnal species may appear at the illuminated waterholes while several species of nightjars hawk insects around the lodge lights. There is also a waterhole, as well as a salt-lick at Ngulia Lodge which attracts a wide variety of animals after dark including Leopards.

Outside Tsavo West's boundaries

As you approach Tsavo West from the direction of Amboseli National Park and Oloito-kitok you pass the Sheitani Lava Flow just before you reach the Chyulu Gate. Here, visitors can park their cars and explore the flows, formed comparatively recently in geological terms. The more adventurous may even wish to climb to the rim of Mt Sheitani.

Lake Jipe, which lies on the western

Baobab Tree *Adansonia digitata*

The Baobab tree is one of the most characteristic sights in Tsavo. Sometimes known as the 'upside-down tree', it has a swollen trunk and branches which appear leafless for much of the year, adding to its resemblance to a tree turned upside down with its roots exposed. The fruit and leaves are eaten by native people and the bark yields a strong fibre. At one time, Baobabs in Tsavo were subject to considerable damage by Elephants who were thought to be obtaining water from them in times of drought. Today, visitors can still see tree trunks which bear the scars.

boundaries of the park and straddles the border with Tanzania, provides an interesting contrast to the arid country that surrounds it. Fringed by reed-beds and waterside vegetation it is home to a wide variety of waterbirds, including several species of egrets and herons as well as African Skimmer, Egyptian Goose, African Spoonbill, Black-winged Stilt and Pied Kingfisher.

Staying in Tsavo West

The best-known place to stay is Kilaguni Lodge which lies at the crossroads of roads leading south from the Mtito Andei Gate and east from the Chyulu Gate. Continue east along the road towards the Tsavo Gate and you will come to the Ngulia Lodge, which boasts fantastic views down over the

Agama Lizards (Agama agama) are colourful and conspicuous.

African Elephant *Loxodonta africana* H 3.5m

Elephants are the largest land mammals, bulls reaching 3.65m at the shoulder and sometimes weighing more than 5 tonnes. They bear ivory tusks (modified teeth) which are used in defence, courtship and feeding but have also been the major cause of their destruction. At one time the Elephant population in Tsavo was vast, numbering in excess of 50,000 animals, the herds being the pride of East Africa. So many animals were present at one stage that they had a noticeable effect on the vegetation, damaging mature trees and preventing new growth. Culling the herds was seriously proposed, not without considerable controversy, but in the end their demise came about as a result of the guns of ivory poachers and not those of the wildlife authorities. Today less than 10% of the original number survive in Tsavo.

edge of an escarpment and is worth a visit even if you do not plan to stay there.

For less cossetted, and cheaper, accommodation visitors can use the Ngulia Safari Camp, near the lodge of the same name, or the Kitani Safari Camp which is near both Kilaguni Lodge and Mzima Springs. At these sites, all your requirements for a night under canvas can be provided. For a more rudimentary stop, there is a campsite just outside the Chyulu Gate. Here, basic toilet and washing facilities are located although these are frequently wrecked by local troops of Baboons. Also outside the park are the Taita Hills Lodge and the Salt Lick Lodge near the road to Voi, both of which offer first-class accommodation at a price.

Tsavo East

For the most part, the 11,747km² that is Tsavo East remain largely unexplored and unexplorable to most visitors to Kenya. The terrain is rough and untamed and all roads north and east of the Galana River are closed except by special permission. Nevertheless, those parts of Tsavo East that can be visited offer superb scenery and a rich variety of wildlife.

Access to Tsavo East is usually from the main Nairobi-Mombasa road (A 109). There are gates at Mtito Andei, Voi and Buchuma. From the gates, roads lead to the lodges and safari camps. The Sala Gate close to the Galana River marks the eastern boundary of Tsavo East where visitors can leave and follow the C 103 all the way to Malindi.

The most noticeable feature of the park is the Yatta Plateau which runs parallel to the Nairobi-Mombasa road. It is made up of the eroded and weathered remains of a lava flow from Ol Doinyo Sapuk which lies close to Nairobi. The Galana River, on which lie the

Lugard Falls, cuts across the park from west to east on its way to the coast at Malindi, where it is renamed the Sabaki River.

What to see in Tsavo East
Driving along the roads in Tsavo East you are likely to encounter much the same species as in its western counterpart. Mammals should include Zebra, Impala, Giraffe and perhaps even Beisa Oryx. Look for Lilac-breasted Roller, Golden-breasted Starling, White-bellied Go-away Bird and Striped Kingfisher perched beside the road.

One of the most spectacular places to visit in Tsavo East is Mudanda Rock, a great out-crop of reddish rock close to the main road between Voi and Manyani Gate. The rock is sign-posted from this road and visitors can climb from the car-park and get superb views over the surrounding land and see the water-hole and wildlife at its base.

The Lugard Falls lie on the Galana River as you drive east on the C 103 from Manyani, just beyond the confluence of the Tsavo and Athi Rivers. The falls are particularly spectacular when in spate and support a sizeable population of Nile Crocodiles at their base. These can also be seen at the Crocodile Tented Camp which lies further down the road to Malindi, just beyond the Sala Gate. Also beyond the gate, and outside the boundaries of the national park, lies the Galana Game Ranch which is a privately owned game reserve.

Staying at Tsavo East
A dirt track leads from the Mtito Andei Gate to the Athi River, on the other side of which lies the Tsavo Safari Camp; a boat ferries visitors across. A prior booking must be made in Nairobi before attempting this trip.

Voi Safari Lodge lies close to the Voi Gate and overlooks two waterholes from its hill-side vantage point. Aruba Lodge, which is close to the man-made Aruba Dam, can be reached either from Voi Gate or from Buchuma Gate to the south.

8 CHYULU HILLS NATIONAL PARK	
Location:	SE of Nairobi adjacent to the Mombasa road
Access:	Rough tracks, suitable only for four-wheel-drive vehicles; scope for hill walking
Terrain:	Rough grassland; pockets of hill forest
Specialities:	Sunbirds, Secretary Bird
Accommodation:	Camping; bring plenty of supplies, including water

Getting there
The Chyulu Hills National Park lies between Amboseli and Tsavo about 150km south-east of Nairobi. The hills run roughly parallel to the main Nairobi–Mombasa road. To reach them leave Nairobi on the A 109 Mombasa road and at Sultan Hamud turn off south down the Pipeline Road (C 102) that leads eventually to Oloitokitok. At Makutano turn off left and follow the dirt track that climbs up the Chyulu Range and runs along the chain. The road eventually descends and joins the C 103 near Kilaguni Lodge. The surface of the track is only suitable for four-wheel-drive vehicles.

About the park
The Chyulu Hills are comparatively recent in origin, having been formed as a result of volcanic activity about 500 years ago. Within the approximately 500km² that comprise the national park, the hills rise to 2081m (6827 feet). The Chyulus are contiguous, at their

Adjoining Tsavo National Park, the Chyulu Hills comprise rolling uplands and remnant pockets of highland forest. Mists hang over the hills at dawn but are soon burnt away by the East African sun. The Chyulu Hills receive comparatively few visitors and offer good opportunities for trekking and camping.

south-eastern end, with the borders of Tsavo The scenery and vegetation of the Chyulu Hills contrast markedly with nearby parks such as Tsavo and Amboseli. The rolling slopes are covered in green grassland and there are remnant pockets of the evergreen hill forest that once cloaked the range. The whole scene looks distinctly English in places and areas where Bracken grows in profusion could pass, at a superficial glance, for downland areas of Surrey. It is not until you see antelopes or exotic sunbirds that the illusion is shattered.

One of the reasons why the Chyulu Hills are so popular with the Masai people is the presence of a plant called *Miraa*. Known locally as the 'stay-awake plant', its leaves are harvested and sold to be chewed as a mild stimulant.

Wildlife of the Chyulu Hills
Since people wander freely through the Chyulus, game animals tend to be hard to see. However, the birds are more conspicuous and Secretary Birds are often seen walking through the long grass ever-alert for the snakes that make up their diet. Trees and bushes should be searched for Cinnamon-chested Bee-eater, Black Cuckoo Shrike, Red-faced Crombec, Rufous Chatterer and White-browed Coucal.

Sunbirds galore
Beside the track you will often see large clumps of red flowering spikes, rather reminiscent of the familiar garden plant, Red Hot Poker. This is *Leonotis mollisima*, a favourite source of nectar for sunbirds. A good way to see them is simply to find a likely looking clump of flowers and wait. Sunbirds are not particularly wary birds if you keep still and you may encounter several species in a few minutes; likely candidates include Golden-winged, Variable, Tacazze, Olive and Malachite Sunbirds.

Staying in the Chyulu Hills
The only way to stay in the Chyulu Hills is to camp. Since there is little or no surface water available, visitors are advised to take plenty with them. Nights can be extremely damp and chilly and so warm, dry clothing is also advisable. However, despite the inconveniences, the scene at dawn, with mist and clouds rolling off the forest-clad slopes, is a memorable one.

9 MASAI MARA NATIONAL RESERVE	
Location:	W of Nairobi, adjacent to the Tanzanian border
Access:	One good road through the reserve; other tracks can be explored in dry weather; four-wheel-drive vehicle advisable
Terrain:	Open grassy plains; pockets of acacia woodland; Mara River
Specialities:	The 'big five'; Hunting Dogs, Spotted Hyenas, spectacular Wildebeest and Zebra migration
Accommodation:	Lodges, tented camps and campsites; book in advance

Getting there

Although many people choose to fly to the Masai Mara, there being daily scheduled flights from Nairobi as well as private planes for hire, most visitors drive there from the capital. The roads get steadily worse as you approach the reserve and a four-wheel drive vehicle is strongly advised.

To reach Masai Mara, leave Nairobi on the Nakuru Road (A 104) heading northwest. Turn left onto the B 3 and head towards Narok passing through vast prairies of cultivated fields. At Narok stop for fuel, and then continue on your journey. Beyond Narok the going becomes slow and you have a choice of two routes. The most straightforward is to turn left onto the C 12 just beyond Uwaso Ngiro (it is sign-posted to Keekorok Lodge and Cottar's Camp) and enter the reserve by the Olemelepo Gate. Alternatively, ignore this turning and continue straight on to reach the western end of

Above: *Masai Mara National Reserve, Kenya's best known wildlife location.*
Opposite above: *map of Masai Mara National Reserve.*
Opposite below: *Hippopotamuses (Hippopotamus amphibius) sunbathing.*

the reserve at the Mara River and enter by the Ololfolo Gate.

About the park

The Masai Mara National Reserve is Kenya's best known wildlife location both for the variety of species that it holds and the numbers. The 'big five' (Lion, Leopard, Buffalo, Elephant and Black Rhinoceros) are all here and between July and August countless hundreds of thousands of Wildebeest and Zebra congregate in the reserve.

Masai Mara lies in south-west Kenya with the Tanzanian border as its southern boundary. It forms an extension of the Serengeti Plains of Tanzania and indeed is contiguous

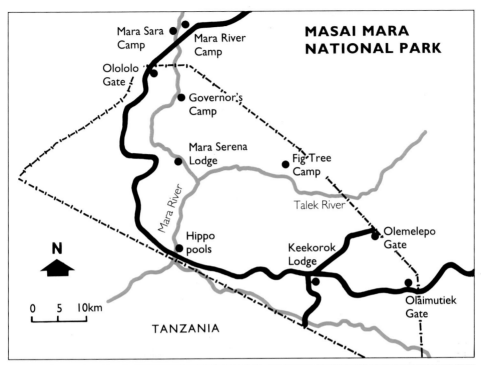

MASAI MARA NATIONAL PARK

Mara Sara Camp
Mara River Camp
Olololo Gate
Governor's Camp
Mara Serena Lodge
Fig Tree Camp
Mara River
Talek River
Hippo pools
Keekorok Lodge
Olemelepo Gate
Olaimutiek Gate
N
0 5 10km
TANZANIA

with the Serengeti National Park (*see* p.140). To the west of the reserve lies the Esoit Olololo Escarpment while to the north and east the Mara merges into the Loita Plains and Loita Hills. The Sand River runs along the southern boundary of the reserve, the Mara River runs from north to south through the reserve with the Talek River joining it in the centre of the reserve.

By comparison with Tsavo National Park, the Masai Mara is small, occupying a modest 1670km^2. However, its size belies its importance to wildlife since it holds arguably the greatest concentration of game animals anywhere on Earth. The reason for its importance lies in the fact that it adjoins the Serengeti, allowing Wildebeest and Zebra in particular to follow their annual migration cycle in search of new growth of grass after the rains.

The scenery in the Masai Mara is quintessentially East African. Most of the land is grassland which for much of the year is dry and golden brown in appearance. Here and there, acacia bushes dot the vista and in places, especially along the water courses, there are stands of woodland.

The spectacle of numbers

If you want to see vast herds of game animals, then the Masai Mara National Reserve is the place to visit. However, the huge numbers of animals are not present all year round and so you should time your trip accordingly. The best time to visit is from July until October, with the greatest numbers in July and August, when up to 2 million Wildebeest, 400,000 Zebra, 500,000 gazelles and tens of thousands of other species of antelope will be present.

The story starts in the southern Serengeti in December and January after the seasonal rains have promoted a new growth of grass

and provided surface water for drinking. The plain's animals congregate here for the next few months and the Wildebeest give birth to their calves. However, by April and May the grassland is parched and the herds begin to move northwards finally concentrating in the Masai Mara in July and August; here the rivers provide a constant supply of water and there is grazing, albeit of a marginal nature.

Man has undoubtedly contributed to the scale of this spectacle ,.as changes in land use on the Loita Plains and to the west of the reserve have reduced the land available for the herds and have had the effect of concentrating them in the Mara. Regrettably, in 1989 and 1990, the Wildebeest and Zebra failed to arrive in their usual numbers. It is to be hoped that this was just a 'natural' and temporary variation, although there is some suggestion that habitat disturbance in Tanzania may have interrupted their migration.

River crossings

Not only are visitors to the Masai Mara in July and August treated to the spectacle of vast numbers of game animals but, with luck, they can also witness the mass river crossings for which the area is also renowned. During their brief stay in the reserve the herds effectively do a circuit and in so doing have to cross the Sand, Talek and Mara Rivers. The animals are understandably nervous about this. Many are trampled and drown and there are unseen dangers, such as Crocodiles in the water and predators lying in ambush on the far bank of the river.

The same crossing points are usually used each year and these are well known by park guides. However, if visiting on your own it is still possible to see a crossing. One way is to simply watch where other vehicles are congregating beside rivers. The animals themselves also give clues to their intentions.

Above: the spectacle of Zebra and Wildebeest crossing the Mara River on migration.
Right: White-backed vultures (Gyps bengalenis) are one of four species of vulture regularly seen at 'kills' in East Africa. Despite their unattractive appearance and grizzly habits, they are fascinating to watch. They also fulfil a vital role in cleaning up carcasses on the East African plains. Within minutes of a kill occurring, vultures will appear on the scene.

From first light Wildebeest, Zebra and Topi, in that order of abundance, begin to gather on the riverbanks, nervously sniffing the air in anticipation. More and more gather until by mid-morning there may be several thousand. There is no retreat now for those nearest the bank and eventually, as if by some signal, they all charge into the water.

Seldom more than a dozen abreast, it may take half an hour for the crossing to be completed. After it is all over, the riverbanks are dotted with the corpses of those animals that did not make it, yet the vast majority of the migrating game cross unscathed.

Game mammals may appear to spend most of their time feeding. However, watch a group of Common Zebras, for example, for a while and you may see other patterns of behaviour: these two are engaged in mutual grooming. This not only helps keep their coats in good condition but also establishes bonds between the two animals.

Mammals at other times of year

Although it is only from July to September that the vast herds of Wildebeest and Zebra are present in the Masai Mara, you can always expect to see these species in smaller numbers, whatever time of year you visit. The best area for these, and most other smaller game animals too, is in the Mara Triangle, the south-western sector of the park bordered to the east by the main road through the reserve.

The best way to see game in the Masai Mara is to follow the course of the main track starting from wherever you happen to be staying. The main road runs from the Ololo-lo Gate down to the Mara New Bridge near the Tanzanian border, past Keekorok Lodge, and on to the Olemelepo and Olaimutiek Gates to the east. There is usually little need to leave the main route since there is always plenty to see from the road, although you may wish to do so if you find something especially interesting.

In addition to Wildebeest, Zebra, Impala, Thomson's Gazelle and Grant's Gazelle, keep an eye open for Topi. Males of these attractive antelopes characteristically stand on grassy knolls surveying their territory and advertising their presence. Elephants too are

regularly encountered, often in the vicinity of riverine forest or acacia scrub, and rhinos prefer the central area of the reserve between Keekorok and Mara Serena Lodges.

The Mara's predators

With this abundance of game, it is not surprising that predators also thrive. Many of the prides of Lions and groups of Cheetahs are partly nomadic, moving to some extent with the migrating herds, so their numbers may fluctuate. However, visitors would be unlucky not to see both species and they can usually be viewed at close quarters.

Leopards are also regularly seen in the Masai Mara although their habits are far less predictable than the other cats and sightings

Black-backed Jackals (Canis mesomelas) are rather retiring animals.

Leopard *Panthera pardus*
L 110–190 (head and body)

The Leopard is one of the animals that visitors to East Africa most want to see; most fail to do so, however. Although comparatively common and widespread, they are rather secretive creatures and largely nocturnal in habits. Leopards hunt by stealth, preferring to ambush prey, such as Impala, gazelle and Baboon, from a rocky outcrop or overhanging branch. Their spotted coat is one of the most beautiful of all cats and they can be told from Cheetahs by the comparatively thick-set build.

The preferred habitat of the Leopard is rough ground with plenty of tree cover and rocky outcrops in which they rest and rear their young. They are, however, adaptable animals and are regular visitors to mature gardens on the outskirts of Nairobi, where they feed on, amongst other things, domestic cats and dogs!

Saddle-bill Stork
Ephippiohynchus senegalensis L 168

The Saddle-bill Stork is one of East Africa's most magnificent and easily recognized birds. It stands over 1.5m tall and is resplendent in black-and-white plumage. The most distinctive feature, however, and the one after which it is named, is the bill; it is huge and brightly marked. The bill is long and slightly curved upwards. It is bright red in colour but has a black band or 'saddle' across the middle and there is a yellow plate near the base on the upper mandible. The legs are mostly black but the 'knees' and feet are red.

Saddle-bill Storks are generally solitary, except where feeding is particularly good. They are usually seen near swamps or riverbanks where they catch fish and frogs.

are, consequently, usually only by chance. They are occasionally found resting in trees during the daytime and visitors fortunate enough to witness this should count themselves extremely lucky.

Masai Mara has a healthy population of Spotted Hyenas whose loud unearthly calls carry far on still nights. Although mostly nocturnal in habit, they are sometimes seen scavenging at the remains of Lion or Cheetah kills. Silver-backed Jackals are often encountered and the reserve is probably the best place in Kenya to look for Hunting Dogs, a species that has declined markedly in recent years in East Africa, partly due to persecution by man and partly as a result of disease.

Birds

Do not be fooled into thinking that the Masai Mara is only good for game animals; it

is a rewarding location for both the dedicated birdwatcher and casual observer alike. On the open plains you can find four species of vulture, Secretary Bird, Ground Hornbill, Anteater Chat and many more species, while swamps and wet areas may harbour Saddle-bill Stork, Hammerkop, Wattled Plover and Egyptian Goose. The trees and bushes are also full of birds; look for Black-chested Harrier Eagle, Green Wood-hoopoe, Lilac-breasted Roller, Spot-flanked Barbet and Blue-eared Glossy Starling.

Ballooning in the Masai Mara
The most unusual way to see the game herds of Masai Mara is from the air. Each morning, balloons take to the air from Keekorok Lodge, Mara Serena Lodge and Governor's Camp, each carrying ten or so passengers. For a couple of hours you glide silently over the plains, the animals below seemingly dis-interested in the vast shapes overhead. Vehicles follow the progress of the balloons on the ground and upon reaching *terra firma*

Dry bush country near Narok, on the way to the Masai Mara, typical of many arid parts of Kenya.

again, the intrepid travellers are met with a champagne breakfast. The experience is un-doubtedly unique but, needless to say, it does not come cheap.

Staying at Masai Mara
In Masai Mara you can either stay in one of the two main lodges or opt for a luxury tented camp or more basic self-service arrangements. The Mara Serena Lodge lies in the western sector of the reserve while the Keekorok Lodge is in the south-east; both offer first-class accommodation. Luxury camps include Governor's Camp and Little Governor's Camp, both near the Olololo Gate, and the Mara Sopa Lodge near the Olaimutiek Gate in the east. Intrepids Camp and Fig Tree Camp lie on the Talek River within the reserve boundaries.

Outside the borders of the Masai Mara, there are tented camps at Cottar's Camp to the north-east, where night drives can be

Hell's gate lies to the south of Lake Naivasha in Kenya's Rift Valley.

arranged, and beyond the Olololo Gate there are the following near the Mara River: Kichwa Tembo Camp, Mara Sara Camp, Mara River Camp and Mara Buffalo Camp. More adventurous visitors try their luck at camping in the bush outside the reserve boundaries if a suitable and discrete area can be found.

Outside the Masai Mara

The Masai Mara's mammals and birds are not confined by the boundaries of the reserve and many can be seen *en route*. While almost any area of natural habitat may be productive, one in particular, the Loita Hills, is worth considering as a diversion. The hills lie to the east of Masai Mara and are crossed by a road between the C 12 and the C 11 roads; numerous unmarked tracks, suitable only for four-wheel-drive vehicles, can also be explored. Unless you are sure of your route, however, do not stray far from main tracks and always retrace your steps.

You should see plenty of game, including Buffalo and Impala, and birds such as Brown Parrot, Crested Francolin, Emerald- spotted Wood-dove, Nyanza Swift, Tropical Boubou, which duet making bell-like sounds, and Slate-coloured Boubou, whose call sounds like a dripping tap.

10 HELL'S GATE NATIONAL PARK	
Location:	NW of Nairobi, S of Lake Naivasha
Access:	Rough trail through the gorge
Terrain:	Steep-sided gorge; geysers
Specialities:	Bearded Vulture, Verreaux's Eagle
Accommodation:	None

Getting there

Hell's Gate National Park lies 13km to the south of Lake Naivasha in the Great Rift

Valley. To reach it, take the Naivasha road (A 104) north-west from Nairobi. Just before you reach Naivasha, turn left onto the road which runs around the southern edge of the lake. Turn left off this road to reach the park entrance which is marked by a towering pinnacle of rock known as Fischer's Tower.

Proceed through the gorge on foot until you reach another rocky outcrop (Ol Basta) at which point it is recommended that you retrace your steps back to the entrance. The area has earned something of a reputation as bandit country; although the Kenyan authorities appear to have dealt with the problem, it might be advisable to travel in a small group rather than alone. Do not leave anything in your car and preferably do not leave it unattended.

About the park

Hell's Gate National Park is a dramatic gorge carved through red, volcanic rock which was once the outlet for a lake that embraced both Lakes Naivasha and Nakuru. There is plenty of evidence that the area has volcanic origins: Fischer's Tower is the remains of an ancient volcanic plug and in the gorge itself, subterranean geothermal activity manifests itself in the form of geysers.

The gorge is beloved of rock climbers while the whole area is renowned for its bird life. There are a few mammals in the gorge itself and out on the plains beyond there is some game.

Wildlife of Hell's Gate

At the entrance to the park, scan the ground for game animals and birds such as Secretary Bird, Anteater Chat, Schalow's Wheatear and several species of larks. The cliffs beyond usually hold more of interest, however. The rocks are home to colonies of Rock Hyraxes.

They can be rather difficult to spot unless they move. You may have to spend some time scanning the rocks carefully to see one. Also on the rocks, nimble-footed Klipspringers stand on tiptoe on rocky vantage points.

Of even more interest are the breeding birds of the gorge. Large numbers of swifts breed here (look for Nyanza and Little Swifts in particular) and Ruppell's Vultures have a sizeable colony. Lucky visitors may spot a Verreaux's Eagle circling overhead or even one of Hell's Gate's breeding Lammergeiers (Bearded Vultures).

11 MOUNT LONGONOT NATIONAL PARK	
Location:	NW of Nairobi
Access:	Tracks lead to the rim of the crater
Terrain:	Volcanic crater; scrub woodland
Specialities:	Stunning views
Accommodation:	None

Getting there

Mount Longonot is clearly visible to the west of the main Nairobi-Nakuru road (A 104). There are various tracks which lead to the crater rim but visitors may wish to consider hiring a guide in Longonot village. It may take six or seven hours to reach the summit so the trip should be planned carefully in advance.

About the park

This is mainly a location for those interested in walking and spectacular views. However, visitors usually come across a few game animals on the wooded slopes. Several species of weavers are found in the area and birds of prey circle overhead.

12 LAKE NAIVASHA

Location:	85km NW of Nairobi
Access:	Road around perimeter; shoreline access in many places
Terrain:	Freshwater lake, swamps and reed-beds
Specialities:	Hippopotamus; waterbirds in abundance
Accommodation:	Lodges, bandas and campsites

Getting there

Lake Naivasha lies north-west of Nairobi and is situated to the west of the main Nakuru road (A 104). A few kilometres before you reach the town of Naivasha, turn left onto Moi South Lake Road which runs around the southern shores of the lake. Stop frequently to scan the water and shoreline for birds. The remaining areas of dry scrub can also yield birds and game animals. The bus service between Nairobi and Nakuru passes through Naivasha town.

About the lake

Despite the fact that Lake Naivasha has suffered more than other rift valley lakes from interference by man, it remains one of the best freshwater habitats in Kenya. It also lies

White-backed Duck (Thalassornis leuconotus).

within easy striking distance of Nairobi and can easily be reached in a few hours. Not surprisingly, it is one of the most popular destinations for people seeking a pleasant day out from the capital.

Lake Naivasha is a shallow lake, being seldom more than 4m deep, and covers an area of roughly 150km^2 although this varies considerably according to rainfall. Its margins are fringed in many places by dense beds of Papyrus while Water Lilies grace the surface of the open water. Channels and lagoons also dot the edge of the lake and add to the variety of habitats. Although much of the surrounding land has been cultivated in recent years, there are still patches of scrub and these harbour a good range of dry-country birds.

Lake Naivasha's wildlife

Among the game animals that can be found around the shore of Lake Naivasha are Zebra, Buffalo, Impala and Giraffe. Hippopotamuses, which are common residents of the lake, make nocturnal forays onto land to graze the vegetation. Usually, all that remains by daylight are their footprints and droppings.

Bird life is much more prolific around the lake margins. Herons and egrets are particularly noticeable and regularly encountered species include Great, Intermediate, Little and Cattle Egrets and Grey, Purple and Goliath Herons. African Darters and Long-tailed Cormorants fish the waters and compete with White and Pink-backed Pelicans. The latter two species can be distinguished by size and colour: the White Pelican is the larger bird and its white plumage contrasts with the Pink-backed's rather greyish plumage and pink rump.

Spoonbills, storks and ibises are usually present in good numbers but flamingos are

*The African Jacana (*Actophilornis africanus*) is adept at walking on floating vegetation.*

*The Blacksmith Plover (*Vanellus armatus*) is found around the margins of lakes and swamps.*

generally found in small numbers and may be absent altogether if feeding conditions do not suit them. African Jacanas, sometimes called Lilytrotters, live up to their name and pick their way across the surface vegetation, and large numbers of waders can be found feeding around the shores. Crowned Plovers, Blacksmith Plovers, Black-winged Stilts and Avocets can be found throughout the year but from October to March their numbers are swollen by migrant species from northern Europe. Curlew Sandpiper, Little Stint, Ruff and Marsh Sandpiper are among the birds to look out for.

Lake Naivasha also has its fair share of birds of prey. African Marsh Harriers can be found throughout the year and during the northern hemisphere's winter, Montagu's,

Marsh and Pallid Harriers may all turn up. Ospreys can be seen fishing in Lake Naivasha's waters but pride of place must go to the African Fish Eagles that reside here.

Crescent Island

Crescent Island is a privately owned wildlife sanctuary, easily explored in a day, which can be visited by either hiring a boat from Lake Naivasha Hotel or taking one of their regular excursions. The island gets its name from its shape; it is part of the rim of an extinct volcano. Most of the time Crescent Island is an island, but occasionally the water level in the lake drops sufficiently for it to be joined to the main-land by a causeway.

Once visitors have landed on Crescent Island, they can walk freely and observe the

African Fish Eagle *Haliaeetus vocifer* L 76

The African Fish Eagle is one of the most striking birds to be found in East Africa. It is often seen perched on dead branches over water, its distinctive plumage making identification easy. The head, shoulders, chest and tail are white, the belly is chestnut and the wings are dark. Its loud call, which sounds rather like a gull, is far-carrying and familiar to anyone who has spent any time in the bush. When it calls, the Fish Eagle throws its head back; it even does this in flight.

As their name suggests, African Fish Eagles feed primarily on fish and are adept at plucking them from the surface of the water with their talons. They will also take small birds and even mammals, however, if the opportunity arises. Fish Eagles are common around most East African lakes and along major watercourses.

wildlife. The species of birds present are similar to those at other parts of the lake but they generally provide closer views. There is a small crater lake on the island. Mammals are present and Zebra, Thomson's Gazelles and Waterbuck can be found.

Threats to Lake Naivasha
Over the years, Lake Naivasha has suffered considerable interference by man. American Bass were introduced to promote the fishing and have had an adverse effect upon the native species. Water Hyacinth was another introduction which has not been welcomed. It is a most prolific water plant and, if left unchecked, could blanket the water surface. The land surrounding Naivasha is used increasingly for commercial agriculture and flowers, fruit and vegetables are grown in abundance. Irrigation schemes also rob the lake of part of its lifeblood.

Staying at Lake Naivasha
Along the southern shores of the lake there are several places for visitors to stay. Heading west along the Moi South Lake Road you first come to the Lake Naivasha Hotel; farther on is the Safariland Lodge. Campsites are available at the Safariland Lodge and at Fisherman's Camp.

13 LAKE NAKURU NATIONAL PARK	
Location:	150km NW of Nairobi
Access:	Tracks suitable for vehicles along the W shore
Terrain:	Alkaline lake surrounded by acacia woodland; Baboon Rocks nearby
Specialities:	Greater and Lesser Flamingos, waterbirds, Defassa Waterbuck
Accommodation:	Lodges and campsites

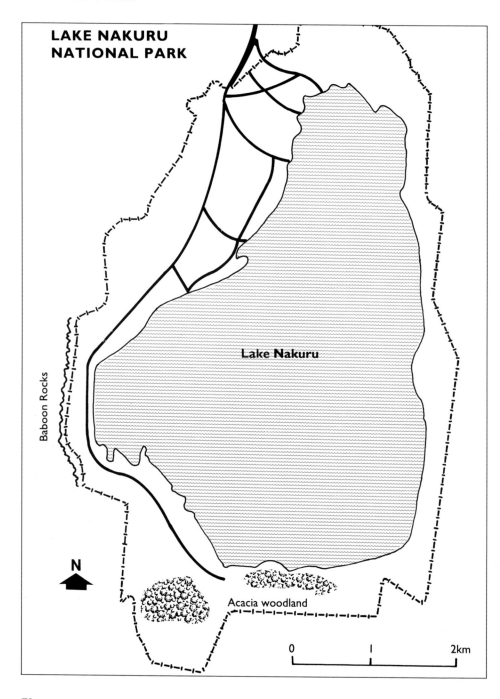

**LAKE NAKURU
NATIONAL PARK**

Baboon Rocks

Lake Nakuru

N

Acacia woodland

0   I   2km

Spectacular views of Lake Nakuru from the nearby Baboon Rocks.

Getting there

To reach Lake Nakuru National Park, take the main Nakuru road (A 104) from the capital which, in part, follows the edge of the rift valley escarpment, with some stunning views .The best access point is from Nakuru town. A road leading to the park gate is signposted in the town. It continues along the west side of the lake with tracks at several points leading to the lake shore. Once visitors have driven to the lakeside, they are permitted to walk along the shore. A track also leads up to Baboon Rocks along the west side of Nakuru from where magnificent views of the lake and pink masses of flamingos can be had, assuming the flamingos are present.

Opposite: *map of Lake Nakuru National Park.*

About the lake

Lake Nakuru is a shallow, alkaline lake in Kenya's rift valley which was designated a national park in 1960. Initially the park comprised the lake and its immediate surroundings but now it has been extended to include savannah scrub to the south. Today, the national park encompasses an area of 200km^2.

The national park was established mainly in an attempt to protect the flamingos for which the lake is famous. Needless to say, the 400 or so other species of birds that frequent Lake Nakuru at different times of the year also benefit, along with the mammals of the park.

Flamingos at Lake Nakuru

Few people can fail to be awe-struck by their first sight of Lake Nakuru. There are birds as

Dawn over Lake Nakuru with its Greater and Lesser Flamingos is unforgettable.

far as the eye can see across the shallow surface and it is difficult to believe that so many can co-exist in one location. Waterbirds of all shapes and sizes are here but of course it is the flamingos that are the most striking birds of Nakuru.

Both Greater and Lesser Flamingos occur here but the numbers and proportions of each species vary from year to year and even from month to month. If feeding conditions are particularly good there may be as many as 2 million flamingos here, with an estimated one-third of the entire world's population of Lesser Flamingos being present on occasions. However, in contrast in 1991, most of the birds had deserted Nakuru for more suitable conditions at Lake Bogoria.

The reason for the flamingos' presence at Lake Nakuru, and indeed their occasional absence, is food. Nakuru's waters are warm, alkaline and slightly saline due to the limited rainfall and evaporation by the sun. These conditions do not suit most forms of aquatic life but a certain blue-green alga, which makes up the diet of the flamingos, thrives.

Reliance on these unusual water conditions does have its drawbacks. If prolonged periods of heavy rain and dull weather occur, the slightly saline waters of the lake become diluted and the algae cease to flourish. Conversely, in periods of drought, the lake has even been known to dry up. Both these extremes soon drive the flamingos away in search of feeding at one of the other rift valley lakes.

Flamingos do not usually breed at Lake Nakuru. In fact the breeding habits of flamingos throughout the world are notoriously unpredictable and mysterious. However, beside the road which runs south along the west side of the lake can be seen abandoned colonial nest mounds which remain from one attempt at breeding in the past.

With all this wealth of bird life, it is perhaps not surprising that the other thing to hit visitors on their first trip to Lake Nakuru is the smell! The shore is caked in a mixture of droppings, feathers and the remains of the inevitable casualties of this crowded lifestyle. Marabou Storks and other scavengers have a field day.

Lake Nakuru at dawn

Dawn breaking over Lake Nakuru is an unforgettable experience and is something that every photographer will want to record. It is best to be in position on the shoreline by 6.15am to give yourself time to compose your picture properly; a tripod is an invaluable aid as you wait. Before long, an orange glow taints the horizon and the sun appears, reflected in the still water and myriad flamingos. Be warned, however; the sunrise does not last long on the equator and within a few minutes the orange glow has gone.

To photograph the dawn, visitors are advised to camp in one of the lakeside campsites, even though this means braving the rather insanitary lavatory conditons; Njoro campsite is best. Campers should also be aware of the Vervet Monkeys that frequent these camps. They have the rather unsavoury habit of sitting on top of tents and urinating down the sides and many of them are quite capable of opening the zips on the tents. Brightly coloured objects left lying around prove to be an irresistible temptation to many of them and so photographers should be warned not to leave film boxes lying around.

Birdwatching along the shores of Lake Nakuru

Once you have witnessed the spectacle of hundreds of thousands of flamingos glowing in the sunrise over the lake, you will now want to see what other wildlife Nakuru has to offer. The best plan is to drive down the west side, pausing where tracks allow access close to the shoreline. Drive slowly and pause frequently because there is always something to see. Towards the southern end of the lake there are a few abandoned boat-houses in the water which are often covered with roosting egrets and herons including Night Herons.

Mingling with the flamingos along the shoreline will be White and Pink-backed Pelicans. These birds have thrived at Lake Nakuru since the introduction of a species of fish, *Tilapia grahami*, which is tolerant of the high water temperatures and low oxygen content that prevail at Nakuru. Great, Intermediate and Little Egrets, Yellow-billed Storks and African Spoonbills can also be found in large numbers along the shores of the lake.

On the open water Cape Teal, Maccoa Duck, African Pochard and White-backed Ducks dot the surface and tree stumps often have perched African Darters or African Fish Eagles. Grey-headed Gulls also feed around the lake's margins and flocks of White-winged Black Terns, Whiskered Terns and Gull-billed Terns hawk insects over the surface.

Not all of Lake Nakuru's birds are as large as the flamingos and egrets; large numbers of waders also frequent the shoreline although the exact species present depend upon the time of year.

Black-winged Stilts and Avocets are both striking in appearance and are present all year round at Nakuru, along with Blacksmith, Three-banded and Kittlitz's Plovers. Their numbers are swollen by visitors from Europe and Asia which spend the northern winter in East Africa. Little Stint, Ruff, and Marsh and Curlew Sandpipers are among the most frequently encountered species.

Yellow-barked Acacia woodlands fringe Lake Nakuru and offer shelter for campsites.

Greater Flamingo
Phoenicopterus ruber L 135

Wildlife of the surrounding land

Wildlife interest at Lake Nakuru is not confined to the aquatic environment by any means and there is plenty of bird life and game to be seen in the surrounding scrub and woodland. Defassa Waterbuck, Bohor Reedbuck and Bushbuck are usually found in the swamps adjacent to the lake while among the Yellow-barked Acacias, look for Zebra, Impala, Thomson's Gazelle and the occasional Giraffe. Lucky visitors have even seen a Leopard resting in the trees in the daytime.

Lake Nakuru National Park has also been established recently as a sanctuary for Black Rhinos and fences help keep them in and poachers out. The only other large mammal likely to be seen in the park is the Hippopotamus. Considerable numbers live in the

The Greater Flamingo is one of two species of flamingo that occurs on the Rift Valley lakes, the other being the Lesser Flamingo. They can be immediately recognized by their pink plumage, long legs, long neck and flattened, down-curved bills. Their pink coloration is derived from their diet. The main feature for distinguishing the Greater from its smaller relative is the pink bill tipped with black. Flamingos feed in a characteristic manner with their neck down and their head and bill upturned. With rapid movements of the bill plates they filter minute plants and animals from the water.

Greater Flamingos have an extensive distribution worldwide, being found in Europe and in the Americas as a different race. However, their greatest concentration occurs in the Rift Valley lakes of Kenya and Tanzania.

lake's waters, tending to concentrate towards the southern end. The only reminders of their night-time emergence from the lake are their footprints and dung around the muddy margins.

Birdwatchers will also find plenty of scope in the acacia woodlands that surround the lake. Around the campsites, Fiscal Shrikes and parties of Arrow-marked Babblers are often seen while more extensive searching should reveal Blue-eared Glossy Starling, White-breasted Tit, Fork-tailed Drongo, White-browed Robin-chat, Little Bee-eater and Emerald Cuckoo. Smaller birds can occasionally be found mobbing Pearl-spotted Owlets among the foliage while, after dark, the owlets can be located by their we-*ooo* we-*ooo* calls.

Baboon Rocks

The western shores of Lake Nakuru are flanked by a steep outcrop of rock known as Baboon Rocks. From the summit, which can be reached by a track, superb panoramic views along the length of the lake can be had. If flamingos are present in good numbers, the entire shoreline will appear pink, a truly astonishing sight. Verreaux's Eagles are occasionally seen circling overhead and Bateleurs ride the updraughts off the cliff. These latter raptors appear to have no tail when seen in flight, but are nevertheless exceptionally aerobatic fliers. Parties of swifts can also be seen in the skies above, and the rocks are home to Cliffchats which are often seen near the parking area at the summit. Males in particular of this species are very distinctive with black and red plumage and conspicuous white shoulder patches.

Menengai Crater

If you are staying at Nakuru for a few days, it is worth taking a trip to Menengai Crater which lies about 8km to the north of the town. Visitors can hike up to the rim, visiting

Marabou Stork
Leptoptilos crumeniferus L 152

Marabou Storks are arguably among the most grotesque of East Africa's birds. Standing over 1.5m tall, with black and rather grubby-looking white plumage, they are reminiscent of undertakers as groups of them huddle around a corpse.

For all their rather unappealing looks, they fulfil a vital role in the African ecosystem in scavenging the dead remains of mammals and birds. They are versatile and adaptable feeders as well; Marabous are not averse to catching frogs and fish if the opportunity arises and will raid nesting quelea colonies and follow locust swarms too.

As a result of their rather unsavoury feeding habits, Marabous have rather dirty bills and the bare facial skin and neck ruff often become stained. Adult birds develop a huge throat sac which can be inflated.

Hyrax Hill, a prehistoric site, on the way. Alternatively, there is a track which can be driven up to a viewing point.

Staying at Lake Nakuru
Lake Nakuru Lodge and the Sarova Lion Hill Lodge lie outside the park boundaries and both provide excellent accommodation. There are also several campsites along the western shores of the lake for which you pay at the park entrance; facilities are rudimentary. Added wildlife interest is provided by the bats that roost in the toilet sheds.

14 LAKE BOGORIA NATIONAL RESERVE	
Location:	NW of Nairobi; 65km from Nakuru
Access:	Road down W side of lake
Terrain:	Soda lake; hot springs; semi-desert
Specialities:	Flamingos, waterbirds
Accommodation:	Campsites

Getting there
Lake Bogoria National Reserve lies roughly 200km north-west of Nairobi. To reach it from the capital, follow the main Nakuru road (A 104) along which you will have superb views of the Rift Valley escarpment. At Nakuru, turn right onto the B 4 which runs past Menengai and is sign-posted to the town of Marigat. The road bears right at Kampi ya Moto and passes through Mogotio towards Marigat and Lake Baringo.

From an altitude of about 2000m (6560 feet) at Nakuru, the road descends 1000m (3280 feet) down the slope of the Rift Valley to Lakes Bogoria and Baringo below; from Mogotio onwards the temperatures begin to rise and the landscape becomes more arid.

Lake Bogoria National Reserve is set against the eastern wall of the Rift Valley.

From the B 4, there are two routes into the park, the more northerly point of access being the most suitable for ordinary cars. Continue along the B 4 until just before Marigat and then turn right following the signpost to the Loboi Gate. From here you can follow the lakeside down to the hot springs on the west side of Lake Bogoria. The track on the east side of the lake, in the shadow of the Laikipia Escarpment, is only suitable for four-wheel-drive vehicles.

If you have a four-wheel-drive vehicle, you may like to take an alternative route and approach the lake from a southerly direction. At Mogotio turn right onto a dirt road that leads to the village of Maji ya Moto. Through the village is the southern gate to the park with the lake beyond.

About the reserve

Lake Bogoria National Reserve covers an area of 107km² and comprises not only the soda lake but also the surrounding dry-country vegetation. The scenery and setting are spectacular; the steep-sided Laikipia Escarpment, on the eastern shores of the lake, provide a stunning backdrop for the steaming waters of Bogoria dotted with pink flamingos.

Prior to Kenya's independence, Lake Bogoria was known as Lake Hannington after the missionary Bishop Hannington. He stopped here briefly towards the end of the last century on his way to Uganda where he eventually met an untimely end. Now the lake goes by its traditional name.

Lake Bogoria and the surrounding land are a testament to the forces of nature at work beneath the ground. The lake itself lies close to the eastern slopes of the Great Rift Valley, monumental forces having created this great cleft across East Africa. Around the western shores of the lake, hot springs and geysers burst to the surface. The water is heated to incredible temperatures by the underlying magma and sulphurous steam fills the air.

Surrounding the geysers and vents, the rocks are often covered in colourful algae that can tolerate the extreme conditions.

Birds

As with most of Kenya's Rift Valley lakes, the flamingos are the star attractions of Lake Bogoria. Thousands often congregate in the shallow waters and feed close to the shores. The sight of large numbers of these elegant birds feeding peacefully in the lake, shrouded by a veil of mist, is worth the trip in itself.

Wildlife of the surrounding land

The National Reserve lies between 1000m and 1500m (3280 and 5920 feet) above sea level and the equatorial sun bakes this arid region. Around the lake shore there is grassland but most of the land is covered in thorn scrub. By careful searching, visitors may find bustards and larks, and see birds of prey and vultures circling overhead.

Game animals include Klipspringers, which frequent the rocky slopes to the south and east of the lake, Dikdiks and Grant's Gazelles. However, the reserve is best known

Lake Bogoria offers some of the best opportunities in East Africa to see Greater Kudu (Tragelaphus strepsiceros). These elegant antelope stand nearly 1.5m tall at the shoulder and have characteristic vertical stripes on their flanks. Only the males possess the long, spiral horns. The Greater Kudu is a scarce animal and it is also very wary, making it difficult to see.

One of the main attractions for visitors to Lake Bogoria is a trip to the hot springs which lie along the western shores of the lake. Geothermal activity in the underlying rocks heats the water to incredible temperatures. When it reaches the surface, geysers and hot springs are the result and the air is full of sulphurous smells.

for its population of Greater Kudu, an antelope that is difficult, if not impossible, to see anywhere else in Kenya.

Greater Kudu are large and attractive animals with grey-brown coats bearing vertical white stripes; these afford them good camouflage among the shadows of dense vegetation. Males possess impressive spiralled horns and tend to live a solitary life whereas the hornless females are often seen in groups of five to ten animals. Despite their size (males can weigh as much as 300kg) they are capable of enormous leaps even from a standing start. Although they are often encountered in the bush, best views are had when they come to drink in the open.

Getting the most from Lake Bogoria National Reserve

Early morning, from dawn until 10am, is the best time of day to watch the wildlife of Lake Bogoria. The mammals and birds are at their most active, the light is better for photography but most importantly, the temperatures are more bearable. During the middle of the day it can get incredibly hot and at this time of day nothing but the flamingos seem to have any energy.

Staying at Lake Bogoria

At the present time the only way to stay within Lake Bogoria National Reserve is to camp. There are three campsites in the park, all towards the southern end of the lake: Acacia, Riverside and Fig Tree Campsites. Of these, the latter is probably the best and is the only one to have water available, although the Acacia Site is in a lovely setting. If planning to camp it is advisable to take plenty of water. Lake Bogoria Lodge lies just outside the reserve boundaries near Loboi Gate.

15 LAKE BARINGO	
Location:	Roughly 240km NW of Nairobi
Access:	Tracks around shores of lake; boat trips
Terrain:	Freshwater lake
Specialities:	Goliath Heron and other waterbirds
Accommodation:	Hotels and campsites

Getting there

Lake Baringo can be reached by leaving Nairobi on the main Nakuru road (A 104). At Nakuru town, bear right onto the B 4 which is sign-posted to Marigat and passes Menengai on the right. At Kampi ya Moto, the road bears right; bear left and you will come to Eldama Ravine. After Mogotio, the road begins its descent to the bed of the Rift Valley in which Lakes Bogoria and Baringo lie. Lake Baringo lies on the east side of the B 4 about 20km north of Marigat. The route is straightforward and, by Kenyan standards, the road surface is good. You will, however, notice a considerable change in the temperature since Lake Baringo lies about 1000m (3280 feet) closer to sea level than the capital. Consequently, daytime temperatures can soar.

About the lake

Lake Baringo is a shallow freshwater lake which nestles in Kenya's Rift Valley. It is the most distant in the chain of accessible lakes which runs north from Nairobi before you reach the vast, arid Suguta Valley separating them from Lake Turkana on the Ethiopian border.

Unlike most of the other Rift Valley lakes, with the exception of Lake Naivasha, the waters of Lake Baringo are silt-laden and murky. Feeding conditions may not be suitable for flamingos but vast numbers of other

The European Roller (Coriacas garrulus) is a colourful and conspicuous visitor.

waterbirds find them ideal. Herons, egrets, waders and ducks occur in abundance and the lake has healthy populations of Nile Crocodiles and Hippopotamuses.

Lake Baringo does not enjoy status as a national reserve or national park and consequently activities such as water skiing, windsurfing and fishing, which are not always compatible with wildlife conservation, can be enjoyed here. Fortunately, the local people appreciate the value, in commercial as well as environmental terms, of the lake's natural resources and the need to preserve them.

Birds

Lake Baringo is an excellent place for watching wading birds. Visitors at any time of year are likely to see Blacksmith, Spur-winged and Three-banded Plovers, Black-winged Stilts and Avocets, but from October until March a number of other species, refugees from the European winter, may turn up. Some of these stay throughout the winter while others occur on passage to and from lakes further south in the African continent. With some luck the following may be seen: Wood, Marsh and Common Sandpipers, Ruff and Greenshank.

Egrets and herons are also much in evidence around the margins of the lake, cashing in on the abundant fish life of Baringo. Goliath Herons, in particular, are associated with the lake since they have a breeding colony on Gibraltar Island, which is one of the largest in Africa. These are the biggest of Africa's herons, standing over 1.5m tall, with a mostly grey plumage but rufous on the head, neck and breast. They are superficially similar to the Purple Heron, which also occurs here. However, when seen side-by-side the larger Goliath Heron appears nearly twice the size and it lacks the black crown and neck markings of its smaller relative.

A Little Egret (Egretta alba) rests on a dead branch around the lake margin.

Namaqua Doves are seen feeding on the ground, sometimes right beside the road, and Fawn-coloured Larks also find food in this dusty terrain. Birds of prey, Madagascar Bee-eaters and Lilac-breasted Rollers perch on exposed branches and the foliage should be searched for White-browed Sparrow Weavers, Grey-headed Bush Shrikes and Silverbirds. The latter are attractive birds, silver-grey above and red below and often move around in pairs. The Baringo area is one of the most reliable in Kenya for finding this rather local species.

To the west of Lake Baringo lies a steep escarpment which is the haunt of a different range of birds. Verreaux's Eagles, often seen in pairs, and Bataleurs ride the thermals and updraughts and keen-eyed observers may see a variety of other birds of prey. Another speciality of the region is Hemprich's Hornbill which nests on the cliffs. It is superficially similar to the Crowned Hornbill, a bird of highland forest, and has a red bill, dark upperparts, white underparts and two pairs of white feathers in its tail.

Hippopotamuses and crocodiles

With its abundance of tilapia fish, it is no wonder that the lake supports a thriving population of Nile Crocodiles, which can often be seen from the shores of Baringo and from boat trips across its surface. Although lying motionless and inactive for much of the time, crocodiles are extremely aware of their surroundings and are adept at snatching a passing meal. Although some consider the Baringo Crocodiles to be safe, it might be wiser to avoid tempting fate by swimming with them.

Hippopotamuses too are easy to see at Lake Baringo. They spend much of the day immersed in the water with only their eyes and nostrils exposed. At night, however, they emerge from the water to graze the vegetation around the shore and they can be seen sometimes on land at dawn or dusk.

Wildlife of the surrounding land

The dry acacia woodland that surrounds the lake in many places has lost much of the game it once held but it is still good for birds.

Staying at Lake Baringo

Visitors seeking accommodation at Lake Baringo have a number of alternatives. On the lake shore, Lake Baringo Club offers excellent facilities with the bonus of having birdwatching right on the doorstep. It can arrange tours birdwatching trips, boat trips on the lake and excursions farther afield. Island Camp is, as its name suggests, situated on Ol Kokwa Island on the lake. It is reached by boat and offers luxury tented accommodation. Basic camping facilities are available at Robert's Camp on the shores of the lake near the Lake Baringo Club.

Opposite: *montane vegetation in the Aberdare highlands.*

16 ABERDARES NATIONAL PARK

Location:	Roughly 180km N of Nairobi
Access:	Network of roads through park
Terrain:	Mountain forest, Bamboo; high moorland
Specialities:	Afro-alpine plants, Bongo
Accommodation:	Lodges, campsites

Getting there
To reach the Aberdares National Park from the capital, take the A 2 which runs north-east towards Thika. By-passing the town, the road continues on towards Nyeri. The A 2 avoids Muranga by taking a wide detour to the east and passes Sagana and Karatina. At Kiganjo, turn left to Nyeri from which several park gates can be reached.

The best known road enters at the Kiandongoro Gate, climbs into the highlands and leaves by the Mutubio Gate travelling on towards Gilgil and Nakuru; a network of other roads and tracks cross the park. Many of these, however, are closed during the rainy season and only four-wheel-drive vehicles are permitted to drive some of the higher tracks.

About the park
The Aberdares National Park was created in 1948 and occupies an area of 767km² of high moorland. The mountain range is part of the central highlands of Kenya and is the country's third highest park after Mt Kenya to the east and Mt Elgon to the west, rising in places to over 3900m (13,000 feet) above sea level. The park's western border is marked by the eastern slopes of the Great Rift Valley and within its boundaries, Ol Doinyo Lesatima rises to 3997m (13,114 feet), Il Kinangop, in the south, to 3906m (12,815 feet), Maratini Hill to 3698m (12,133 feet) and Table Mountain to 3791m (12,438 feet).

Two of the Aberdares' wildlife viewing lodges, the Ark and Treetops, are probably better known to the world in general than the park itself; they lie in the eastern sector known as the Salient.

Highland climate
The climate and vegetation of the Aberdares are in sharp contrast to lower-lying areas of Kenya and are a welcome change for visitors travelling from Samburu or Meru to the north or from the dry, dusty plains of Amboseli. The lower slopes are covered in dense montane forest which supports a rich growth of ferns and mosses. These are most apparent along the gorges carved by the regions many rivers.

As you approach the treeline, the forests become dominated by Bamboos and *Hagenia*, and provide an almost impenetrable sanctuary for the park's game animals. Above this the landscape opens out into vast stretches of grassy moorland, dominated by huge tussocks of grass and an interesting range of Afro-alpine plants. Many of these, such as the spurges, groundsels and lobelias have evolved into species which reach tree-like proportions, dwarfing their more modest-sized relatives found elsewhere in the world.

Famous visitors
The Aberdares National Park is probably as well known for its famous visitors as for its wildlife. Celebrities and royalty alike have visited to experience the night-time wildlife viewing facilities at the Ark and Treetops. It was after a night of game watching at Treetops that Elizabeth II learnt of her father's death and her accession to the throne.

Opposite: *map of Aberdares National Park.*

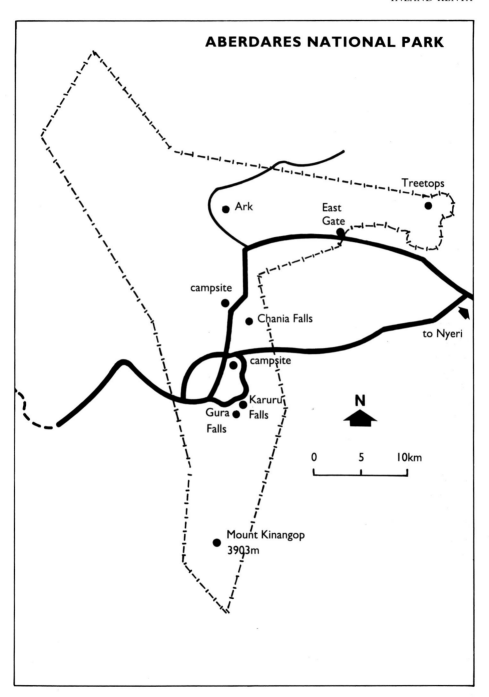

ABERDARES NATIONAL PARK

Ark

East Gate

Treetops

campsite

Chania Falls

campsite

Karuru Falls

Gura Falls

to Nyeri

N

0   5   10km

Mount Kinangop
3903m

Nearby, to the west of the park, is the Wanjohi Valley, otherwise known as Happy Valley, which became notorious in the 1930s and 40s as a playground for rich and titled ex-patriot settlers. Its story is documented in James Fox's book *White Mischief*.

Game mammals

The Aberdares holds a surprising range of game mammals although these are not always easy to see due to the dense forest cover. For those who can afford them, the Ark and Treetops offer superb opportunities to watch creatures visiting waterholes and salt-licks after dark. However, most visitors can only drive around the park's roads and tracks during daylight hours but they still manage to see plenty of species.

Elephants are found within the borders of the Aberdares National Park and occasionally stray outside despite an extensive ditch along the boundary; here they inevitably come into conflict with local farmers. Buffalo, Eland, Waterbuck and Reedbuck also occur and there are also small numbers of Black Rhinoceroses in the park which are sometimes seen on the open moorland.

Of particular interest are the park's Giant Forest Hogs, which are similar in overall appearance to Warthogs but nearly twice as heavy, and Bongos. These are attractive forest antelopes that have rufous-coloured coats with vertical white stripes on the flanks. They are largely nocturnal and rather secretive but are occasionally encountered in the Bamboo forests. Consider yourself extremely lucky if you see one.

Birds

As you drive through the highland forests, stop from time to time to look for birds. With luck you may see Olive Pigeon, Red-eyed Dove, Bronze-naped Pigeon, Silvery-cheeked Hornbill, Ayre's Hawk Eagle, Hartlaub's Turaco and Cinnamon-breasted Bee-eater.

As you climb above the forests and reach the open moorland, scan for the red flower spikes of *Leonotis*, somewhat resembling Red-hot Poker, which will attract feeding sunbirds. In this zone you should also look for Alpine Swift, Augur Buzzard, Mountain Buzzard and Mountain Chat.

Natural Wonders

In addition to its wildlife interest, the Aberdares National Park also offers spectacular views and contains some impressive waterfalls. Gura and Karuru Falls in the southern sector of the park plunge 300m (985 feet) and 275m (902 feet) respectively while the

Thomson's Falls lie near the Aberdares National Park and are well worth a visit.

86

Chania Falls, on the Chania River, lies in the centre of the park. The best-known waterfall in the Aberdares lies outside the boundaries of the park, however. Thomson's Falls are at Nyahururu to the north of the park.

Getting the most from
the Aberdares National Park
If you are not visiting Treetops or The Ark, the best way to explore the park is to camp in one of the designated sites. Failing that, stay in one of the lodges outside the park and make a very early start. Game animals are best seen early in the morning, especially those with essentially nocturnal habits.

Start off in the moorland/Bamboo zone and work down to the forest as the day progresses. Although the birds are most active at dawn, there is still plenty to see throughout the day. If the weather is good, you may opt to search for the specialities of the open moorland; visitors can stray a short way from the road in this zone.

Staying in the Aberdares
The two best-known places to stay in the Aberdares are Treetops, whose base is the Outspan Hotel in Nyeri, and The Ark,

whose base is the Aberdares Country Club in Mweiga. Both bases are outside the park itself and also offer accommodation. Within the park, there are two designated campsites; camping was, for a time, suspended due to the attentions of the park's Lions!

17 MOUNT KENYA NATIONAL PARK	
Location:	About 190km N of Nairobi
Access:	Several passable tracks lead to the high moorland; thereafter, trails followed on foot; you must have a guide
Terrain:	High moorland; mountain peaks; glaciers
Specialities:	Afro-alpine flora, Black-fronted Duiker, Mountain Chat
Accommodation:	Lodges outside the park; mountain huts on slopes

Getting there
Take the A 2 which heads north-west from Nairobi. The road passes close to Thika and

Mt Kenya is the country's highest mountain reaching 5199m (17,057 feet) at its summit. Above the treeline it is home to some extraordinary plants, the so-called Afro-alpine flora, with many well-known groups of plants reaching giant proportions. Point Lenana at 4985m (16,355 feet) is readily accessible and does not require special climbing skills to be reached.

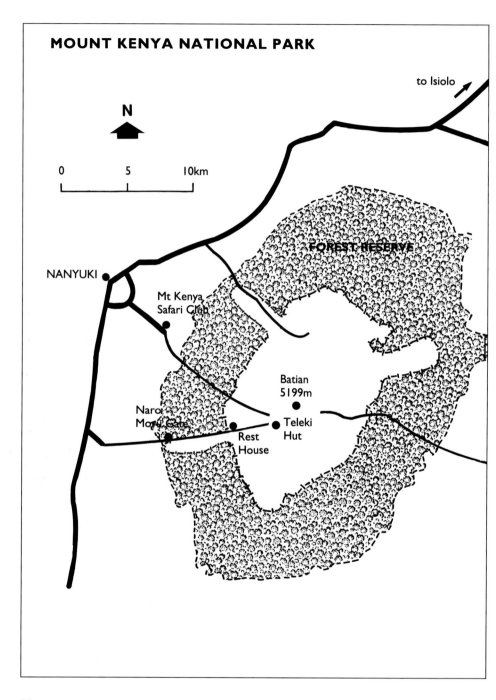

MOUNT KENYA NATIONAL PARK

N

0   5   10km

to Isiolo

NANYUKI

Mt Kenya
Safari Club

FOREST RESERVE

Batian
5199m

Naro
Moru Gate

Teleki
Hut

Rest
House

by-passes Muranga before bearing west around the base of Mt Kenya and heading north to Nanyuki. Several tracks allow access to the national park, which lies above the 3100m (10,200 feet) contour line, and the best of these are accessible from the A 2 to the west. Another route, Carr's Road, approaches from the east.

From the town of Naro Moru, a track to the right leads past the River Lodge and on to the Naro Moru Gate. At Nanyuki the Burguret Route leads past the Mount Kenya Safari Club and into the park while to the north of the town, the Sirimon Track ascends the mountain in a south-easterly direction. Carr's Road climbs the road from the east side; the route starts from Chogoria village, reached from the Embu to Meru road (B 2).

These tracks lead to the high moorlands and are accessible, at most times of the year, to four-wheel-drive vehicles. Beyond these tracks the journey must be continued on foot; it cannot be attempted alone and a guide and even porters should be seriously considered. Only one of the climbs, to Point Lenana, can be attempted by hikers rather than climbers. The driest times of year, which are also the best for views, are January and February, and July to October.

About the park

The first view most people get of Kenya as they fly in from Europe is of the snow-capped summit of Mt Kenya emerging from a veil of clouds which often cloak the highlands. To many, the idea of permanent snow and even glaciers on the equator seems as extraordinary today as it did last century when reports of its existence were sent back to Europe. The first European to see it was the missionary Johanne Krapf, who first saw it in December

Opposite: map of Mount Kenya National Park.

1849. However, the notion was dismissed by many leading geographers. Mt Kenya is Africa's second highest mountain and the highest in Kenya.

The mountain itself, volcanic in origin, straddles the equator with the highest point lying slightly to the south of the line. At the summit, there are not one but several peaks, the highest two peaks being Nelion at 5192m (17,034 feet) which is only narrowly exceeded in altitude by its sister Batian at 5199m (17,057 feet); they are all that remains of a once vast volcanic plug. A third peak, Point Lenana, at 4985m (16,355 feet) is more readily accessible and does not necessitate climbing abilities.

Mount Kenya National Park was created in 1949 and covers an area of 717km². Study a map and the area looks roughly elliptical in shape with two projections, salients, to the west and north-west; these are Naro Moru and Sirimon respectively.

The national park is buffered from changes in land use by the surrounding land which now comprises the Mount Kenya Forest Reserve. All the forest between the 1600m (5250-feet) contour line and the national park boundary at 3100m (10,170 feet), an area of more than 2000km², has acquired this status and, together with the national park, the whole area has now been declared a UNESCO Biosphere Reserve.

This land protection not only benefits the wildlife and vegetation of the Mt Kenya area but has far wider effects as well. Mt Kenya is the largest watershed in the country and hence the health of its forest and moorland are of national importance.

Habitats of the national park and forest reserve

Your ascent of Mt Kenya will begin with a trek, or more likely a drive, through the montane forests on its lower slopes that are the Mount Kenya Forest Reserve. Huge trees, often festooned with epiphytic plants, are dominant here giving way eventually to forests of *Hagenia* and Bamboo. Inside the national park boundaries you pass the tree-line and come upon open moorland. This is characterized by huge tussocks of grass and the appearance of giant plants such as lobelias and groundsels. As the ascent continues, the flora becomes more impoverished and stunted as you approach the snowline above which glaciers and permanent snow prevail.

Mount Kenya Forest Reserve
The forest reserve harbours some of the best montane forest in Kenya and certainly some

Highland forest cloaks the lower slopes of Mt Kenya and lies within the boundaries of the Mount Kenya Forest Reserve.

of the most accessible. A drive or walk up any of the main routes to the national park, on the Sirimon Track, or Burguret or Naro Moru Routes, passes through magnificent stands of trees. Along the Sirimon Track species such as Juniper and *Podocarpus* predominate and at higher altitudes *Hagenia*, an extremely long-lived tree, and Bamboo occur. Ferns, including species of tree ferns as well as the more modest-sized ground dwelling species, and mosses are abundant, and the best way to appreciate these and other members of the forest community is along steep gorges and ravines.

Above the 3000m (9840-feet) contour, the forests become more open and scrubby, with *Hypericum* (St John's Wort) predominating; flowering plants and shrubs are found in abundance. It is not until you climb above about 3300m (10,825 feet) that the forests give way to the open moorland.

Wildlife of Mount Kenya's forests
Many of Mt Kenya's forest mammals are rather difficult to see, taking advantage of the deep cover, but Syke's Monkeys and Black-and-White Colobus Monkeys are generally rather conspicuous. The latter species is particularly attractive with black and white fur and a long bushy tail, and these monkeys are capable of spectacular leaps from branch to branch. Dawn and early morning offer the best opportunities for game watching, when there is a chance of seeing that elusive forest antelope, the Bongo. Despite their size, Mt Kenya's Elephants and Buffaloes can be remarkably difficult to find and Bushbuck and Giant Forest Hogs are more likely to be encountered.

Bird life in the forests is prolific and many of the more characteristic species can be seen in the vicinity of the Naro Moru River Lodge. Along river courses, look for the

When the light is right, Violet-backed Starlings (Cinnyricinclus leucogaster) have an amazing iridescence on their backs.

Giant Kingfisher which certainly lives up to its name. Marshy areas beside the water provide feeding grounds for the Green Ibis, a rare bird which can only be found here and in the Aberdares. This species should not be confused with the somewhat similar Hadada from which it differs in having a shaggy crest.

Hartlaub's Turaco, a colourful bird that is found throughout the highlands of Kenya, is common although rather unobtrusive but Olive Pigeons, Silvery-cheeked Hornbills and Red-fronted Parrots are easier to find. At higher altitudes, where the forest opens out, flowering bushes and shrubs should be searched for sunbirds; several species may be found including Eastern Double-collared, Tacazze and Malachite.

Mount Kenya's open moorland and the Afro-alpine flora
Above the 3350m (10,990-feet) contour, the forest disappears, being replaced by open moorland; this is characterized by large tussocks of grass. As you climb higher, some of the more spectacular Afro-alpine flowers begin to appear. Many grow to giant proportions and are spectacular in appearance, a result of having evolved to cope with the mountain's extreme environment.

On the mountain, daytime temperatures may soar before the sun becomes obscured by the inevitable cloud and mist and, because of the thin air, ultraviolet radiation is harsh. However, after dark, temperatures can plummet with several degrees of frost, even below the snowline. Only on the equator can these extremes be encountered on a daily basis and it is no surprise that the flora is unique.

The most striking feature about many of the Afro-alpine plants is their size: lobelias and groundsels may exceed 6m in height. Groundsels have evolved an intruiging way of overcoming heat loss at night: leaves that die are not shed but instead remain attached to the plant and help insulate it. Lobelia flowers are almost encased and protected by the calyx so that sunbirds require all their ingenuity to feed on the nectar.

Wildlife of the open moorland
The most frequently encountered mammal above the treeline is the Rock Hyrax, those on Mt Kenya belonging to a different subspecies from those found elsewhere in Kenya.

Rock Hyraxes (Procavia capensis) are endearing creatures.

These endearing creatures are often particularly bold around mountain huts where they become accustomed to man's presence.

Black-fronted Duikers can also be found at these high altitudes. Like other duikers, these charming antelopes are rather retiring and generally nocturnal in their habits. However, they are sometimes seen at dawn or dusk. Mt Kenya Giant Mole Rats are common on the open moorland but signs of their activity are more often seen than the animals themselves. Look for ridges on the surface of the ground marking the passage of their underground tunnels. If you are lucky, you may see a bold individual break the surface.

The bird life of the open moorland has a lot in common with similar altitudes in the Aberdares. Mountain Chats perch conspicuously and Alpine Swifts, Nyanza Swifts and the occasional Scarce Swift can be seen overhead. Sunbirds feed on the flowering spikes of Afro-alpine plants. In particular, look for the Scarlet-tufted Malachite Sunbird, a speciality of Mt Kenya, and also Tacazze and Golden-winged Sunbirds. Augur and Mountain Buzzards are among the birds of prey of the area and Montane Francolins are occasionally seen foraging in the vegetation.

Safety and getting the most from Mount Kenya

Whether you intend to climb to the summit or birdwatch at lower altitudes in the forests and on the moorland, Mt Kenya should never be underestimated. Remember that the open moorland does not occur below about 3350m (10,990 feet); the air is thin even at this altitude. Above that, breathing becomes difficult and if time permits it is sensible to allow a day or so at this altitude to acclimatize; the Meteorological Station provides an ideal first stop on the Naro Moru route for this purpose. Never rush things since your physiology will pay for it in the long run. At the slightest signs of altitude sickness (headaches, nausea, etc.) stop and rest, and consider descending to a lower altitude. It should be noted that numerous cases of pulmonary oedema (fluid on the lungs), some of which are fatal, occur here each year, a direct result of doing too much too soon.

To get the most from a trip to Mt Kenya you need to allow time. Not only because there is so much to see but also because the weather can be rather fickle. As a general rule, which also applies to many other mountainous areas near the equator, the day often starts with clear blue skies. However, within a few hours, clouds start to build up and by midday the mountain tops are shrouded in mist and cloud. You should, therefore, make the most of good weather as it will probably not last. It also goes without saying that you should bring clothing appropriate to the changeable and extreme climate of these uplands. Another point to remember is that, because the air is thin, the effects of the sun's ultraviolet radiation can be severe. Apply suntan lotion liberally to any exposed areas of skin.

Staying at Mount Kenya

When visiting Mount Kenya National Park, most people stay first of all for a few days in one of the lodges that border the park and the forest reserve. From there, they plan their expedition to the highland areas, booking accommodation in the mountain huts and hiring guides.

The Naro Moru River Lodge lies to the west of the park and can easily be reached from the main road. It lies on the most popular route into the park, the Naro Moru Route. Mount Kenya Safari Lodge lies near Nanyuki. On the east side of the mountain,

the Meru Mount Kenya Lodge lies at the park boundaries and can be reached from Chogoria and the Meru Road.

Another excellent place to stay is the Moutain Rock Lodge at Naro Moru, where there are chalets and a campsite. Birdwatching trips can be arranged to the forest reserve and national park and birdwatching around the Lodge itself is good. Look for Hadada Ibis, Violet-backed Starling, White-eyed Slaty Flycatcher and sunbirds galore.

Exploring the national park

There are a number of routes into the park itself, many of which are accessible to the park boundaries at least to four-wheel-drive vehicles. The highland areas and stunning Afro-alpine flora and scenery can be explored easily but to attempt an ascent of one of the main peaks Batian or Nelion requires not only experience and skill at rock climbing but the assistance of a guide. As such, it is beyond

Several days trekking are required to reach the higher slopes of Mt Kenya.

the scope of this book. Point Lenana, however, can be reached by hikers willing to tackle the hard slog although even for this comparatively modest route you will need to set aside at least five days (three for the ascent and two for the descent).

The Naro Moru Route starts from the River Lodge and climbs to the Meteorological Station inside the park boundaries. This is a popular destination for expeditions organized by the River Lodge; basic accommodation can be booked at the station through the River Lodge. Proceed beyond this point on foot, allowing two or three overnight stops in huts further up the track before an attempt is made on Point Lenana. From the Meteorological Station, it will take a day's hike to reach Mackinder's Camp, passing through the Vertical Bog, an area of marshy ground, and up the Teleki Valley. Beyond that, visitors often make one more stay in the Austrian Hut, five to six hours beyond, before climbing Point Lenana the following morning.

The Sirimon Track approaches Mt Kenya from the north-west and leaves the main road near Nanyuki. A rough track, accessible to four-wheel-drive vehicles, climbs to the park gate and the open moorland beyond.

The Chogoria Route approaches from the east, with Meru Mount Kenya Lodge at its start inside the park boundaries; the lodge itself is worth visiting for the variety of game it attracts to its waterholes. Several huts lie on the route towards the summit.

18 TANA RIVER

Location:	On A 2 between Thika and Sagana
Access:	Viewable from the road bridge
Terrain:	Muddy river and lush riverine margins
Specialities:	Hippopotamuses, waterbirds
Accommodation:	None

About the river

If travelling to or from one of the national parks or reserves north or north-east of Nairobi, you may well travel on the A 2, often referred to as the Great North Road. A wide sweeping road now by-passes the town of Muranga and crosses the River Tana by a large road bridge. This makes an excellent spot to pause on your journey and stretch your legs and see some interesting wildlife.

The muddy banks of the river are much frequented by people. However, not only human footprints adorn the mud: Hippopotamuses too are found in these waters and

emerge at night to graze the surrounding vegetation, leaving their footprints and droppings!

During the daytime, views of Hippos are generally restricted to backs, noses and ears in the murky water. However, the views of the birds are more impressive. Great and Little Egrets stalk fish in the shallows and Pied Kingfishers hover and plunge-dive for fish from overhanging perches. Mudbanks, exposed by receding waters, are home to waders which are especially numerous during the northern hemisphere winter. Look for Marsh Sandpiper, Little Stint, Snipe, Greenshank, Ruff and Common Sandpiper. Long-legged Black-winged Stilts feed in deeper water, able to wade to a greater depth. A telescope can be a useful birdwatching aid if viewing the river from the bridge.

A view from the road bridge of the Tana River, haunt of egrets and waders.

19 MERU NATIONAL PARK

Location:	Roughly 320km NE of Nairobi
Access:	Network of tracks throughout the park
Terrain:	Dry bush; acacia woodland; riverine forest
Specialities:	Reticulated Giraffe, Grevy's Zebra, Somali race of Ostrich
Accommodation:	Several lodges and campsites

Getting there

To reach this park, leave the capital on the A 2 heading north-east. The road passes by Thika and takes a long sweep around Muranga. After Sagana, the destination is Meru but there is a choice or routes: either continue on the A 2 around the western flanks of Mt Kenya, passing through Naro Moru and Nanyuki or take the C 73, joining the B 6 through Embu and on towards Meru. To reach the park, take the road from Embu to Maua, which is tarmacked, and then on to the Murera Gate of Meru National Park. For those who prefer not to drive, Meru can be reached by plane, from Nairobi.

About the park

Meru National Park straddles the equator, and covers an area of roughly 870km^2 to the north-east of Mt Kenya. It was established as a reserve in 1959 prior to its subsequent designation as a national park. Although scenically, it is one of the most attractive national parks in Kenya, it receives comparatively few visitors. Despite this, however, it has a good network of roads and a choice of lodges and campsites. An area in the north of the park has been designated a wilderness

area and is only accessible on foot, and then only with permission and in the company of a ranger.

As well as more widespread species of birds and game mammals, it holds species more usually associated with more northerly territories: Reticulated Giraffe, Grevy's Zebra, Vulturine Guineafowl and the Somali race of Ostrich all occur. Meru National Park is also fortunate in having nearby reserves which serve to hold similar species of birds and mammals.

Despite its undoubted wildlife attractions, Meru National Park is probably best known as the territory of Elsa the lioness, made famous by the writings of Joy Adamson. Her camp still remains in Meru but sadly the story of the Adamsons has an unhappy ending: both Joy and her husband George met with brutal and untimely ends, murdered in the Kenyan bush they loved. Regrettably, a similar fate befell the park's White Rhinoceroses, introduced and once a major attraction in Meru. They were supposedly protected by armed guard day and night but were gunned down by poachers in 1988.

Meru's varied habitats

For such a comparatively compact national park by Kenyan standards, Meru shows a

Pied Wheatears (Oenanthe leucomela) *are migratory visitors to dry areas of bush.*

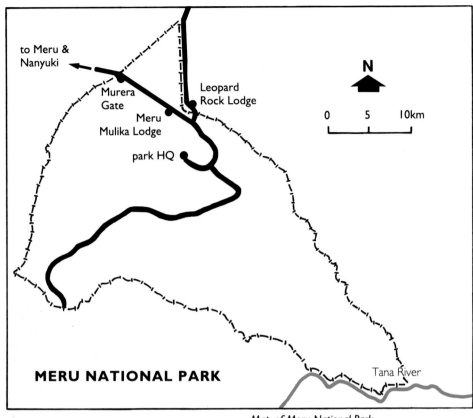

to Meru & Nanyuki

Murera Gate

Leopard Rock Lodge

Meru Mulika Lodge

park HQ

N

0   5   10km

MERU NATIONAL PARK

Tana River

Map of Meru National Park.

surprising variety of habitats and vegetation. This is partly due to the change in altitude within the park, the land rising from around 300m (1000 feet) along the Tana River in the south-east to over 900m (3000 feet) in the north of the park, but is also due to the rainfall pattern: considerably more rain falls in the west of the park than in the east. The presence of near-permanent rivers, most notably the Tana River, within or on the borders of the national park, adds to the variety. The Tana runs along the south-eastern boundary, the Kiolu Sand River crosses from west to east joining the Tana at the boundary and the Bwatherongi and Rojewero Rivers cut through the centre of the park.

Grassland and scrub predominate in Meru National Park but differ markedly in character throughout the park. In the west, where the rainfall is highest, the grasslands are often densely wooded while to the east they are much more open. Along the river courses can be found lush growths of riverine forest; they comprise both Duom and Raphia Palms of mature and imposing stature.

Game mammals
If you have already visited open savannah parks you will see some familiar friends at Meru. Grant's Gazelle, Kongoni and Impala all occur and support healthy populations of

*Bohor Reedbuck (*Redunca redunca*), a widespread but comparatively inconspicuous antelope.*

Lions and Cheetahs. Although Common or Burchell's Zebras occur here, visitors should also look out for Grevy's Zebra as well which can be distinguished by the narrower stripes on the flanks. Any Giraffe you see here is going to be a Reticulated Giraffe, the patterns on its skin resembling crazy paving. In drier areas, long-necked Gerenuks can be found, often seen standing on their hind legs feeding on leaves out of reach to other antelopes.

Other unusual mammals seen here include Beisa Oryx and Lesser Kudu. Usually seen singly or more rarely in small groups, the Lesser Kudu are retiring animals that keep to cover. The best way to see them is to search thickets of thornbush, especially in the

early morning. If they keep still, they can be rather difficult to spot. Only the male Lesser Kudus have the characterstic narrow, spiralled horns but both sexes have two white chevrons, one on the throat and the other lower down the neck.

Of the larger mammals, both Elephant and Buffalo occur, often congregating near water where groups of Hippos can also be found. Black Rhinos, although still present in Meru National Park, have suffered badly from poachers.

Birds

Like the game animals of Meru, the birdlife contains species that are familiar from further south in Kenya as well as a few species more characteristic of the northern regions.

Driving across areas of open grassland, you may encounter Ostriches. Although these are the same species as those found in Nairobi National Park and elsewhere in southern Kenya, the neck and thighs of the birds are blue as opposed to pink; they belong to the Somali race of Ostrich. Parties of Yellow-necked Spurfowl can sometimes be seen from the road as well as groups of guinea-fowl which come to areas of water to drink in the evenings. Look closely at each

*Two races of Ostriches (*Struthio camelus*) occur in East Africa. This is a male of the Somali race which is characterized by having blue legs and neck when mature. It occurs in the north of the region and is the typical ostrich found in the dry habitats of Meru National Park and Samburu National Reserve. When alarmed, Ostriches can run at speeds of up to 50kph (30mph).*

Ruppell's Vulture (Gyps ruppellii), recognized by pale spots on its mantle feathers, is a widespread species.

Crowned Plovers and Three-banded Plovers feed around the margins and Malachite Kingfishers can be seen on overhanging perches. From November to March, European Bee-eaters which, like the Rollers are migrant visitors to Meru, are also seen.

There is a chance of seeing that elusive bird, Peter's Finfoot, along some of the quieter watercourses. This species is rather retiring and one of the best ways to see it is simply to find a pleasant, likely-looking spot and wait; you never know, you might be lucky! Whilst waiting, however, do not neglect to scan the trees for species such as Violet Wood Hoopoe, Scimitarbill, Grey-capped Warbler and Sulphur-breasted Bush-shrike.

Joy and George Adamson
Over the years, the names of Joy and George Adamson, and their lioness Elsa, became synonymous with that of Meru. In her book *Born Free*, Joy Adamson told the story of the rehabilitation back to the wild of Elsa and Elsa's Camp is still there in the south of the park beside the Ura River. In her book *The Spotted Sphinx* the story of the rehabilitation of a Cheetah called Pippa is told and Pippa's grave is also found in the park.

Sadly, the story of the Adamsons does not end happily. In 1980, Joy Adamson was murdered at her camp in Shaba National Reserve and George Adamson was ambushed and murdered in Kora National Reserve in 1989 at the age of 83; memories of their conservation work, however, live on.

Rhinoceroses in Meru
At one time, rhinos were a familiar sight in Meru National Park and visitors were almost guaranteed to see at least one during their visit. Sadly, the same is not true today. Black Rhinoceroses, native to the park, were quite common, but the last decade in particular

group you see: in addition to the more common and widespread Helmeted Guinea-fowl, there are also Vulturine Guinea-fowl in Meru. They have bare heads but the neck, chest and mantle feathers are blue, black and white.

Several species of vultures gather at kills in the open areas and birds of prey can be seen perched in bushes; in particular look for Black-winged Kite, Black-chested Harrier Eagle, Pale Chanting Goshawk and Martial Eagle. Sharing similar perches are the park's Lilac-breasted Rollers. Visitors should also look for Broad-billed and Rufous-crowned Rollers and, from November to March, European Rollers which are migrants to the region.

Marshy areas, such as the Mulika Swamp which lies near the Meru Mulika Lodge, attract an interesting variety of birds. Most conspicuous are species such as Crowned Crane, Yellow-billed Stork and Hammerkop but there are plenty of others to look for:

has seen the population here, as in most parts of East Africa, decimated by poaching for their horns.

The story of Meru's White Rhinoceroses is, if anything, more depressing. Introduced from South Africa in an attempt to establish a breeding herd, the rhinos were protected night and day by an armed guard. So trusting were they that they would follow him around like domestic animals. In 1988, the guard was held up at gun-point by poachers and the rhinos slaughtered, and thus the five remaining White Rhinoceroses in the park were gone. White Rhinoceroses are so called not because of their colour but because the name is a corruption of the Afrikaan word for 'wide' which refers to the broad shape of their mouths.

Staying in Meru

Visitors to Meru National Park have a number of alternatives when it comes to accommodation. Near the Murera Gate is the Meru Mulika Lodge which overlooks the Mulika Swamps. Nearby, on the northern border of Meru, is Leopard Rock Lodge, a self-help lodge with bandas. There are also several campsites within the park for the more adventurous.

Neighbouring reserves

Kora National Reserve lies to the south-east of Meru and their boundaries meet at the Tana River. Rahole National Reserve lies to the north of Kora, separated by the Tana. Basandi National Reserve abuts Meru's north-eastern border. There are no facilities for visitors at any of these reserves.

20 SAMBURU AND BUFFALO SPRINGS NATIONAL RESERVES	
Location:	c. 300km N of Nairobi
Access:	Network of tracks through the reserves
Terrain:	Open grassland; acacia woodland; freshwater pools
Specialities:	Reticulated Giraffe, Grevy's Zebra; dry country birds
Accommodation:	Lodges and campsite

Getting there

Samburu and Buffalo Springs National Reserves are the most accessible of the northern territory reserves. To reach them, head

This view of Samburu National Reserve is quintessentially East African. Troops of Olive Baboons regularly use acacia trees as resting places and to keep out of the way of predators. Those which can be seen here had just visited the pools at Buffalo Springs and are now resting before moving off across the plains to forage.

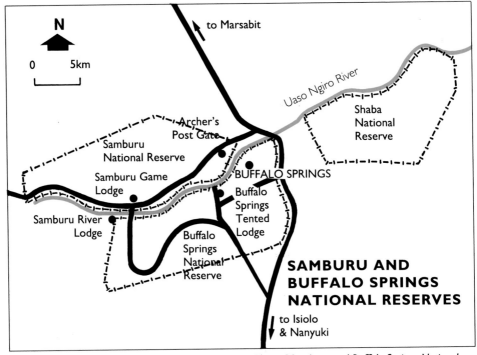

N

0   5km

to Marsabit

Uaso Ngiro River

Archer's
Post Gate

Samburu
National Reserve

Shaba
National
Reserve

Samburu Game
Lodge

BUFFALO SPRINGS

Buffalo
Springs
Tented
Lodge

Samburu River
Lodge

Buffalo
Springs
National
Reserve

**SAMBURU AND
BUFFALO SPRINGS
NATIONAL RESERVES**

to Isiolo
& Nanyuki

north-east from the capital on the A 2, by-passing Thika and skirting to the east of Muranga. Follow the road west around Mt Kenya, passing through Naro Moru and Nanyuki and continue north to Isiolo. Continue north in the direction of Marsabit and turn left either at the Gare Mara Gate or the Buffalo Springs Gate for the reserve of that name, or continue to the Archer's Post Gate for Samburu. From Samburu's West Gate, a road leads west and then north to Wamba. Shaba National Reserve can be reached by turning right at Archer's Post on the A 2. The reserves can also be reached by plane.

About the reserves

Because of their close proximity and the similarity of the terrain, Samburu and Buffalo Springs National Reserves can effectively be treated under the same heading.

Map of Samburu and Buffalo Springs National Reserves.

Samburu National Reserve covers about 165km² of arid thornbush, dry grassland and semi-desert. It is a popular destination together with its sister reserve. The 30km of the southern boundary of Samburu are marked by the Uaso Ngiro River, the single most important feature of the reserve. Part of this border marks the northern limit of the Buffalo Springs National Reserve which can be reached by bridge near the Samburu Game Lodge.

Buffalo Springs National Reserve comprises 130km², the terrain being similar to Samburu. The Uaso Ngiro River runs along the entire length of the northern border and, together with the park's waterholes and swamps, is the focal point of the reserve.

The habitat

The terrain in Samburu and Buffalo Springs National Reserves is rugged and beautiful, with the flat-topped mountain of Lolokwe visible from many parts of the reserves. For the most part, the vegetation is dry grassland dotted with arid thornbush and more extensive areas of acacia woodland. In parts, the landscape grades into semi-desert vegetation, a reminder that here you are on the fringes of Kenya's Northern Territories.

By contrast with the dry habitats, the Uaso Ngiro River provides a permanent source of water which helps maintain the populations of game mammals and birds at comparatively high levels. The waters feed swamps along the river margins and encourage a rich growth of riverine forest made up of some impressive Doum Palms. The Uaso Ngiro River has a most unusual course. With its origins on the slopes of Mt Kenya, the river at first flows north-west before veering eastwards and passing between the two reserves. Thereafter, it meanders eastwards only to become lost in the vast swamps that lie between Habaswein and Hagadera without ever reaching the sea.

Game mammals of the bush

In common with Meru National Park, game drives through Samburu and Buffalo Springs National Reserves yield both species familiar from the southern parks and reserves and a few more usually associated with Kenya's Northern Territories. With a few exceptions, the game animals are drawn to the waters of the Uaso Ngiro River or to the waterholes sooner or later. Therefore, driving along the tracks in the vicinity of the river, especially first thing in the morning, is particularly productive. At this time of day, large mammals, such as Buffalo, Reticulated Giraffe and Elephant, are easy to see.

Reticulated Giraffe *Giraffa camelopardalis*
L 300–400 (head and body), H 450–480

Although the Reticulated Giraffe looks distinctly different from the more widespread Giraffe seen in southern Kenya, many experts now consider them to be races of the same species. The Reticulated Giraffe has a beautiful chestnut coat which is broken by neat, narrow white lines that delineate geometric patterns of colour. In size and shape there is little to separate the two races. Giraffes stand over 4m tall and live in herds of 2–20 animals.

They browse vegetation from trees and shrubs, aided by their long necks. Although their necks are proportionally much longer than any other mammal, in fact they contain exactly the same number of vertebrae, that is seven. Reticulated Giraffes are most easily seen in Meru National Park and Samburu National Reserve. However, their distribution continues northwards to Turkana and beyond.

Grevy's Zebra *Equus grevyi*
L 250–260 (head and body)

Grevy's Zebra is an attractively marked species which is noticeably larger than its common relative. The flanks and legs are covered in narrow stripes which become broader along the neck. Unlike the Common or Burchell's Zebra, the belly lacks stripes and is pure white. The ears are also rather large and boldly marked; they are rounded in shape with a black margin and white tip.

Grevy's Zebra prefer arid bush country and can survive well in semi-desert habitats. They generally live in small herds of 5–20 animals but, unlike Burchell's Zebra, they are never seen in the vast herds. In the East African region, Grevy's Zebra is only found in the north of Kenya, its range continuing on into Ethiopia. Samburu and Meru offer the most accessible opportunities for seeing this species which can also be found around Lake Turkana and at Marsabit.

White-throated bee-eaters (Merops albicollis) are common along water courses in Samburu and Buffalo Springs.

Since they do not need to drink, Gerenuks can be found almost anywhere in the dry thornbush. These graceful, long-legged and long-necked antelopes are sometimes found in small groups. Pairs of dikdiks feed close to cover and these tiny creatures are among the most engaging of all the antelopes. With the abundance of game life that the waters of the Uaso Ngiro encourage, there is no shortage of predators in either Samburu or Buffalo Springs National Reserves. Lions and Cheetahs are often encountered and there is a better than average chance of seeing a Leopard.

Both Common or Burchell's Zebra and Grevy's Zebra are found in the reserves and can be separated by comparing the size of the stripes, those of Grevy's being narrower. Impala, Common Waterbuck, Beisa Oryx, Grant's Gazelle and Bushbuck may also be encountered near the water but keep a wary eye open for predators.

Birds of the bush
The largest and most conspicuous bird of the open thornbush country is the Ostrich; the blue-legged, blue-necked Somali race is found here. Kori and Buff-crested Bustards are also occasionally seen and visitors should look for gamebirds such as Yellow-necked Spurfowl, Crested Francolin and flocks of both Vulturine and Helmeted Guinea-fowl.

102

Birds of prey are much in evidence in Samburu and Buffalo Springs. Pale Chanting Goshawks perch conspicuously, ever alert for small mammals and lizards on the ground, and Little Sparrowhawk, Long-crested Hawk Eagle, Black-winged Kite and Black-chested Harrier Eagle can also be found. Most spectacular, however, are the Martial Eagles which are sometimes seen perched on the tops of trees. Using this as a vantage point, they swoop down on their prey which can include animals as large as dikdiks and Baboons, although hyraxes and gamebirds feature more prominently.

Woodland, especially in the vicinity of water, is usually rich in bird life and worth investigating. Pearl-spotted Owlets roost inconspicuously during the daytime but more in evidence are species such as White-headed Mousebird, Bearded Woodpecker, South African Black Flycatcher and White-bellied Go-away Bird.

Close to water
The presence of the Uaso Ngiro River and the clear waters of Buffalo Springs undoubtedly have a pronounced effect upon the wildlife of Samburu and Buffalo Springs, influencing both the abundance and diversity of life in the reserves. In particular, the swamps and marshes attract birds that are seldom seen away from water.

Many of the parks' mammals need water and regularly come to drink. It is not surprising that the river, swamps and waterholes are important locations for game watching. The river is also the permanent haunt of Nile Crocodiles which can often be seen sunbathing on the banks. These reptiles are an ever-present threat to the animals that come to drink.

Waterbirds, such as Green Heron, Goliath Heron and Hammerkop are visitors to the swamps and banks of the river, and African Fish Eagles sometimes put in an appearance. Three-banded and Crowned Plovers are often seen and keen-eyed observers may also find Water Dikkops in cover near the water's edge. Visitors from Europe will be struck by the resemblance of these rather extraordinary-looking birds to Stone Curlews; they are in fact closely related, but are greyer in colour. They are found throughout East Africa on rivers and lake shores.

Many animals, including these Olive Baboons (Papio anubis) must have regular access to water. Early mornings and late afternoons are favourite times for visiting waterholes like this one in Samburu and Buffalo Springs National Reserve. While drinking, the baboons are vulnerable to attack by predators; some members of the troop usually stand guard.

Staying at Samburu and Buffalo Springs National Reserves

Within the boundaries of the reserves and close by, there are three lodges available to visitors. In Samburu itself, the Samburu Game Lodge lies close to the river while on the other bank, just outside the boundaries of Buffalo Springs, is the Samburu River Lodge. Within the borders of this reserve, and not far from the waterholes of Buffalo Springs, is the Buffalo Springs Tented Lodge. There are also several campsites in both reserves near the river, most without facilities.

OL Doinyo Lenkiyo Mountains and Samburu Country

To experience a real taste of the bush and bush people, drive to Maralal from Samburu. From the A 2 which continues north to Marsabit, turn off left to the north of Archer's Post on the C 79. From the town of Wamba, you can climb the nearby Lolokwe Mountain or continue on the C 79 west. The terrain is stunning and Maralal has the feel of a real frontier town.

Shaba National Reserve

A short distance to the east of Samburu and Buffalo Springs National Reserves lies the Shaba National Reserve. To reach it turn right off the A 2 between the Buffalo Springs Gate and Archer's Post; this leads to the Natorbe Gate. The reserve comprises roughly 240km² of arid thornbush country grading to acacia woodland; the northern boundary of Shaba is marked by the Uaso Ngiro River. The reserve's name is derived from the volcanic cone of Mt Shaba in the south of the reserve from which there are some fine lava flows. Visitors can stay in the Shaba Sarova Lodge and there are campsites.

Shaba National Reserve was where Joy Adamson returned her Leopard 'Penny' to the wild; the exact spot, a spring, is christened Penny's Drop. Sadly, Shaba is also the place where Joy was murdered in 1980.

21 MARSABIT NATIONAL RESERVE AND NATIONAL PARK	
Location:	550km N of Nairobi; 270km N of Isiolo, nearest town Marsabit
Access:	Rough tracks from the main road (itself rough)
Terrain:	Volcanic peak covered in dense forest; surrounded by arid semi-desert
Specialities:	Elephant ('large tuskers'), Greater Kudu, desert birds
Accommodation:	Lodge and three campsites

Getting there

Before contemplating a trip to Marsabit National Reserve by road, it should be appreciated that this not a journey to be undertaken lightly. To reach the reserve involves at least 550km of driving, the last 270km of which from Isiolo are on extremely poor roads and across arid, semi-desert terrain with no facilities whatsoever. This stretch of the journey alone can take seven or eight hours. It is with good reason, therefore, that the provincial authorities require travellers to obtain a permit from Isiolo and travel in a convoy of at least two vehicles appropriate to the conditions. The vehicles must be fully provisioned.

To reach Isiolo, follow the directions for Samburu and Buffalo Springs National Reserves (*see* page 99). From the town, continue north on the A 2 passing the reserves and Archer's Post. Beyond the settlement, most of the country is arid thornbush until you pass through the eastern sector of Losai National Reserve, an area of forested hills. Thereafter, the road crosses the inhospitable wastes of the Kaisut Desert before you enter the Marsabit National Reserve and arrive at the town of the same name.

Many visitors choose to fly here from Nairobi but, whichever mode of transport is used, the benefits of reaching this out-of-the-way reserve are well worth the effort.

About the park

Marsabit National Reserve covers an area of more than 2000km² in Kenya's Northern Territories. Surrounded by desert, parts of the reserve are somewhat incongruous: dense forests cloak the higher reaches of the volcanic mountain and grade, at lower altitudes, into acacia woodland and arid thornbush. The reserve incorporates Marsabit National Park whose boundaries just embrace the mountain slopes.

Marsabit's unusual environment

By comparison with the surrounding lands, the mountain vegatation of Marsabit is lush and green. Its luxuriance is a testament to how profound an effect altitude can have on climate, even at a local level. Mt Marsabit rises to an altitude of 1531m (5023 feet); although not a great height in itself, it is high enough for clouds to form each evening. These remain through the night and the following morning creating a damp, cool environment in which forests, festooned with epiphytic plants, thrive. The western slopes of the mountain have considerably more cloud and rain than the eastern slopes and, consequently, support far more lush forests.

Within the reserve, Lake Paradise, at the

Leopard Tortoises *(Testudo pardalis) are widespread in East Africa. They usually remain concealed in the undergrowth.*

bottom of one of the volcanic craters, is a well known location and a haunt of large-tusked Elephants. There is a crater swamp at Sokortre Dika which is just south of Marsabit town and close to Marsabit Lodge.

Away from the climatic influences of the mountain, the vegetation becomes more and more arid. At the fringes of the deserts, many arid-country species of birds can be found.

Game mammals

Marsabit's lush, forested slopes serve as an oasis of green in this otherwise arid region. Consequently, game mammals are here in unusual abundance although they are not always very easy to find among the dense vegetation.

Marsabit National Reserve harbours Reticulated Giraffes which have taken to living in the forest, their normal habitat being open thornbush. However, it is for its Elephants that the reserve is particularly well known. A considerable number live on the mountain slopes and the population is one of the least affected by poaching. As a consequence,

Top: *the Lappet-faced Vulture (Torgos tracheliotus) is the largest vulture seen at kills.*
Bottom: *Beisa Oryx (Oryx gazella) are adapted to life in arid environments.*

many of the animals have immense tusks, a sight increasingly rare in the wild these days. One animal in particular, known as Ahmed, was particularly renowned for his tusks; he died a few years ago of old age, perhaps one of the last 'big tuskers' to have had a natural fate in recent years.

Marsabit is also known for its now thriving population of Greater Kudu, large and elegant antelopes with long, spiralled horns. At one time the herds almost died out due to rinderpest, but inoculation of domestic animals in the region appears to have aided their comeback. Search for them on the edge of the forest on the lower slopes of the mountain. As you move into more arid terrain, you should search for Gerenuk, Beisa Oryx and Grant's Gazelle, although these can be rather difficult to spot as they feed amongst the dry scrub, remaining fairly well hidden.

Birds
Because several different habitat types are found in Marsabit, a surprisingly wide variety of birds can be found in a comparatively small area. The crater swamps near Marsabit Lodge and Lake Paradise attract wetland birds such as ducks, herons and waders. The exact species present is dependent partly upon the time of year, migrants and winter visitors occuring from November to March, and on the water levels at the time. Most bird life is concentrated around the margins of the lake and swamp.

The evergreen forests which cloak the mountain slopes harbour birds such as Narina's Trogon, Yellow-whiskered Greenbul, Grey Apalis, Robin Chat and several species of sunbirds and weavers. Birds of prey are much in evidence in Marsabit. Look for species such as Crowned Hawk Eagle and Mountain Buzzard, with many more species found in the drier areas on the lower slopes.

Fischer's Finch Lark (Eremopterix leucopareia) is a common dry-country species, usually seen in small flocks.

22 LAKE TURKANA	
Location:	N Kenya, on Ethiopian border
Access:	Roads and tracks to parts of shoreline; boat trips to islands
Terrain:	Alkaline freshwater lake surrounded by desert and semi-desert scrub
Specialities:	Nile Crocodile, migrant waterbirds
Accommodation:	Lodges and campsites

Most views are those of birds in flight, which can pose identification problems.

The fringes of Marsabit grade into semi-desert and desert, those regions to the north being especially interesting. Some of the desert and arid-country birds can be found within the reserve from roads and tracks. Cream-coloured Courser, Masked Lark and Chestnut-bellied Sandgrouse are among the most typical of the desert species and fortunate visitors may even see Heuglin's Bustard or the Somali race of Ostrich, the males with their characteristic blue legs and neck.

Staying in Marsabit

Within the reserve there is one lodge, Marsabit Lodge, which is close to Sokortre Dika Crater Lake. There are also campsites in Marsabit.

Losai National Reserve

Those adventurous enough to drive to Marsabit will travel the Great North Road (A 2) to and from Isiolo. The road passes through the eastern sector of Losai National Reserve which, although largely inaccessible, may be worth a stop *en route*. It is not recommended, however, that visitors stray from the road.

Getting there

Most visitors to Lake Turkana choose to fly there, thus saving the three or four days it takes to drive there from Nairobi. However, with planning and considerable preparation, it is possible to drive all the way and those adventurous (some would say foolhardy!) enough to undertake this journey are sure to find it exciting and not uneventful.

Lake Turkana runs roughly north–south. There are roads leading to parts of the western and eastern shores. However, there are no roads between the two, the route being blocked by the Suguta Valley to the south.

For the route to the western side of the lake, take the A 104 north-west from Nairobi to Nakuru. Here, take one of two routes: either continue on the A 104 to Kitale, at the foot of Mt Elgon, and then head north-east through Kapenguria and Sebit until you reach the B 4. Thereafter you head north through Lotongot towards Lodwar. Alternatively, turn off at Nakuru in the direction of Marigat and Lake Baringo on the B 4. After Lomut, head north through Lotongot to Lodwar. From Lodwar, a road heads north-east to Lokwa Kangole on the shores of Ferguson's Gulf. Here you can get a boat to Lake Turkana Fishing Lodge.

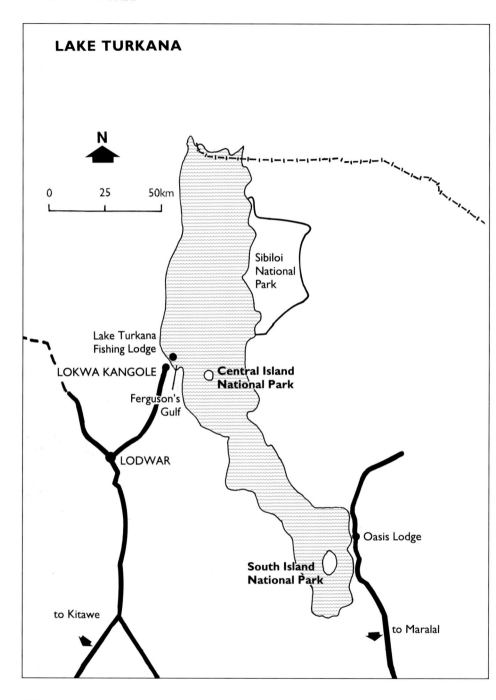

LAKE TURKANA

N

0   25   50km

Sibiloi
National
Park

Lake Turkana
Fishing Lodge

LOKWA KANGOLE

**Central Island
National Park**

Ferguson's
Gulf

LODWAR

Oasis Lodge

**South Island
National Park**

to Kitawe

to Maralal

Opposite: *map of Lake Turkana and its environs.*
Above: *Lesser Flamingos (Phoenicopterus minor) in Crater Lake on Central Island National Park, Lake Turkana.*

To reach the east side of the lake, the best route is to head north-west from Nairobi and turn off on the C 77 through Nyahururu to Maralal. Continue north to South Horr and on to Loyangalani and the Oasis Lodge.

About the lake

Lake Turkana is the northernmost of the Rift Valley lakes of Kenya; its northern shores lie just over the border within Ethiopia. It is over 250km long, and up to 45km wide, and covers more than 6000km². Lake Turkana is Africa's fourth largest lake and is fed by the waters of Ethiopia's River Omo; there is no outflow, evaporation off the surface compensating for the huge input. The lake is a watery oasis in the surrounding desert landscape,

rich in wildlife and archaeological interest.

The deserts which border Lake Turkana are among the harshest environments in Kenya, with daytime temperatures sometimes soaring to 50°C or more. Nevertheless, desert wildlife still survives although the natural history interest of the region is understandably focused on the lake. Turkana is famed for its fishing, Nile Perch regularly exceeding 100kg in weight, and for its Nile Crocodiles, as the lake has the biggest concentration of these reptiles in East Africa. Waterbirds also congregate here and the lake plays passing host to hordes of migrants from Europe and Asia, many of which use the Rift Valley as a migration route.

Much of Lake Turkana's shoreline is effectively inaccessible. However, there are several areas that visitors can reach without too much trouble. If staying at the Lake Turkana Fishing Lodge, the Ferguson's Gulf area is excellent for birds and boat trips can

The Cream-coloured Courser (Cursorius cursor) lives in arid habitats. It is most easily seen in north Kenya.

Nile Crocodile *Crocodylus niloticus*
L up to 500

The Nile Crocodile is one of Africa's most feared predators and rightly so since this species accounts for more human deaths on the continent than any other. Due to their size they can tackle prey as large as Wildebeest although their diet mainly comprises fish. In some areas, larger crocodiles feed by ambushing game mammals as they come to drink at the water's edge. With large prey, crocodiles generally hold a leg in their jaws and spin in the water until it is torn from the carcass.

Crocodiles were once thought to be cannibalistic. This unjustified assertion probably came about as a result of their excellent parental care being witnessed. Female Crocodiles lay a batch of eggs in the sandy bank of a river where they are incubated by the heat of the sun. When they are about to hatch, the young make a faint call from within the egg which alerts the mother. She guards them as they hatch, from would-be predators such as monitor lizards and birds of prey, and often carries them gently in her mouth to the water's edge.

be arranged from here to Central Island National Park. From Oasis Lodge, visitors can reach South Island National Park and permission can sometimes be arranged to fly in and visit Sibiloi National Park further up the eastern shore.

Ferguson's Gulf
Although the area does not have the status of a national park or reserve it is in effect protected by its comparative isolation. Arid-country birds which can be seen *en route* from Lodwar to the lake shore include Heughlin's Bustard, Cream-coloured Courser, Abyssinian Ground Hornbill and Carmine Bee-eater. Around the shores, look for pelicans, Sacred Ibis, herons, waders, such as Black-winged Stilt and Avocet, Caspian Tern and African Skimmer. The number of waders and terns build up from November to March (the northern hemisphere winter), but numbers and the variety of birds are greatest during migration times. The flocks of Marsh Sandpipers and White-winged Black Terns can be particularly impressive.

around which crocodiles and waterbirds breed. Take care when in the vicinity of the crocodiles.

Central Island National Park
The island can be reached by boat from Ferguson's Gulf and contains crater lakes

South Island National Park
South Island lies at the southern end of the lake opposite Oasis Lodge and Loyangalani.

It too boasts nesting crocodiles and water-birds and is a popular location with fishing enthusiasts.

Sibiloi National Park

Reaching Sibiloi National Park overland is an expedition in itself and the few people who visit this remote location generally do so by plane. Its chief claim to fame is as the site where Richard Leakey, son of the late Dr Louis Leakey and now head of Kenya's Parks Department, found the remains of some of our earliest ancestors. These were *Homo habilis*, a tool-making ancestor, and *Homo erectus*, our ancestor that first walked upright.

23 LAKE VICTORIA AND RUMA NATIONAL PARK

Location:	c. 300km W of Nairobi; nearest town Kisumu
Access:	Boat trips and ferries on lake; network of tracks around national park
Terrain:	Freshwater lake; grassland and scrub
Specialities:	Hippopotamuses, Roan Antelope
Accommodation:	Hotels in Kisumu; camping in the park

Getting there

Lake Victoria lies to the west of Nairobi and can be reached by public transport (coach, train and plane) as well as private vehicle. Kisumu is Kenya's third largest town and a good centre from which to explore the lake and its environs. Head north-west from Nairobi on the A 104 to Nakuru. Beyond Nakuru, turn left onto the B 1 to Kericho at which point the road bears north-west to Kisumu. From the town, roads around the lake margin allow exploration.

About the lake

Lake Victoria is the largest freshwater lake in Africa and one of the sources of the Nile. A wide variety of birds, such as ducks, herons, egrets and storks, are found around its shores and its waters support populations of Nile Crocodiles and Hippopotamuses. At one time, Lake Victoria harboured many endemic species of fish, particularly cichlids. Unfortunately, modern man has upset the balance of nature somewhat by introducing the voracious Nile Perch which has effectively been the downfall of many other species of fish. In addition, there is also the looming spectre of commercial overfishing of the stocks.

Kisumu is a thriving town on the north-eastern shores of the lake from which ferries depart and boat trips can be arranged. There is more cultural interest than natural history interest in the town although visitors may like to see Hippopotamuses near the Sunset Hotel at Hippo Point. For wildlife interest, visitors should try to get to Ruma National Park to the south-west.

Ruma National Park

Formerly called Lambwe Valley National Park, this park was specially created to protect a population of Roan Antelopes. Much of the land bordering Lake Victoria has been colonized by man but the area of the park remained wild partly due to its Tsetse Flies which transmit sleeping sickness.

The park comprises an area of 120km² of open grassland with patches of acacia woodland. If you do not intend to camp in the park, the most convenient place to stay is in Homa Bay. In addition to Roan Antelope, the reserve harbours Jackson's Hartebeest, Oribi and numerous species of birds. Ostriches, as well as Giraffes and Zebras have been introduced.

Roan Antelope *Hippotragus equinus*
L 240–265 (head and body)

The Roan is one of the largest of the East African antelopes, standing nearly 1.5m tall at the shoulder. Both sexes have horns, those of the male being larger; they arch backwards over the head but are not as curved as in their close relative, the Sable Antelope. There is a mane down the back of the neck and a fringe of hairs on the throat. They have thickset bodies and hides that are a sandy-brown colour. The markings on the face are most distinctive, being a bold mixture of black and white.

Roan Antelopes are one of the most endangered of Kenya's many antelopes. Apart from the population in the Ruma National Park, the only other place that they can be found is in the Shimba Hills. They live in groups of five to ten animals and are wary creatures, keeping to the cover of wooded grassland wherever possible.

24 KAKAMEGA FOREST NATIONAL RESERVE	
Location:	W Kenya; c. 40km N of Kisumu
Access:	Forest paths and tracks
Terrain:	Tropical rainforest
Specialities:	Great Blue Turaco, Black-and-white Colobus
Accommodation:	Limited camping; forest lodge

Getting there
Kakamega Forest National Reserve lies to the east of the town of Kakamega in western Kenya. From Kisumu, on the shores of Lake Victoria, drive north on the A 1 for about 30km. Approximately 10km before Kakamega town, turn right at a sign onto a dirt road. After about 12km, turn left to the forest station.

About the forest
Kakamega Forest is unique in Kenya. It is the last remnant of a tropical rainforest that was once much more extensive, stretching westwards all the way to the Congo. Isolated by changes in climate and cultivation of much of the surrounding land, it is destined to remain a forest island. Kakamega is West African in origin and West African in character: many of its birds, mammals, insects and plants are found nowhere else in Kenya.

Kakamega Forest's status as a national reserve goes some way to protecting this fragile environment from the fragmentation of the surrounding habitat by farming and forestry; the reserve covers just 97km². However, having reserve status is no cause for complacency. Because of its isolation, anything that is lost, be it tree, bird or mammal, will never be replaced.

The forest lies at an altitude of around 1600m (5250 feet) and receives an annual rainfall of at least 250cm which qualifies it as true rainforest. The abundance of life in the forest, which is not always immediately obvious, is astonishing.

Getting the most from Kakamega Forest
When you visit Kakamega, do not expect the same sort of experience as you would in an open savannah reserve. Large mammals are almost absent; forests in general support fewer large mammals than open grassland and those in Kakamega have long-since been hunted by the surrounding peoples. Even the birds can be difficult to see; you will hear calls everywhere but a fleeting glimpse in the foliage may be all the view you get.

Kakamega is a place for the dedicated birdwatcher, one who is willing to put effort, and more especially time, into the endeavour. The rewards are definitely worth it, however, and some of the most exciting birds in East Africa can be seen here. If birds are thin on the ground, then there is always something else to see. The plant life is luxuriant and amazing and there are monkeys and a host of insects to discover.

The first couple of hours after dawn provide the best opportunities for bird and mammal watching when things are at their most active. Many of the birds are forest-canopy dwellers and visitors will have to resign themselves to getting a stiff neck. Try to find a clearing or forest ride to get a good view. If you find a likely looking spot, wait and see what comes to you.

Birds that live nearer the forest floor can be equally challenging to locate. Although not necessarily shy, many remain motionless and concealed if disturbed. Therefore, walk slowly along forest trails looking for any sign of movement and listening for the tell-tale rustling of leaves or calls. If something attracts your attention, stand still and wait to see what appears rather than trying to get closer. You may even find that some of the birds are curious about you, so long as you give them no cause for alarm. Forest clearings provide excellent opportunites for watching birds in the tree canopy and at the forest edge.

Birds
Some of the forest species will be familiar to anyone who has already been birdwatching in the Kenyan Highlands and even in Nairobi City Park; Narina's Trogon, Cinnamon-chested Bee-eater, Klaas' Cuckoo, Golden-rumped Tinkerbird and Striped Kingfisher are all widespread.

Although seeing new species at Kakamega is usually fairly slow-going, it is undoubtedly

The Blue-eared Glossy Starling (Lamprotornis chalybaeus) *has a shiny, blue plumage making it extremely eye-catching.*

worth the effort. Perhaps the most spectacular and colourful of the forest residents are the turacos, large birds with long tails. Of the four species which can be seen in Kakamega, Hartlaub's Turaco is widespread with a mainly green plumage, rufous on the wings and conspicuous black-and-white markings on the head. The Black-billed Turaco, a mainly green-plumaged bird, and Ross's Turaco, a deep-purple bird with yellow face and bill, and red crown, are more local. The last species, the Great Blue Turaco, is extremely local and Kakamega is the only place where you are likely to see it in Kenya. It has blue upperparts, yellow and orange underparts and a conspicuous crest; it is altogether a most striking bird.

Other colourful birds of the forest include the parrots. Brown Parrots which in fact have grey-brown upperparts, green underparts and yellow on the shoulders and crown, are widespread in Kenya and throughout much of east and central Africa, but Grey Parrots are restricted to the west of the country with Kakamega as a stronghold. They have pale grey plumage and a striking red tail.

Another speciality of the forest is the Blue-headed Bee-eater which has a rather subdued plumage when compared to some of its relatives. It can sometimes be seen

*The Grey-headed Kingfisher (*Halcyon leucocephala*) is often seen away from water.*

perched on branches overhanging forest clearings when its deep-blue plumage, chestnut mantle and red throat can be seen. Forest clearings should also be searched for Crowned Hawk Eagle, Black and White-casqued Hornbill, Red-headed Malimbes (weaver-like birds with a red crown and nape) and sunbirds.

A quiet walk along a forest trail may yield African Thrush, Snowy-capped Robin-chat and perhaps some of Kakamega's primates. Blue Monkey and Black-and-white Colobus Monkey have been recorded although they can be difficult to see. As you proceed along the paths, always keep an eye on the forest floor in front of you since Gabon Vipers occur at Kakamega. These masters of disguise spend much of their time lying in wait for birds and small mammals, camouflaged among the fallen leaves; forest paths are an ideal habitat for them. Although these are not aggressive reptiles, they will certainly bite if trodden on.

After dark

As dusk approaches, there is a chance of seeing one of Kakamega's nocturnal residents. The Red-chested Owlet is known from this forest. If seen well, it has a rufous chest and white collar, although you are more likely to catch a glimpse of its round-winged shape in flight. Bat Hawks have also been recorded here. The flight silhouette resembles that of a typical falcon and they catch swallows and bats just as the light is fading.

Staying at Kakamega

Kakamega is close enough to Kisumu and Kakamega town, both of which have hotels, for day trips to be made to the forest. There is also limited and basic rest house accommodation at the forest station.

25 MOUNT ELGON NATIONAL PARK

Location:	c.420km NW of Nairobi; nearest town Kitale
Access:	Rough tracks and trails
Terrain:	Forested slopes, open moorland, caves
Specialities:	Cave-visiting Elephants, Afro-alpine flora
Accommodation:	Lodges nearby, campsites inside park

Getting there

The nearest town to Mt Elgon is Kitale which lies roughly 400km north-west of Nairobi. It can be reached by public transport but is also accessible on good roads from the capital. Take the A 104 which heads north-west from the city towards Nakuru. Continue on to Eldoret and near Lesuru turn right onto the B 2 to Kitale. Mt Elgon provides a superb backdrop to the town, the summit lying less than 50km to the west. Access to the national park is by one of three gates, the easiest of which to find is the Chorlim Gate. This is reached via a turning off the C 45 Endebess road, 25km from Kitale; in good weather, it is possible to drive most of the way up through the forest in a four-wheel-drive vehicle. There is another gate at Kimilili which lies to the west of Kitale on the C 42.

About Mt Elgon

Mt Elgon is Kenya's second highest mountain after Mt Kenya to the south-east. Like its sister mountain, it is also an extinct volcano whose crater rim straddles the Kenyan-Ugandan border. At its highest point, the broad rim reaches 4321m (14,177 feet). This is on the Ugandan side of the border, but since the Kenyan side reaches 4310m (14,140 feet) the difference is hardly noticeable.

Mount Elgon National Park protects only a small area of the mountain's flanks on its eastern slopes. It covers an area of 170km² and ranges between 2500 and 4300m (8200–14,100 feet) in altitude. As a consequence, the national park harbours a surprising variety of habitats for such a small area, from montane forest to open moorland and the zone of Afro-alpine plants above.

Like most of East Africa's mountains, many of the plants, such as Senecio amblyphyllus shown here, found in Mt Elgon's Afro-alpine zone, are endemic to this location. This means that they are found nowhere else in the world. Many Afro-alpine species grow to a great size and have leaves and flowers coated in hairs to help prevent frost damage.

Mt Elgon is one of the least visited of Kenya's national reserves and parks. Partly because of its distance from Nairobi, it is not on the main tourist route and consequently there are relatively few visitor facilities. However, for many people this is part of the appeal of Mt Elgon, a park where you can explore and enjoy the scenery and wildlife in isolation. The park is most easily explored during the dry seasons, from November to March and June to July.

Mt Elgon's wildlife

Although you can drive through the forest as far as the open moorland, visitors may choose to walk all the way. The first habitat to be encountered is the montane forest. This has similarities with the wooded slopes of Mt Kenya and the Aberdares and the wildlife is similar. Look for Mountain Buzzard, Crowned Hornbill, Hartlaub's Turaco and Narina's Trogon.

Mammals are also well represented in Mt Elgon's forested slopes but are always difficult to see. Considering their size, Elephants are particularly elusive and live up to their reputation for being quiet creatures. African Buffalo also occur on the slopes. Both these large mammals are rather unpredictable, especially if surprised or confronted. Visitors should be prepared to back-off quickly if they are encountered. Black-fronted Duikers and Waterbuck are shy forest residents and are seldom seen other than by chance, but Black-and-white Colobus Monkeys are more conspicuous as they leap through the tree-tops.

The open moorland and Afro-alpine zone

Above the treeline the forest is replaced first by Bamboo and then by open moorland where huge tussocks of grass predominate. With increasing altitude, the Afro-alpine plants for which Mt Elgon is famous, begin to appear. Many of these are characterized by their giant forms, species of lobelias, groundsels and heathers reaching several metres in height.

Salt caves and Elephants

Although Mount Elgon National Park is well known for its stunning Afro-alpine flora and scenery, it is probably best known for the Elephants that visit some of its caves in search of salt. This curious phenomenon, unique among Kenya's Elephants, can occasionally be witnessed by lucky visitors and the caves themselves are worth inspecting for their interesting inhabitants.

The lower slopes of Mt Elgon are riddled with caves in the lava. A few of them, most notably Kitum Cave, are famous for having attracted generations of Elephants to feed on salts. Indeed, it is probably true that the Elephants themselves have actually enlarged and lengthened Kitum cave to its present dimensions.

Mt Elgon's Elephants visit this cave in small groups, generally arriving at the mouth around dusk. So familiar are they with the subterranean route that they negotiate hazards and obstacles in complete darkness until they reach the end of the cave. Here they use their tusks to gouge salts and minerals from the rock face.

Staying at Mt Elgon

If you wish to explore Mount Elgon National Park at length then the only way to do it is to camp. There are no lodges within the park but nearby is the Mt Elgon Lodge. Alternatively, you could stay in the Loikitela Guest House between the park entrance and Kitale or at Kitale Hotel in the town itself. You will then need your own transport to get to and from the park.

26 SAIWA SWAMP NATIONAL PARK

Location:	25km NW of Kitale
Access:	Platform viewing hides
Terrain:	Swamp forest.
Specialities:	Sitatunga
Accommodation:	None

Getting there

Saiwa Swamp National Park is more than 400km from Nairobi and is generally only visited by people already in western Kenya at sites such as Mt Elgon and Kakamega Forest. From Kitale, drive north-west on the C 46 which leads eventually to Lodwar and Turkana. Turn right after 25km at the village of Kipsain and follow the track for 5 km until you reach the reserve. Trails within the reserve lead to tree platforms from which the inundated swamp can be viewed.

About the swamp

Saiwa Swamp is Kenya's smallest national park and comprises an area of only 1.9km². The main feature of the park is, as its name suggests, the swamp habitat dominated by bulrushes and other aquatic plants. A river winds its way through the wetland, the area being surrounded by forest. Saiwa Swamp is largely inaccessible. However, elevated tree platforms have been erected from which the wildlife of the park can be viewed.

The chief reason for establishing Saiwa Swamp National Park was to protect its resident population of Sitatunga which may number as many as 100 animals. This antelope is on the eastern edge of its distribution in Kenya and Saiwa Swamp is the only site where visitors stand a reasonable chance of seeing one. They are largely nocturnal and extremely shy creatures. Their preferred habitat of swamps and marshes does not help

observing them, nor does their habit of hiding in Papyrus and almost submerging when alarmed. Fortunately, at Saiwa Swamp, the viewing platforms afford good vantage points, but even so you may need to wait some time to see a Sitatunga.

Sitatunga have brown coats, transverse white stripes on their backs and twisted horns not unlike those of a Bushbuck. The most unusual features, however, are the hooves which are extremely elongated, an adaptation for life in an aquatic environment.

In addition to the Sitatunga, there are several other interesting mammals to look out for at Saiwa Swamp, notably Pottos, relatives of the Bushbaby, and Spotted-necked Otters. Small groups of Brazza's Monkeys also live in the swamp forest. Because of their retiring habits, the platform viewing hides are ideal for watching them without causing disturbance.

Bird life is also rich and varied in the national park. Waterbirds, such as herons, egrets and ducks, can be seen and a variety of cisticolas occur.

Visiting Saiwa Swamp

There are no opportunities for staying at Saiwa Swamp and most visitors travel from accommodation in Kitale (Kitale Hotel) or nearer Mt Elgon.

East Africa's cisticolas can be difficult to identify. This is a Winding Cisticola (Cisticola galactotes).

2. COASTAL KENYA

INTRODUCTION

Most people's image of coastal Kenya is of beach holidays with white sands, palm trees and bronzed bodies. It is certainly true that the majority of visitors to this region are there simply to enjoy a relaxing holiday. However, in doing so they miss a wide variety of coastal wildlife. The two approaches to having a holiday on the coast, wildlife watching and beach relaxation, are not necessarily mutually exclusive and many visitors successfully combine the two.

Do not expect to find the same game-watching opportunities on the coast that inland Kenya has to offer. Its attraction lies in the coral reefs, mangrove swamps and extraordinary variety of bird life that frequents the shores. However, there is always an exception and in this case the Shimba Hills National Reserve is the odd one out. Here, just a few kilometres inland from Mombasa, there are good game-watching opportunities and open-country birds to be seen.

Although almost anywhere on the coast has its attraction, one area in particular stands out from the rest. The stretch of coast from Watamu north to Malindi and the mouth of the Sabaki River has the best of everything. There are superb coral reefs offshore while the shore is fringed with sandy beaches, sand dunes, mudflats and mangroves. There is even a remnant pocket of coastal tropical forest to add an extra dimension. Although there are a few unusual mammals to see on the coast, most of the interest lies in the marine life and the coastal birds.

Opposite: extensive mangrove swamps still survive on the Kenyan coast.

27 MALINDI-WATAMU BIOSPHERE RESERVE

Location:	100km N of Mombasa
Access:	To shore on foot; snorkelling and boat trips to view coral reefs
Terrain:	Coral reefs; sandy beaches, mudflats and mangroves
Specialities:	Crab Plover, migrant waders, marine life
Accommodation:	Numerous hotels in Malindi and Watamu

Getting there

Malindi and Watamu can be reached by driving north from Mombasa on the B 8 coastal road. After the mouth of Kilifi Creek has been crossed by ferry, the road continues north past Mida Creek. Just beyond the creek there is a turning to the right which leads past the ruins of Gedi to Watamu and on to the mouth of Mida Creek. Follow the B 8 north and you will come to Malindi. The northern shores of Mida Creek can be explored on tracks leading from the main road. Visitors can explore the shores freely and take boats out to the edge of the coral reef.

The journey from Mombasa is straightforward if you have your own vehicle and there are buses which regularly run along this route. If you travel by train from Nairobi to Mombasa, you will be besieged at the station by hordes of drivers of both taxis and minibuses; a very reasonable rate for the trip can usually be negotiated.

About the biosphere reserve

The Malindi-Watamu Biosphere Reserve was created in 1979 and comprises four previously separate designated sites which may cause a little confusion. At the northern end

of the reserve is the Malindi Marine National Park, 6km² encompassed by the much larger Malindi National Marine Reserve. At the southern end is the Watamu National Park which is surrounded by the Watamu National Marine Reserve. The biosphere reserve therefore stretches from Malindi, south to the southern side of Mida Creek.

Habitats of Malindi and Watamu
For the marine biologist, the Malindi and Watamu area has got everything. There are long, sandy beaches interspersed with rocky outcrops which provide rock pools at low tide and anchorage for seaweeds lower down the shore. Shallow waters lead out to coral reefs which are rich in marine life and buffer the shores from the pounding Indian Ocean. By way of contrast there is Mida Creek, an almost land-locked lagoon which empties

Mida Creek, which lies at the southern end of the Malindi-Watamu Biosphere Reserve.

out at low tide to expose vast areas of mudflats. Bird life is abundant and varied and the edge of the creek is fringed in mangrove providing yet another marine habitat.

Coral reef
Malindi and Watamu are a snorkellers paradise. With just the aid of a mask and a lung full of air, a whole new world opens up. Add the use of a snorkel and you will have hours of pleasure watching the colourful reef inhabitants.

Corals are the backbone of this rich but fragile ecosystem. They are tiny animals which form hard calcareous cases for protection and support of their soft bodies. As individuals they may be small but they live colonially forming the massive reefs so characteristic of the coast. New colonies build on old ones and so the reef grows. Never be tempted to buy ornamental coral or products made from it, as by doing so you would be contributing to the destruction of this beautiful habitat.

Coral reefs provide shelter not only for the coral polyps that made them but also for a vast array of marine creatures. Fish are there in colourful abundance and, where not hunted or disturbed, become tolerant of human visitors and sometimes even inquisitive. Starfish, sea anemones, sea urchins, sea cucumbers and many other exotic creatures will also capture your interest.

Mida Creek

Mida Creek is one of the most exciting birdwatching spots on the Kenyan coasts. Throughout the year there are herons, egrets, waders and terns in abundance but the numbers of resident birds is boosted by migrants from Europe and Asia which flock here outside the breeding season. Many species arrive as early as August and stay until the following April.

Mida Creek is fringed with mangroves and those along the northern shore in particular provide a natural hide from which to view the mudflats, not that the birds are particularly wary of man, and fishermen can be seen out in the creeks working alongside herons and gulls. The northern shore can be reached by tracks from the main road. In this area you will seldom spend much time alone, since birdwatchers exert a curious fascination for the local children.

An alternative view of the creek can be had by continuing south from Watamu until you reach the spit at the mouth of the creek. Tracks lead a short way along the shore in either direction and plenty can be seen from the road on the way. As the tide is changing,

Crab Plover *Dromus ardeola* L 35

This is one of the most distinctive of Kenya's waders. With striking black-and-white plumage, it is superficially similar, at a distance, to an Avocet. However, a closer view will soon reveal the difference: Crab Plovers are bulky birds which have large and heavy black bills. Although a few can be seen throughout most of the year along the Kenyan coast, they do not breed there. Instead, most fly north to islands in the Red Sea where, unusually for waders, they excavate holes in the sandy ground in which to nest.

this is an excellent spot to watch waders flying in and out of the creek to and from roosting spots.

Perhaps the most outstanding wildlife feature of Mida Creek is the number and variety of waders that it supports. Arguably the most elegant are the Crab Plovers which stalk the mudflats in search of crabs and other invertebrates; with their black-and-white plumage, they are certainly the most striking. Whimbrel, Curlew, Greenshank and Grey Plover are non-breeding visitors that are present from August or September until April or May.

Smaller waders also dot the surface of the mudflats at low tide. Both Greater and Lesser Sandplovers occur in considerable numbers, several thousand being present at times, which provides a rare opportunity to compare these two similar species side-by-side. Curlew, Common and Marsh Sandpipers, Little Stint and Ringed Plover are also usually present in good numbers, and there is always the chance of seeing something more unusual, such as a Terek or Broad-billed Sandpiper.

Mangroves

Fringing the shores of Mida Creek are dense swathes of mangroves. These trees are found throughout the tropics and are specially adapted to a life partly immersed in seawater. The environment is indeed harsh for a land plant: the roots have to contend with being buried in choking, anaerobic mud and are twice daily both immersed in salty seawater and exposed to the air. Several different species are found around Mida Creek, each with a different tolerance of exposure to air and immersion in seawater. Consequently, each grows at a different level on the shore. Mangroves are important agents in the creation of new land; their tangled roots trap silt and mud, which leads to the formation of dry land. One of the best places to explore the mangroves is from the northern side of the mouth of Mida Creek; a path leads westwards for a short way around the shore.

A male fiddler crab (Uca sp.) vigorously defends the entrance to its burrow on the mudflats.

The surrounding land

When visiting Mida Creek, it is worth paying some attention to the surrounding land as well as to the mudflats. Little Purple-banded Sunbirds can be seen visiting flowering plants and Striped Swallows and Ethiopian Swallows rest on overhead wires. These same perches are used by Zanzibar Sombre Greenbuls, which are rather dull birds but with colourful songs, and by Lizard Buzzards which scan the ground below for insects, lizards and small mammals.

Staying at Watamu-Malindi

There are numerous hotels and beach chalets in the Malindi and Watamu areas. One of the most convenient for exploring the Mida Creek area is Seafarers at Watamu

28 MALINDI AND THE SABAKI RIVER	
Location:	110km N of Mombasa
Access:	Open access to beach and sand dunes
Terrain:	Sandy beach and dunes, estuary with mudflats and mangroves
Specialities:	Wading birds, Madagascar Pratincole
Accommodation:	Numerous hotels and beach chalets in Malindi

Getting there

Malindi is a thriving coastal resort north of Mombasa. Drive north on the coastal B 8 passing Kilifi Creek and Mida Creek. There are regular coach services from Mombasa and minibuses and taxis can be negotiated at Mombasa railway station.

About Malindi and the Sabaki River

Malindi provides an often welcome opportunity to unwind from the rigours of a safari.

Here the pace can be more relaxed even though the birds in particular are just as exciting. Although Malindi is a beach resort like many others, it has the advantage of being close to an excellent area for wildlife. The shores of the Indian Ocean are invariably productive, but combine this with extensive sand dunes and the estuary of the Sabaki River and the site becomes outstanding.

At one time, Malindi had a rather ugly reputation for mugging and street robbery. Nowadays, however, the local police appear particularly vigilant and visitors should not be unduly concerned. It might, however, be tempting providence a little to wander back from the Sabaki River on your own after dark, laden with cameras and binoculars.

The Sabaki River

The Sabaki River is one of Kenya's most important watercourses. It starts life in the hills near Nairobi and then flows south-east through Tsavo National Park. After tumbling over Lugards Falls, it becomes the Galana River and finally, where it empties into the sea, it is called the Sabaki River. At its mouth, extensive mudflats are exposed at low tide which attract large numbers of waterbirds.

Exploring the area

Walk north from Malindi town along the road which runs parallel to, and closest to, the coast, looking for African Palm Swifts and Indian House Crows on the way. About a kilometre from the town, the road bears left; continue straight ahead on a track signposted to the golf course.

Birds of the golf course

Once you have passed the clubhouse, you will see the greens on your right. If you arrive early enough in the morning you should find Blackhead Plovers which get scared off by the first golfers. Further on, the track bears to the right and passes between two pools which harbour African Jacana, egrets, Squacco Heron and Goliath Heron. Before you reach the first of the sand dunes, you come to a larger lake on the left. African Pygmy Goose has been seen here and there are usually Openbill Storks, egrets and Long-tailed Cormorants to be found.

To the north of the town of Malindi lies an extensive area of sand dunes which stretch to the mouth of the Sabaki River. A wide range of resident and migrant birds can be found by searching the brackish and freshwater pools and the dune scrub. At the mouth of the river, extensive mudflats and mangroves support herons, gulls, terns and waders.

123

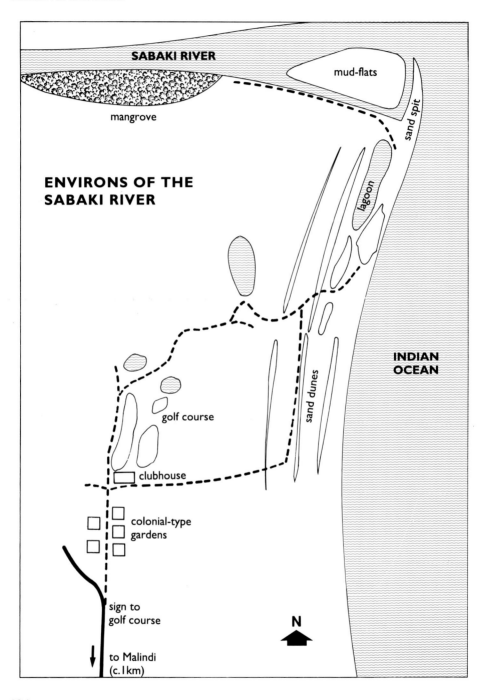

SABAKI RIVER

mud-flats

mangrove

sand spit

**ENVIRONS OF THE
SABAKI RIVER**

lagoon

INDIAN
OCEAN

sand dunes

golf course

clubhouse

colonial-type
gardens

sign to
golf course

N

to Malindi
(c.1km)

The sand dunes

Once you reach the sand dunes, paths radiate in all directions so follow any one that heads vaguely northwards; the dunes are a vast and wonderful place for the naturalist to explore. Sand dunes are not a static environment and present a variety of different habitats. Closest to the sea, the dunes are constantly shifting, forming great ridges of sand with hollows between. Inland, the sand soon becomes colonized by plants which gradually stabilize the surface. The farther away from the sea, the older the dunes are and the more stable they become. Eventually scrub and finally woodland predominate and mask the maritime origins of the habitat.

Many of the hollows between the dunes harbour wet flushes and lagoons on which herons and waders bathe and feed. Some of the more stable dunes have been colonized by patches of lush vegetation, such as Morning Glory, which is adorned by colourful pink, funnel-shaped flowers. Bushes and scrub develop in some of the drier areas.

Some of the birds that are found in the sand dunes are extremely colourful. Zanzibar Red Bishops, for example, are striking with red-and-black plumage. They are resident along the coast while the equally attractive Carmine Bee-eater is a visitor from September until March, sometimes in sizeable flocks. As their name suggests, they have deep carmine-red plumage but their bluish faces and long tail streamers are also noticeable. By contrast, a few species are sombre and difficult to locate. The Mozambique Nightjar, for example, has a plumage which provides superb camouflage as it rests by day among the ground vegetation. You are unlikely to see one before you flush it as you walk through the dunes. However, you may be lucky enough to watch where it lands so that you can creep closer for a better view without disturbing it.

As you walk past some of the lagoons you will see waders such as Black-winged Stilts and Spur-winged Plovers feeding; the plovers nest here so be careful where you tread, especially if you see a distressed bird. Larger lagoons may harbour preening Crested Terns and, if you are fortunate, a few African Skimmers. These curious, tern-like birds have bills with the lower mandible longer than the upper. They fly low over the water with the

Opposite: *map of the environs of the Sabaki River.*
Right: *the Spur-winged Plover (Vanellus spinosus) is a widespread bird in East Africa and is commonly seen on the dunes at Malindi. Here it occasionally breeds, making a shallow scrape in the sand in which to lay its eggs. The 'spur' on the wing, from which the species gets its name, is only visible in flight and even then it is difficult to see.*

125

lower mandible just breaking the water surface. If it touches a fish, the bill snaps shut and the prey is caught.

Pratincoles also occur in small numbers but, from July to September, there are also large flocks of Madagascar Pratincoles, often more than a thousand strong, to be found as well. Madagascar Pratincoles, like common Pratincoles, are unusual waders with a swallow-like silhouette in flight. They both have red underwings but Madagascar Pratincoles are much smaller and shorter-tailed and lack the neat black line that defines the pale throat of their relatives.

The mouth of the Sabaki River

Continuing northwards, you will eventually come to the mouth of the Sabaki River. The state of the tide will greatly affect what you see and how well you see it. At low tide, the birds are often spread out over the mudflats and rather distant. At high tide, they may fly off to roost elsewhere. Therefore, the best time for birdwatching is on a rising tide; sit quietly on the sand and let the water push the birds towards you.

The mudflats are treacherous so do not be tempted to walk on them to get closer to the birds. There is also another danger: with the almost perpetual wind that blows along the coast, dry sand often gets blown onto the mud nearest the shore giving the impression of dry land. Exercise extreme caution near the edge of the mud since if you fall in it is unlikely that anyone will come along to pull you out.

Waders galore

From August until the following April or May, the mouth of the Sabaki River is a wonderful place for the birdwatcher, especially one who is interested in waders. Hundreds of Greater and Lesser Sandplovers

can be present. The sand plovers, together with Ringed Plovers, are non-breeding visitors, present in numbers only from September until April. They join the resident White-fronted Sand Plovers and Kittlitz's Plovers and often feed together.

Larger waders are represented by Whimbrel, Curlew and Greenshank and there are several smaller species to be found as well. Curlew Sandpipers are common and recognized by their long, downcurved bills and white rumps in flight, and Marsh Sandpipers are also easily found. With patience, you should also find Little Stint, Wood Sandpiper and Sanderling feeding on the mudflats. Highlights, however, for many birdwatchers are the Terek Sandpipers and Broad-billed Sandpipers which are also found here in small numbers. Terek Sandpipers are easily recognized by their long, upcurved bill which is somewhat reminiscent of that of an Avocet. The Broad-billed Sandpiper has a straight bill with a broad, downcurved tip.

Waders are not the only birds of interest out on the mudflats. Great Egrets, Little Egrets and Grey Herons stalk fish and crabs and African Spoonbills and Sacred Ibises can also be found. African Fish Eagles regularly hunt here and look distinctly out of place when seen standing on the bare mud.

Whimbrel (Numenius phaeopus) *are visitors to the East African coast during the northern winter.*

Waves continually pound the sandy beach which runs north to the Sabaki River. At its mouth, the force of the river's current and that of ocean meet and a sand spit juts out into the Sabaki as a continuation of the beach. This provides an ideal roosting spot for birds at high tide and an excellent opportunity for the birdwatcher to compare species. A telescope is advisable to enable identification without having to get too close to the birds.

Gulls and terns

Sooty Gulls are much in evidence on the sand spit and birds of different ages and in different plumages often sit side-by-side. A careful inspection of each bird is often a good idea since White-eyed Gulls occasionally turn up. Several species of tern can also be found; when they are not roosting on the sand spit they fish offshore between the breakers. Caspian Terns are the largest and most distinctive: they are gull-sized and have immense orange-red bills. Crested and Lesser Crested Terns are slightly smaller species but are larger than the White-cheeked and Roseate Terns that roost with them. Smallest of all is Saunder's Little Tern which looks positively minute when seen beside a Caspian Tern.

Mangrove wildlife

At the mouth of the Sabaki River, a track leads a short way upriver along the southern bank. The way is eventually blocked by muddy creeks and mangroves but gives the visitor an excellent opportunity to watch the mangrove wildlife at close range. Fiddler Crabs, males brandishing their colourful and outsize single claw, panic at your approach and retreat to their mud burrows. Sit quietly for a few minutes and they will soon emerge again and resume feeding. They do so by picking particles off the surface of the mud with their small pincers, a most laborious task. The colourful pincer that each male bears is used to advertise his presence both to rival males and to females.

Equally endearing are the Mudskippers that abound among the mangroves. These unusual fish spend much of their time out of water, using their pectoral fins and tails to literally 'skip' across the surface of the mud. They have elongated bodies and bulging eyes with which they keep a wary eye open for fish-eating birds and other potential predators.

The way back

The sand dunes and mudflats of Malindi have enough of interest to keep most people occupied for a full day. It is worth setting off back to Malindi before it gets dark to avoid getting lost, but if you leave too early you may miss some of the area's specialities. Boehm's Spinetails, a type of swift, sometimes come low as dusk approaches and fruit bats take to the air. Smaller species of bats, as well as late roosting swallows, sometimes fall victim to Bat Hawks which take to the wing at this time of day.

29 GEDI NATIONAL PARK	
Location:	100km N of Mombasa
Access:	Tracks and trails lead around the ruins and surrounding forest
Terrain:	Ancient ruined city and tropical forest
Specialities:	Giant Land Snail, Yellow-rumped Elephant Shrew, Mottled-throated Spinetail
Accommodation:	None

The ruins at Gedi offer archaeological interest combined with forest wildlife.

Getting there

To reach Gedi from the south, take the B 8 coastal road northwards from Mombasa heading to Malindi. Just beyond Mida Creek, take a turning to the right which is sign-posted to Watamu and the ruins are then sign-posted a short distance from this junction. If you are staying in Malindi or Watamu, the national park is a short drive from these centres, lying about 20km south of Malindi. Buses frequently pass by on the main coastal road and matatus will take you to the gates of the park.

About the park

Apart from the wildlife interest that abounds in the forests and ruins of Gedi, there is plenty of archaeological note as well. Gedi, sometimes written 'Gede', was an early Islamic city that dates back to the thirteenth century. Today it lies several kilometres inland, but in its heyday it was a coastal settlement harbouring a rich community that traded extensively with Asia and Arabia.

Mystery surrounds Gedi's past, however, because in the seventeenth century it was suddenly, and seemingly peacefully, abandoned to the encroaching forest. The remains and finds tell archaeologists much about the day-to-day life of its former inhabitants but little about their sudden departure.

Gedi was only rediscovered comparatively recently this century. The 18ha site has been largely cleared of the lush vegetation that had choked and covered the ruins, allowing easy exploration of the wells, mosque, tombs and other buildings. An information centre displays some of the artifacts discovered and interprets them in the context of the city's past.

Gedi's wildlife

The forests that surround the ruins of Gedi provide welcome shade from the fierce coastal sun. Many birds and mammals also find refuge in the area but seeing them can be quite a challenge. If you visit during the middle of the day when tourists are coming and going, you could come away having seen only a handful of species. However, an early morning visit can be far more productive, although the species do not show themselves easily.

Birdwatching at Gedi, and mammal-watching too, require patience and stealth. Many tracks and paths radiate from the ruins through the forest. Follow one, pausing at regular intervals to listen and look around you. Birds and mammals on the forest floor sometimes give their presence away by rustling sounds as they feed or move. In the tree canopy, many of the birds remain silent and are only located when they move from perch to perch. Some, such as Narina's Trogon, remain motionless for long periods of time, their plumage providing excellent camouflage among the dappled leaves.

As you walk among the ruins, keep a look out for the Mottled-throated Spinetails, a type of swift, that nest in some of the wells. It is also worth watching overhead through clearings in the forest for Palmnut Vultures, sometimes referred to as Vulturine Fish Eagles, which soar over the canopy.

Birds of the forest floor include Spotted Ground Thrush, which is difficult to see elsewhere in Kenya, and African Pitta. This latter species, a non-breeding visitor to Gedi, is one of the most elusive and sought-after of African birds. Despite its bright colours, it is secretive and keeps to dense cover. It is usually seen either by pure luck or by patient observation: find a likely looking spot of dense undergrowth and wait to see if anything emerges. If you are lucky, the reward will make the wait seem worthwhile.

Among the dense foliage of the trees, Retz's Red-billed Shrike, Scaly Babbler and Nicator, a babbler-like bird with green plumage and a hook-tipped bill, can sometimes be found while Silvery-cheeked Hornbill and Green Pigeon are usually more conspicuous.

Wildlife interest around the ruins at Gedi is not confined to birds. Several species of Duikers live in the forest along with Suni, Kenya's smallest antelope. All are difficult but not impossible to see as they hide in the foliage. The Suni are a comparable size to one of Kenya's most unusual animals, the Yellow-rumped Elephant Shrew, which also lives here. They are rather nervous creatures and are most easily seen by sitting still and waiting.

Giant African land snails are among the most conspicuous residents of the forest floor around Gedi. The shells of these enormous molluscs may exceed 20cm in length and the body is so large that it cannot be retracted into the shell when the animal is disturbed. They often make a considerable noise as they rustle through the dry leaves, but not so Gedi's snakes. Most retreat long before visitors get the chance to see them, but one, the Black Mamba, is less cautious and not

Giant African land snails (Achatina sp.) *are a frequent sight as they crawl across the forest floor.*

without good reason. Mambas can exceed 2m in length and have deadly venom. They are also not intimidated by man's presence and have been known to be actively aggressive. They move very fast, and if you come across one of these snakes you are advised to give it a wide berth.

30 ARABUKU-SOKOKE FOREST RESERVE

Location:	c.100km N of Mombasa
Access:	Tracks and paths the forest; caution: it is easy to get lost
Terrain:	Tropical, coastal forest
Specialities:	Yellow-rumped Elephant Shrew, Amani Sunbird, Sokoke Scop's Owl, Sokoke Pipit
Accommodation:	None

Getting there

The Arabuku-Sokoke Forest stretches northwards from Kilifi Creek to Mida Creek and is bounded on its eastern side by the coastal B 8 road which is the road from Mombasa to the south. Access is along various tracks which lead from the main road but an often-used route is about 5km south of the turning to Watamu and the Gedi ruins. This is not sign-posted and it might be advisable to ask directions or to hire a guide.

About the forest

The Arabuku-Sokoke Forest is the largest and most important remnant of the native tropical forest that once ran the length of the Kenyan coast. It is similar in character to the forest that surrounds the ruins at Gedi but covers a far greater area. Not surprisingly, therefore, it harbours far more endemic creatures than neighbouring Gedi.

Sokoke's wildlife

Although rich in wildlife, the casual visitor to Sokoke may come away having seen very little. As with tropical forest areas elsewhere, those at Sokoke have to be 'worked' with a degree of determination and dedication before its potential can be realized

To get the best from Sokoke, try to arrive early in the morning and walk slowly along forest tracks and paths. It is easy to get lost and therefore it is best to stick to main trails and try to head in the same direction. There are still a few Elephants left in Sokoke, so be prepared to back-track if you suddenly come across one of these surprisingly silent creatures.

Butterflies and other insects are abundant along the forest rides, especially where these are open enough for sunlight to filter down to the forest floor. It is in clearings like this that the Sokoke Pipit lives, one of several birds endemic to the forest. Lucky visitors may also see a Spotted Ground Thrush or an African Pitta, feeding unobtrusively on the ground, or even a Duiker or Yellow-rumped Elephant Shrew.

Forest clearings also provide an opportunity to observe the tree canopy above and keen-eyed observers should look for the endemic Amani Sunbird and Clarke's Weaver as well as Nicator, Zanzibar Puff-back Shrike and Fischer's Turaco.

Another of the forest's endemic birds, Sokoke Scop's Owl, is, however, far more elusive. Shy and retiring by day, this bird is usually only located by its monotonous call which is uttered after dark. Birds can sometimes be lured by imitations or play-backs of the call but an excursion into Sokoke after dark should not be undertaken lightly and certainly not without a guide. Never underestimate the ease with which visitors get lost in the forest.

31 TANA RIVER PRIMATE RESERVE

Location:	c.240km N of Mombasa
Access:	Boat tours
Terrain:	Riverine forest
Specialities:	Tana Mangabey and other primates
Accommodation:	Campsite and lodge

Getting there
The reserve is a long way north of Mombasa or 130km north of Malindi on the B 8. It lies on the east bank of the Tana River to the north of Garsen. Visitors who wish to stay on the reserve should check in advance about current access and accommodation.

The reserve's wildlife
Tana River Primate Reserve comprises 169km² of riverine forest. Within its boundaries, the meandering river and its oxbow lakes are fringed with unspoilt forest and are home to a wide range of mammals and birds.

The reserve was established primarily to protect its populations of seven species of primates, in particular the Tana Mangabeys and Red Colobus Monkeys that live here. The former is a subspecies of the Crested Mangabey and may number less than 1000 individuals. Although the animals are now fully protected, loss of their specialized riverine habitat surrounding the reserve has effectively isolated them and the reserve will thus remain their last stronghold.

In addition to these two species, Baboons and Syke's Monkey also occur and there are Hippopotamuses and Nile Crocodiles in the river. The river acts as a magnet for many of the game animals that live in the savannah which borders the riverine forest and Elephants, Zebras, Giraffes and Waterbucks can also be seen.

32 ARAWALE NATIONAL RESERVE

Location:	c.250km N of Mombasa
Access:	No access road; four-wheel-drive vehicle essential
Terrain:	Savannah and thornbush
Specialities:	Hunter's Hartebeest
Accommodation:	None

Getting there
Arawale National Reserve lies some way inland from the coast, 150km north of Malindi. It can be reached by following the B 8 northwards as far as Hola where a ferry crosses the Tana River.

About the reserve
Arawale is the only reserve in Kenya where Hunter's Hartebeest can be found, a rather shy species of antelope which bears lyre-shaped horns. It is generally found in small groups of up to twenty individuals. Also present in the reserve are Grevy's Zebras, Elephants, Lesser Kudus and Giraffes.

33 DODORI NATIONAL RESERVE

Location:	c.280km N of Mombasa
Access:	Dhow
Terrain:	River floodplain
Specialities:	Waterbirds, Dugong
Accommodation:	Campsite

Getting there
Dodori National Reserve lies close to the coast between Lamu and Kiunga. It can be reached by taking the B 8 coastal road northwards passing through Malindi. At Garsen, turn eastwards on the C 112 towards Lamu and then on to Mangai, from where there is access to the reserve.

About the reserve

Dodori National Reserve comprises over 870km² of coastal forest, riverine forest, mangroves and savannah and is best explored by boat.

The channels and waterways are home to waterbirds in abundance and are a refuge for the endangered and persecuted Dugong. This gentle aquatic mammal eats sea grasses and other marine and estuarine vegetation and is a fast-declining species.

The reserve also harbours good numbers of Topi which breed here in comparative safety. Also present are Elephants, Lesser Kudu and Zebras to add to the game interest. Although camping is available at the one campsite in the reserve, there is an ever-present danger in the area from armed bandits who come across the Somali border. Listen to, and heed, current advice from the authorities at the time of your visit.

Nearby reserves

Dodori National Reserve has two other national reserves as close neighbours. To the north lies the Boni National Reserve while to the south is the Kiunga Marine National Reserve. Unfortunately, both these areas are difficult to reach and, because of the threat of armed attack, visitors are currently advised to stay away.

Boni National Reserve is an area of nearly 1340km² with the eastern boundary of the reserve along the Somalian border. The habitat is a mixture of coastal groundwater forest and grassland and is home to Topi and Elephants among the game animals.

Kiunga Marine National Reserve protects over 250km² of Kenyan coast and is made up of coral reefs, islands, beaches and mudflats. Green Turtles nest here as do thousands of seabirds. The area is also good for visiting migrant waders, terns and gulls.

34 DIANI BEACH	
Location:	35km S of Mombasa
Access:	Beach walks and snorkelling
Terrain:	Coral reef, white sandy beach
Specialities:	Coral reef
Accommodation:	Numerous hotels and beach chalets

Getting there

To reach the Diani Beach, head south from Mombasa on the coastal A 14 and turn off at the town of Ukanda.

Snorkelling is an ideal way to combine wildlife observation with a relaxing beach holiday. Unfortunately, tourists are increasingly damaging the coral reefs they come to admire simply by walking over them.

About the area

Although the Diani Beach area has experienced considerable development in recent years, the 5km stretch of white sandy beach and extensive offshore coral reefs remain largely unspoilt. The same cannot be said, however, for the habitat inland: with the exception of small, remnant patches, most of the coastal forest that once cloaked the region has long-since been felled.

Despite the large numbers of visitors the area receives, visitors can still see a few birds along the shore. Migrant waders include Sanderling, Whimbrel, Common Sandpiper and Curlew Sandpiper and there is even a chance of seeing the occasional Crab Plover. Gulls and terns sometimes rest and preen on the beach.

Snorkelling gear can be rented from most of the hotels in the area and is a major attraction to visitors. Boats will take snorkellers out to the reef proper, although many people chose to swim from the shore since there is plenty to see on the way. If possible, try to wear lightweight shoes to protect the soles of your feet.

Staying at Diani Beach

There are numerous hotels around the Diani Beach area covering the usual range of prices and standards. Beach chalets can also be rented and there are campsites as well.

Ghost crabs (Ocepode sp.) disappear into a burrow at the slightest sign of danger.

Getting there

Access to the park and reserve is by a ninety-minute boat journey from Shimoni. This town lies about 90km south of Mombasa and can be reached by driving south on the coastal A 14 towards the Tanzanian border. At Ramisi, turn off for Shimoni.

About the area

The Kisite Marine National Park and Mpunguti Marine National Reserve are contiguous and comprise 39km². Together they protect a fantastic area of coral reef with all the attendant fish, starfish and marine molluscs.

35 KISITE MARINE NATIONAL PARK AND MPUNGUTI MARINE NATIONAL RESERVE	
Location:	c.90km S of Mombasa
Access:	By boat from Shimoni
Terrain:	Coral reef
Specialities:	Coral reef animals
Accommodation:	None

36 SHIMBA HILLS NATIONAL RESERVE	
Location:	60km SW of Mombasa
Access:	Network of roads and tracks
Terrain:	Grassland, riverine forest and acacia woodland
Specialities:	Sable Antelope
Accommodation:	Campsites available

Getting there

Shimba Hills National Reserve lies to the south-west of Mombasa and is best approached from the town of Kwale. Head south from Mombasa on the A 14 and

branch left onto the C 106 to Kwale; just before the town a rough track leads into the hills.

About the reserve

Shimba Hills National Reserve is an area of over 300km^2 of rolling hill country with fantastic stands of tropical rainforests interspersed with areas of grassland and open woodland.

Wildlife of the Shimba Hills

The Shimba Hills are perhaps best known for their population of Sable Antelope, as they are the only place in Kenya where this species is found. These elegant antelopes, with long, curved horns, are easy to see and often quite approachable. Elephants, Bushbucks and Sunis also occur but are more difficult to see.

Bird life in the Shimba Hills is rich and varied. In the forested areas, look for Palmnut Vultures, also known as Vulturine Fish Eagles, which prefer areas where Doum Palms occur, Fischer's Turaco, Crowned Hornbill, East Coast Akalat and Peter's Twinspot. In more open areas, Red-necked Spurfowl, Carmine Bee-eater and Yellow-throated Longclaw can be found.

Opposite: the Black-headed Heron (Ardea melano-cephalus) is frequently seen well away from water, often feeding in grassland among herds of grazing mammals.
Right: Warthogs (Phaco-choerus aethiopicus) are widespread in Kenya and common in most national parks. Although they can be seen during the hours of daylight, they become most active at dawn and dusk. This one was photographed at dusk as it foraged on the woodland floor.

The White-eyed Slaty Flycatcher (Dioptrornis fischeri) characteristically makes short sallies after insects from its perch. It is often indifferent to humans and can be easily approached.

Staying in Shimba Hills

There is a public campsite which is close to the main gate at Kwale. There is also a lodge just outside the reserve boundaries.

135

3. TANZANIA

INTRODUCTION

Tanzania lies to the south of Kenya and, like its neighbour, offers splendid opportunities for wildlife observation. Although considerable numbers of people visit the northern reserves and parks using Arusha as a touring base, the figures fall well short of those for Kenya. Even fewer people visit the southern half of the country which remains largely undiscovered, and some would say unspoilt, by foreign visitors.

Tanzania is an extremely varied country. The north and south are dominated by highlands, the centre of the country being lower lying. The east is bounded by the Indian Ocean, the coast being considerably less developed than that of Kenya. Tanzania boasts Africa's highest mountain, Mt Kilimanjaro, and borders the continent's largest lake, Lake Victoria, in the north.

Tanzania also boasts what is arguably the most famous wildlife area in the world. The Serengeti National Park, which is contiguous with the Masai Mara Game Reserve in Kenya, harbours millions of Wildebeest and Zebras at certain times of the year together with some of the densest populations of predators, such as Lions, Cheetahs and hyenas.

Like Kenya, Tanzania has considerable archaeological interest, containing some of the earliest remains of man's ancestors. If anything, the sites are even better known than those in the neighbouring country. Olduvai Gorge and the fossil humanoid footprints at Laetoli are powerful indicators that East Africa was the birthplace of man.

Opposite: *although the diet of the Olive Baboon is largely omnivorous, it possesses well-developed canine teeth!*

37 KILIMANJARO NATIONAL PARK

Location:	N of Moshi
Access:	Trails and paths through forest lead to peaks
Terrain:	Rainforest, high moorland, glaciers and ice fields
Specialities:	Afro-alpine flora, spectacular views
Accommodation:	Mountain huts within park; hotels in Moshi

Getting there
The best place from which to explore Kilimanjaro National Park is the town of Moshi. This lies to the south of the mountain and is on the main road from Dar-es-Salaam to Arusha (A 23). It is within easy reach of the Kilimanjaro Airport to the west and a road leads to Marangu, the centre for the park headquarters and the most frequently used gate to the park.

About Mt Kilimanjaro
Mt Kilimanjaro is the highest peak in Africa rising to 5895m (19,341 feet) at Kibo peak. It is also one of the most dramatic mountains in the world, rising from the comparatively flat and featureless plain that surrounds it. Kilimanjaro attracts large numbers of visitors each year, many of whom make the ascent to the summit. However, for those whose interests centre on natural history there is still plenty to see: lush rainforests cloak the lower slopes and harbour interesting birds and mammals while above the treeline, a specialized and fascinating Afro-alpine flora has evolved.

Kilimanjaro National Park protects the higher reaches of the mountain and encircles and area of 756km². A game reserve and

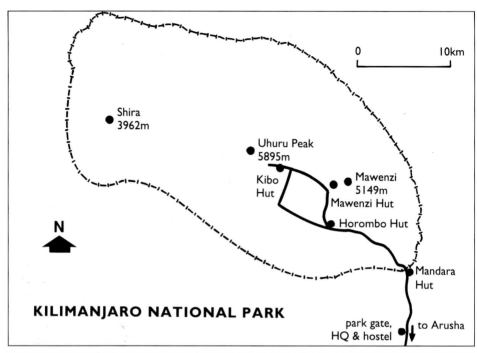

KILIMANJARO NATIONAL PARK

forest reserve protect the lower slopes and forest corridors allow access to the park above.

The first European to conquer Mt Kilimanjaro was Hans Meyer. Nowadays, almost anyone who is reasonably fit and determined can follow in his footsteps and many reach the highest point at Kibo. Mt Kilimanjaro has two other peaks, like Kibo the remains of extinct volcanoes, these being Shira at 4002m (13,764 feet) and Mawenzi at 5145m (16,880 feet).

Climbing Mt Kilimanjaro

Although climbing Mt Kilimanjaro does not require any particular climbing skills, as it is basically a long, steep trek, this is not to say that considerable planning and forethought are not required. The ascent usually takes about five days and cannot be undertaken without hiring a guide. Porters should also be considered and hiring people as well as the necessary equipment and purchase of provisions can be arranged in the hotels in Moshi. Although an ascent can be made at any time of year, most people prefer to attempt it during the months of January, February, August and September when there is the greatest chance of cloudless mornings and evenings, and hence better views.

Unless there are specific reasons for using one of the alternative ascent routes and special permission has been granted, visitors usually start at the Marangu gate where the park headquarters are situated. From here a trail climbs up through the forest to the first stop at the Mandara Hut.

On day two, visitors normally reach the Horombo Hut at over 3800m (12,500 feet)

Opposite above: *map of Kilimanjaro National Park.*

Opposite below: *Mount Kilimanjaro is Africa's highest mountain.*

for the next night's stay. It is worth considering spending a second night at Horombo giving an extra day to explore the surrounding area. This allows you to acclimatize to the altitude and give more than a breathless glance to the fantastic Afro-alpine flora here.

The following day, the Kibo Hut at the base of Kibu peak can be reached. From here, an early start, between midnight and 3am, allows an ascent of the summit by dawn and spectacular views assuming clouds have not formed.

Climbing Mt Kilimanjaro cannot be undertaken lightly and risks and precautions should be carefully considered. There is a real danger from altitude sickness, so heed the early warning signs, such as headaches and sickness, and allow time for acclimatization. Warm and waterproof clothing are essential for the higher reaches of the mountain and it is a good idea to wear several thin layers of clothing that can easily be put on or removed as conditions change during the day's climb. Sunglasses are useful on the ice and snow and sunburn can also be a problem, so use generous quantities of suntan lotion or keep yourself covered up.

Forest wildlife

The montane rainforest that cloaks the lower slopes of Mt Kilimanjaro is lush and verdant as a result of the high rainfall. There are towering *Hagenia* trees, festooned with epiphytic lichens, mosses and ferns. Tree ferns and giant lobelias also reach a great height here.

Forest bird life is easiest to see in the early morning. Both Narina's and Bar-tailed Trogons occur, although they can be hard to spot despite their bright plumage. Silvery-cheeked Hornbills and Cinnamon-chested Bee-eaters, also characteristic of highland forests in Kenya, are more easy to locate since they often perch conspicuously near the tops of

Top: the Red-billed Hornbill (Tockus erythrochynchus) is widespread in East Africa and often conspicuous.
Bottom: a male Bronze Sunbird (Nectarinia kilimensis) feeding its young.

Above the treeline
The high moorland above the treeline is dominated by tussock grassland with outstanding examples of giant heathers, groundsels and lobelias. The plants that grow here are superbly adapted to a life of extremes: during the day temperatures may soar and ultraviolet radiation is intense, while after dark, temperatures can plummet to below zero. Adaptations to this environment include the retention of dead leaves to act as insulation and compact form which helps guard against frost damage.

Eland and Klipspringers are occasionally seen in this high zone but bird life is rather sparse. White-naped Ravens sometimes show an interest in visiting groups and Mountain Chats and Scarlet-chested Malachite Sunbirds, also found on Mt Kenya and the Aberdares, are sometimes conspicuous.

trees or on dead branches. A variety of sunbirds can be found but patient observation is often needed to get a positive identification.

The forests also shelter a variety of mammals, the most conspicuous and noisy of which are the Olive Baboons, Blue Monkeys and Black-and-white Colobus Monkeys. Bushbucks, Elephants, Giraffes and Suni also occur but are difficult to observe well and are usually seen by chance. One of the most interesting mammals found in the forests of Kilimanjaro is Abbot's Duiker. This tiny antelope only occurs in montane forests in northern Tanzania; it has a brown coat, small horns and is generally shy and retiring. Visitors should count themselves extremely lucky if they see one.

38 SERENGETI NATIONAL PARK	
Location:	NW Tanzania, adjacent to the Kenyan border
Access:	Road and several tracks
Terrain:	Grassy plains, acacia woodland, riverine forest
Specialities:	Vast numbers of Wildebeest, Lions, hyenas
Accommodation:	Lodges and public campsites

Getting there
The Serengeti National Park lies in the north-west of Tanzania with its northern boundary along the Kenyan border, contiguous with the Masai Mara Game Reserve.

Opposite: map of the Serengeti National Park.

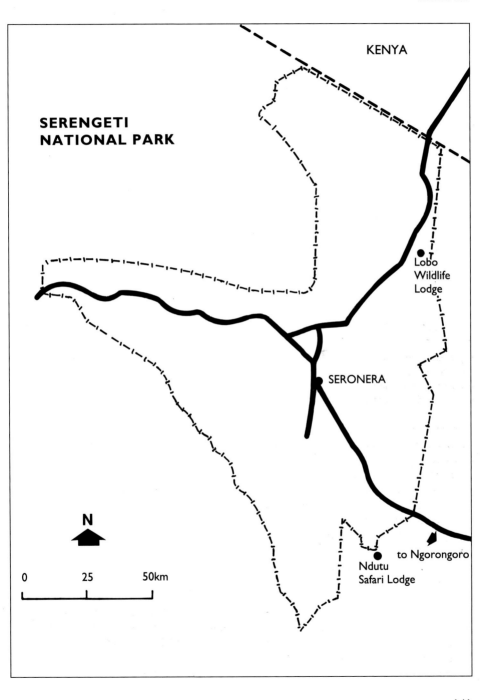

KENYA

**SERENGETI
NATIONAL PARK**

Lobo
Wildlife
Lodge

SERONERA

N

0   25   50km

Ndutu
Safari Lodge

to Ngorongoro

Kopjes and the rolling grassy plains of the Serengeti.

To reach it from Arusha and Kilimanjaro Airport to the east, take the B 142 which heads north-west from the A 104 at Makuyuni. The road passes Lake Manyara, Ngorongoro Crater and Olduvai Gorge before continuing to Seronera Lodge in the heart of the Serengeti where the park headquarters are situated. From Seronera, a road continues west towards the Ndabaka Gate and Lake Victoria and another heads northwards to the Fort Ikoma Gate and on to Musoma. A further road heads north-east to the Bologonja Gate near the Kenyan border and on to Keekerok in the Masai Mara. At present, the border crossing is closed and it is not possible to drive between these two contiguous wildlife areas.

About the Serengeti

The Serengeti National Park is the oldest and largest in Tanzania having been created in 1951 and comprising an area of more than 14,700km^2. It is also famous the world over for both its immense concentrations of game animals, and in particular Wildebeest and Zebra, and its Lion population.

The importance of the Serengeti to wildlife lies not just in the protection afforded by the establishment of the national park boundaries, but also in its role as part of a larger ecosystem that extends beyond the arbitrary boundaries of countries. Game animals do not recognize or respect international boundaries and hundreds of thousands freely move across the Kenyan border into the Masai Mara. The Masai Mara, or more precisely the pasture and permanent water it offers during Tanzania's dry season, are vital to the maintenance of population numbers within the Serengeti itself.

Much of the Serengeti's fame derives from the book *Serengeti Shall Not Die* and the attendant publicity that surrounded it. It was based on the work and studies of the late Bernard Grzimek and his son Michael who performed aerial surveys and population censuses in their zebra-striped aircraft. Sadly, both father and son are no longer alive, but their work has inspired numerous follow-up studies as well as large numbers of visitors.

The character of the Serengeti
Part of the attraction of the Serengeti National Park, both to human visitors and to wildlife alike, lies in the variety of habitats that are found in the area. Not only are there vast, open grasslands (the name Serengeti derives from the Masai word meaning 'endless plain') dotted with rocky outcrops, or *kopjes*, but there are acacia woodlands, marshes and riverine forests as well.

The abundance, variety and distribution of game animals depends in part on the time of year, but there is always plenty to see. Predators, including Lions, Cheetahs, Leopards and Spotted Hyenas, are common and the bird life is abundant. During the northern hemisphere's winter, thousands of birds visit the Serengeti from places as far afield as northern Europe and Asia.

The terrain and vegetation found within the national park is varied, and influenced by factors such as altitude, rainfall and proximity to water courses. Much of the Serengeti is open grassland, green during and shortly after the rainy season but turning golden brown during the dry season. Isolated kopjes dot the horizon and add variety to the otherwise flat terrain.

The open landscape is typical of the south and south-east of the park where the annual rainfall is lower than in the north and west. In these other parts of the Serengeti can be

Common Zebra *Equus burchelli*
L 200–245 (head and body)

The Common Zebra, also referred to as Burchell's Zebra, is one of the most characteristic and easily recognized of Africa's game animals. It is donkey-like in size and appearance, the body bearing a series of black stripes on a white background. In some races of Zebra there is a faint grey line between adjacent black stripes. Zebras live in herds which may number hundreds or thousands of animals in some areas and at certain times of the year; they migrate along with Wildebeest in the Serengeti and Masai Mara.

Zebras have to drink on a regular basis and usually do so early in the morning; much of the rest of the day is spent grazing. They can sometimes be seen engaged in mutual grooming although, during the breeding season, males are bad tempered and fight one another. Zebras emit a characteristic, donkey-like whinny.

found stands of acacia woodland and thorn scrub together with dense forest stands along the watercourses. Many of the plains animals are intimately dependent upon these differing habitats and their movements are tied to the seasonal patterns and differences in rainfall throughout the Serengeti and Masai Mara as a whole.

Game migrations

The Serengeti National Park is justly famous for its incredible concentrations of game animals. Although some species are resident in particular parts of the park, others undertake seasonal migrations which may take them over 800km in a single year. Wildebeest and Zebras are especially known for their migrations and hundreds of thousands of animals are often involved. Few who have witnessed this natural spectacle fail to keep it as a lasting memory.

From November to April, huge herds of Wildebeest, Zebras and Thomson's Gazelles concentrate in the south-east of the park, from Seronera south to Lake Ndutu and eastwards to the Ngorongoro Conservation Area. In excess of a million animals may be concentrated here at this time of year.

This concentration of life on the plains of short grass reaches its peak in April and May, and corresponds to the rainy season which begins in November. There is a fresh growth of grass which provides good feeding for the grazing animals and, not surprisingly, most Wildebeest and many other species produce their young during this period in February and March.

Thanks to the wealth of natural history programmes on television these days, many people have watched the miracle of Wildebeest birth in their homes if not in the wild. Despite this familiarity, to see it in real life is always impressive: within half an hour of being born, the calf can keep up with its mother at a galloping pace, a staggering feat when compared to the young of most other animals. Although the majority of births are successful, there are inevitable casualties and many young Wildebeest, Zebras and Thomson's Gazelles die. Some die of weakness or exhaustion while others fall victim to predators. In both cases, nothing is wasted thanks to the scavengers that thrive in the Serengeti.

Wildebeest and Zebras must drink on a regular basis and so at the start of the dry season in May or June they begin to move

Thomson's Gazelles (Gazella thomsoni) are often referred to as 'Tommies' and are one of the most endearing of East Africa's antelopes. They are common in the Serengeti National Park and form a major part of the diet of many predators, such as Cheetahs and Hunting Dogs. They are at their most vulnerable when mothers have just given birth. However, the young can walk and run very soon after being born.

north in search of water and fresh pastures. Columns of animals work their way north towards the Kenyan border, some of them heading west along the Western Corridor towards Lake Victoria before turning northwards.

The destination of most Wildebeest and Zebras is the Masai Mara Game Reserve in Kenya, most arriving in July and staying until September, although not all the animals necessarily cross the border. In the northern Serengeti and Masai Mara they can find permanent water and comparatively good pastures which provide grazing until they begin the return migration to the southern Serengeti in October.

Other game mammals

Although from June to November the south-east corner of the Serengeti National Park may lack the huge numbers of Wildebeest and Zebras present at other times of the year, there are plenty of other mammals to be seen here as elsewhere in the park. Thomson's Gazelles tend to move in search of fresh grazing but its larger relative, Grant's Gazelle, is more sedentary. Together with other species such as Bushbucks, Waterbucks, Kongoni,

Giraffes, Buffalos and Warthogs, they are most easily seen in the vicinity of watercourses, dry or otherwise, where the vegetation is generally lusher.

The best time of day for observing game animals is in the early morning. Dikdik, which are invariably found in pairs, are sometimes seen browsing low bushes in the early morning sun. These dog-sized antelopes are among the smallest in Africa. In contrast, Eland, the largest of the African antelopes, also occur in the Serengeti, preferring open, grassy plains.

Predators and attendant scavengers

The three big cats, Lion, Cheetah and Leopard, which most visitors to East Africa especially want to see, are as common in the Serengeti as anywhere in Africa. Indeed, on a visit to the park, visitors would be most unlucky not to see both Lions and Cheetahs, as there are estimated to be more than 1000 Lions here, although, as everywhere, Leopards are more elusive.

The Lions of the Serengeti are noted both for the size of the prides, which often number more than twenty animals, and for the numbers of dark-maned mature males. Most of

*The African Buffalo (*Syncerus caffer*) has a reputation for being one of the most aggressive and unpredictable mammals in Africa. Given the large size of a fully grown animal, it is always best to err on the side of caution if you confront one by surprise. Buffaloes love to wallow in muddy swamps but can sometimes be found some way from water. They usually live in herds of ten to fifty animals.*

the prides are fairly sedentary, occupying territories where game is more-or-less abundant throughout the year. However, some are more nomadic, tailing the movements of the migrating herds. Cheetahs prefer the short grassy plains and are most regularly seen from Seronera Lodge southwards. As with

the Lions, kills usually take place just after dawn and early risers can often see the predators feasting on the carcass even if they cannot witness the kill itself.

The way most people see Leopards is resting in a tree during the daytime, although it must be said that even this is a comparatively

Left: Spotted Hyenas (Crocuta crocuta) are generally nocturnal and so are most frequently seen at dawn or dusk. Their loud screams, reminiscent of eerie laughter, are a familiar sound to anyone who has camped in the bush. Below: Cheetahs (Acinonyx jubatus) use their speed to catch prey such as Thomson's Gazelle. They usually hunt at dawn or dusk.

rare observation. Do not be disappointed if you fail to see one; it may take several trips to Africa before you are finally lucky.

After a kill has been made, it is not long before a host of scavengers appear on the scene. Spotted Hyenas are usually among the first and, if it is a Lion kill and the cats are still present, they usually stand their ground until reinforcements arrive. A pack of hyenas can usually drive Cheetahs away from their quarry but on a one-to-one basis the two species have a healthy respect for each other's power. Black-backed Jackals are also soon on the scene along with Marabou Storks and vultures. Up to six species of vulture can sometimes be seen at a kill including Lappet-faced, the most powerfully built, and White-headed, arguably the most elegant, or least inelegant, of the vultures.

Birds

The bird life of the Serengeti is as rich and varied as that of the game mammals. Like the populations of some of the park's mammals, many of the birds are seasonal visitors from either other parts of Africa or further afield.

The grassy plains are home to gamebirds, waders and bustards. Crested Francolins, Harlequin Quails and Red-necked Spurfowls feed unobtrusively in the grass and parties of Helmeted or Crested Guineafowls are sometimes seen in procession. Kori Bustards, the largest of the African bustards, are common and White-bellied, Black-bellied and Hartlaub's are also seen. Pairs of Spotted Stone Curlews rest on broken ground and beside bushes, their plumage providing excellent camouflage, while Senegal, Crowned and Blacksmith Plovers are more conspicuous. From October until April, they are joined by small flocks of Caspian Plovers, visitors from Asia which, towards the end of their stay in the Serengeti, acquire the maroon breast of their breeding plumage.

White Storks and Montagu's and Pallid Harriers are also seasonal visitors to the park, escaping the northern winters in Europe and Asia. The harriers quarter the plains, occasionally dropping to catch an unsuspecting insect, lizard or small mammal. Other birds of prey scan for quarry from acacia trees and these perches are often shared by European, Madagascar and White-throated Bee-eaters and European and Lilac-breasted Rollers.

Crowned Cranes, egrets and herons are attracted to marshy areas and swamps while

*Crowned Plovers (*Vanellus coronatus*) are widespread and common in East Africa. Although often found near water, they are by no means confined to the vicinity of swamps and marshes and sometimes occur on dry grassland. Crowned Plovers get their name from the distinctive markings on their heads.*

areas of woodland, especially along watercourses, are a rich hunting ground for the birdwatcher. Several species of kingfisher can be found along with hornbills, cuckoos, barbets, starlings and weavers.

Staying in Serengeti
There are several lodges and campsites in the Serengeti National Park from which game runs and routes are usually based. However, these generally fall short, in terms of quality and facilities, of Kenyan standards.

The best known lodge is at Seronera in the middle of the park where there are also four campsites and where the park headquarters is situated. To the north-east lies the Lobo Wildlife Lodge near the eastern boundary of the park which also has a campsite. The Ndutu Safari Lodge is situated just outside the south-eastern boundary of the park in the Ngorongoro Conservation Area and is an excellent base from which to see the concentrations of game animals in this corner of the park from November to April.

The Caspian Plover (Charadrius asiaticus) is a winter visitor to East Africa.

39 NGORONGORO CONSERVATION AREA	
Location:	c. 170km W of Arusha; just S of the Serengeti
Access:	Circular route around crater floor of Ngorongoro; roads throughout the larger conservation area
Terrain:	Grassy plains, acacia woodland, volcanic scenery
Specialities:	Black Rhinoceros, Lion, resident game mammals
Accommodation:	Lodges and campsites

Getting there
The Ngorongoro Conservation Area lies west of Arusha and can be reached by taking the A 23 westwards from the town. At Makuyuni, head north-west on the B 142 to Ngorongoro. There is also an airstrip near the rim of the crater.

About the conservation area
Whenever Ngorongoro is mentioned, people immediately think of the crater which is understandably the focal point of the area. However, the crater only represents a tiny percentage of the overall conservation area which covers more than 8000km². The Ngorongoro Conservation Area was established in 1959, much of the land and indeed the crater itself formerly having been part of the Serengeti National Park. The purpose of the re-designation was to afford rights to the native Masai people as well as to protect the area's wildlife.

Today, the conservation area is contiguous with the Serengeti National Park along its north-western boundaries, part of the Serengeti Plain actually lying within the

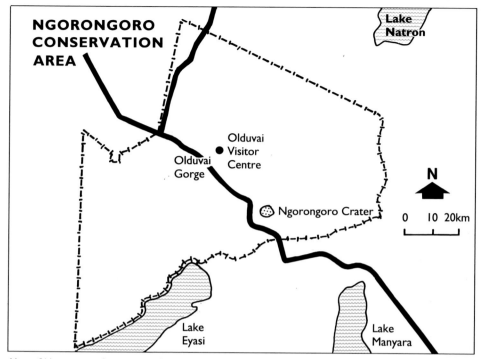

Map of Ngorongoro Conservation Area.

Ngorongoro Conservation Area, and it runs south to Lake Eyasi. Not only is the Ngorongoro Crater embraced within its boundaries but there are also several other craters and Olduvai Gorge, famous for its fossil remains of man's ancestors.

The Ngorongoro Conservation Area as a whole is extremely important for mammals and birds. The Serengeti Plains in the northwest of the area receive hundreds of thousands of migrant Wildebeest, Zebra and gazelles from November to April while species such as Elephants, Hippopotamuses, Black Rhinoceroses, Giraffes and numerous antelopes can be seen throughout the area, although the Ngorongoro Crater undoubtedly provides the best opportunities for observing the large mammals.

Ngorongoro Crater
Ngorongoro Crater has quite justifiably been referred to as the eighth wonder of the world. It is one of the largest complete volcanic calderas, a collapsed volcanic cone, to remain unflooded and is nearly 15km in diameter and 700m (2300 feet) deep in places. It is home to large numbers of resident game mammals and birds and the crater wall provides a superb visual backdrop for the crater's wildlife.

Exploration of the Ngorongoro Crater can only be undertaken in a four-wheel-drive vehicle; ordinary vehicles are prohibited. The descent into the crater is steep but eventually leads to a circular route around the crater floor. This passes Lake Magadi, which is not to be confused with the soda lake of the same name in southern Kenya, and carries on past swamps, rivers and forests before finally

Opposite: Wildebeest (Connochaetes taurinus) *thrive on the rich grazing in Ngorongoro Crater.* **Above**: *Olive Baboon* (Papio anubis) *leaping a stream.*

Grant's Gazelle *Gazella granti*
L 95–150 (head and body)

Grant's Gazelle occurs widely throughout much of Kenya and northern Tanzania, often alongside its smaller relative, Thomson's Gazelle. They are beautifully marked with a pale tan coat and dark lateral stripe and white belly. Grant's Gazelles have extremely variable horns, those of the male being much larger than the fe male. They usually diverge but in some groups of animals they are almost parallel. Grant's Gazelles are found in small groups and prefer open, grassy terrain where they are ever alert for danger.

climbing out of the crater. A tour of the crater offers superb game-watching opportunities and Black Rhinoceroses, Elephants, Wildebeest, Lions, Cheetahs and Spotted Hyenas are often encountered.

Ngorongoro Crater's wildlife

For a comparatively small area, Ngorongoro supports a surprising variety and abundance of wildlife. Because there is permanent water available, the more water-dependent species such as Wildebeest, Zebras and Elephants do not have to migrate and, consequently, stable populations of these species exist. Lions are well represented in the crater and it is one of the best places in Africa to see Black Rhinoceroses at close range.

Lake Magadi, which is a prominent feature of the crater floor, attracts Greater and Lesser Flamingos, often in considerable numbers. Also present around its margins are pelicans, Squacco Heron, Crowned Crane, Saddle-bill Stork and a variety of wildfowl including Egyptian and Spur-winged Geese. Together with many other species of waterbirds, these species can also be found around Mandusi Swamp, Ngoitokitok Springs and Gorigor Swamp where Hippopotamuses and Elephants also occur.

The grassy plains that make up the dominant vegetation on the crater floor are home to Warthogs, Wildebeest, Zebras, Buffalos, Grant's Gazelles and Thomson's Gazelles. Black Rhinos are often seen in the open and Kori Bustards, Ostriches and Secretary Birds also occur. One of the nicest aspects of the grasslands of the Ngorongoro Crater is that they remain green and lush for much of the year. To see game animals and birds in this stunning setting is in marked contrast to many other game-watching areas in East Africa.

If you are an early morning visitor to the crater or fortunate enough to be camping

The Secretary Bird (Saggitarius serpentarius) got its name because the curious feathers on its crown reminded early visitors to the continent of Victorian secretaries with quills tucked behind their ears. It walks with a stately gait through tall grass and uses its long legs to dispatch venomous snakes which make up the bulk of its diet. Secretary Birds are widespread in East Africa.

within its perimeter, you stand a good chance of seeing a recent Lion kill. Vultures, Spotted Hyenas and Black-backed Jackals are soon in attendance and in a surprisingly short time, the skull and a few bones may be all that is left of the prey. If you are lucky, you may see Golden Jackals which are also occasionally attracted to kills. These attractive animals are usually nocturnal in habits but sometimes venture out during daylight hours in Ngorongoro.

The rim of the crater is partly cloaked with highland forest while within the crater itself, two stands of Yellow-barked Acacia or Fever Tree can be seen at Laindi and Lerai Forests. There is a picnic site in the latter area of woodland which affords excellent opportunities for bird and mammal watchers alike. Superb Starlings, Black Kites, Vervet Monkeys and Olive Baboons will announce themselves but other species may require a more prolonged search. Look and listen for Slate-coloured and Tropical Boubous as well as Sulphur-breasted Bush Shrike, White-breasted Tit, White-eyed Slaty Flycatcher and Green Wood Hoopoe, all of which may be seen at this site.

Olduvai Gorge
This site, which lies within the Ngorongoro Conservation Area, achieved worldwide fame when Louis Leakey discovered the fossil remains here of one of our early ancestors, known as Nutcracker Man or *Zinjanthropus boisei*. The remains date back approximately 1.75 million years; the skull of Nutcracker Man is in the National Museum in Dar-es-Salaam and a small site museum illustrates and interprets these finds. Olduvai Gorge can be reached by driving north-west from Ngorongoro Crater towards the Serengeti National Park; a visitor centre is situated a short distance from the main road.

West of Ngorongoro Crater is another archaeological site, Laetoli, where fossilized footprints of an even earlier ancestor of man have been found. These date back over 3.5 million years.

Staying in the Ngorongoro Conservation Area
Around the rim of the crater are sited three lodges, the Ngorongoro Crater Lodge, the Ngorongoro Wildlife Lodge, both of which have views of the crater, and the Ngorongoro Rhino Lodge. Further afield, the Ndutu

Black Rhinoceros *Diceros bicornis*
L 295–360 (head and body)

The Black Rhinoceros is an unmistakable creature which may reach a weight of more than a tonne. The head bears two horns, which are in fact made of modified and compacted hair, the front one of which is usually the larger. Rhinoceroses are vegetarian and generally browse from low bushes. The hooked upper lip of the Black Rhinoceros greatly assists it in this feeding method. They have poor eyesight but acute hearing and a good sense of smell.

Black Rhinoceroses are more unpredictable than their White relatives and will occasionally charge vehicles if approached too closely and startled. They have suffered greatly from poaching over the last few decades and it is debatable whether there would be any left at all in East Africa were it not for the armed protection which vulnerable populations receive.

From a population in the tens of thousands at the turn of the century in Kenya alone, numbers have now been reduced in that country to a matter of a few hundred individuals. The horns which so characterize their appearance are their death warrants, ending up as dagger handles and as supposed medicinal remedies and aids in the Far East. There can be few sadder indictments of values held by some humans than the pathetic fate of so noble a creature as the Black Rhinoceros.

Safari Lodge is on the border with the Serengeti National Park and is ideally situated for watching the migrant herds from November to April. There is a campsite on the crater rim and campsites on the crater floor; the latter need to be booked well in advance and visitors must be accompanied by a ranger.

40 LAKE MANYARA NATIONAL PARK

Location:	c. 110km W of Arusha
Access:	Network of tracks and roads
Terrain:	Soda lake, groundwater forest, grassland, acacia woodland
Specialities:	Tree-climbing Lions, Lesser Flamingo
Accommodation:	Lodge, bandas and campsites just outside park

Getting there
Drive west on the A 23 from Arusha and at Makuyuni turn off north-west onto the B 142. The park lies to the south of the road and the turning is just beyond the village of Mto Wa Mbu.

About the park
Lake Manyara National Park covers an area of roughly 320km², two-thirds of which is the northern half of the lake itself. The alkaline lake lies at an altitude of approximately 1000m (3280 feet) above sea level, and is flanked by the towering western escarpment of the Great Rift Valley several hundred metres above.

The vegetation
For such a comparatively small area, the national park harbours a wide variety of

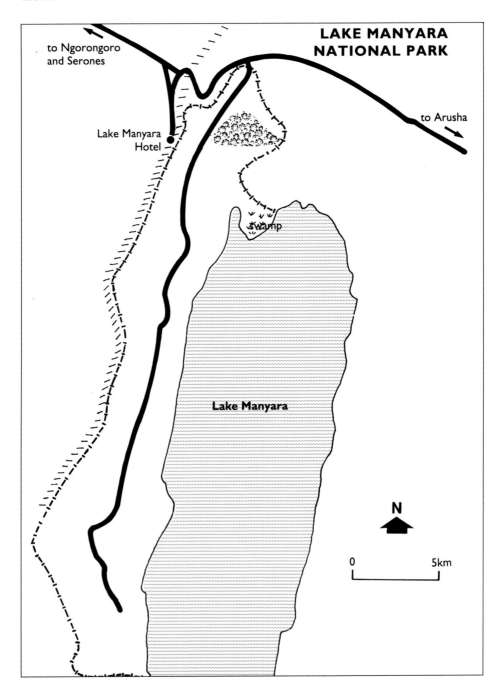

to Ngorongoro
and Serones

**LAKE MANYARA
NATIONAL PARK**

to Arusha

Lake Manyara
Hotel

Swamp

Lake Manyara

N

0   5km

habitats and vegetation types. Most unusual of these is the so-called groundwater forest, an area of lush, tropical woodland centred around the north-west of the lake, which is sustained not by direct rainfall but by springs and run-off streams from the Rift Valley wall which appear at its base. Forest trees include Mahogany, Fig Tree and Tamarind, none of which would survive without this constant water supply.

Elsewhere in the park, areas of open woodland can be found, grading into thorn scrub on the escarpment wall of the Rift Valley. On the northern shores of the lake, in particular, there are swamps and marshes while away from the lake, open grassland predominates. The lake itself is an alkaline soda lake and the conditions often suit large numbers of Lesser Flamingos. Many of the lakes other residents prefer to concentrate around the entry points of streams and rivers where there is a freshwater influence.

The lake's wildlife

Lake Manyara is a paradise for the bird-watcher, the highlight for many people being the large numbers of flamingos that often gather here. Lesser Flamingos usually out-number their Greater relatives but, being the notoriously fussy feeders they are, their numbers can never be guaranteed. However, both White and Pink-backed Pelicans can invariably be found and Yellow-billed Stork, Hammerkop, Squacco Heron and many other egrets and herons are present.

Wildfowl also concentrate around the lake margins and in the swamps with species such as White-backed Duck, Maccoa Duck, Egyptian Goose and African Pygmy Goose. From October to March, Garganey can also be found. These ducks, which have a rattling

Opposite: map of Lake Manyara National Park.

Egyptian Goose *Alopochen aegyptiacus* L 70

This is one of the most widespread and charac-teristic water birds of East Africa. It is usually found in pairs but sometimes occurs in small, loose flocks. It is catholic in its choice of habi-tat, occurring in all sorts of watery places including lakes, streams and rivers. Egyptian Geese have a grey-brown plumage with a dark patch around the eyes, red legs and a prominent white wing patch in flight. They make a loud honking call, especially when alarmed.

Cape Teal (**Anas capensis**)*, a widespread species on East African Lakes.*

flight call, are visitors from Europe and Asia during the northern hemisphere winter.

Several other species of birds are seasonal visitors: White-winged Black Tern, Curlew Sandpiper, Marsh Sandpiper and Ruff sup-plement the numbers of year-round residents such as Crowned, Blacksmith and Kittlitz's

Plovers and Chestnut-banded Sandplover. The latter is a local bird in East Africa, the only other reliable place to see it being Lake Magadi in southern Kenya.

Wildlife interest at Lake Manyara is not confined to bird life. Many game animals, such as Buffaloes, visit the shores and swamps and there is a sizeable population of Hippopotamuses in the lake. These tend to concentrate towards the northern end, especially in the swamps and hippo pool.

Wildlife of the surrounding land

Most of the common game animals that visitors expect to see in East Africa can be found in Lake Manyara National Park, including the 'big five': Lion, Leopard, African Elephant, Black Rhinoceros and Buffalo.

As elsewhere in East Africa, seeing a Leopard is largely a matter of luck. As likely as not, if you see one it will be resting in a tree, but the Lions of Lake Manyara share this habit as well. Precisely why they rest in trees here but are less inclined to do so in other reserves and parks is not known for certain. An obvious benefit of being off the ground is from the cooling effect of the breeze, but it

may also have something to do with avoiding the bites of Tsetse Flies which are prevalent in the area and tend to concentrate their activities closer to ground level.

Driving around the open grassland and acacia woodland surrounding Lake Manyara, mammals such as Warthogs, Burchell's Zebras, Common Waterbucks and Impalas can be seen. Ostrich, Ground Hornbill, Secretary Bird, Yellow-necked Spurfowl and Richard's Pipit are also common in this terrain while the woodland is home to weavers, woodpeckers, cuckoos and starlings as well as Olive Baboons and Vervet Monkeys. A conspicuous feature of the park are the Termite mounds. These are not only interesting in their own right but also play host to family parties of Dwarf Mongooses and pairs of Red and Yellow Barbets.

Staying at Lake Manyara

The Lake Manyara Hotel is situated on the Rift Valley escarpment, overlooking the lake, to the west of the park. It can be reached from the road to Ngorongoro and Serengeti. There are two campsites near the main gate at the northern end of the park.

One of the famous tree-climbing Lions (Panthera leo) of Lake Manyara National Park. Opinions differ as to the reason for this behaviour which is observed far less frequently elsewhere in the region. Perhaps they have learned to take advantage of the cooling breeze provided by the branches or maybe they are avoiding the bites of the park's large Tsetse Flies which are more active at ground level.

41 ARUSHA NATIONAL PARK

Location:	35km from Arusha; 65km from Moshi
Access:	Tracks linking Ngurdoto Crater and Momela Lakes
Terrain:	Lakes, grassland, forested crater
Specialities:	Black-and-white Colobus, waterbirds
Accommodation:	Lodges nearby, hotels in Arusha

A calf African Elephant (Loxodonta africana) *suckling from its mother.*

Getting there

To reach the park drive either east from Arusha towards Moshi on the A 23 or west from Moshi on the same road. Turn off northwards at Usa River on a gravel road which is sign-posted to Ngare Nanyuki. After about 15km a track to the right leads to the Crater Gate entrance to the park. There is another entrance at the Momela Gate further up the road. Arusha National Park can easily be visited as a day trip from Arusha.

About the park

In reality, Arusha National Park comprises not one but three wildlife areas: those known formerly as Mt Meru Game Reserve and Ngurdoto National Park together with the Momela Lakes. It now covers an area of about 140km² but despite its comparatively small size it represents a surprising variety of habitats.

The seven shallow crater lakes at Momela are alkaline in nature; they harbour waterbirds and attract game animals to drink and bathe. Elsewhere in the park there are is acacia woodland and open savannah while a circular road leads around the wooded rim of Ngurdoto Crater. The crater itself is closed and remains the domain of the wildlife. By contrast, Mt Meru is a steep volcanic cone that rises to over 4500m (14,760 feet). Its slopes are covered in dense highland forest which shelters many interesting animals.

In many parts of Arusha, visitors are allowed to walk on foot as there are no Lions around Ngurdoto Crater and Momela Lakes. However, if you wish to walk in the Mt Meru sector of the park, you must be accompanied by an armed ranger.

Mammals

In the north of the park, the Momela Lakes are a focal point for animals of the bush. Early mornings offer the best game-watching opportunities and Giraffes, Elephants, Buffaloes, and Common Waterbucks sometimes

White-browed Sparrow Weaver (Plocepasser mahali).

Male Golden Weaver (Ploceus subaureus) at nest.

WEAVERS

The weavers are a group of sparrow-like birds that are renowned for their nest-making abilities. Males are usually more brightly coloured than females and construct elaborate, woven nests made of grass and other strips of vegetation. The nests are suspended from slender branches and in many species are found in colonies. It is thought that placing a nest in such an inaccessible place protects eggs and young birds from predators, such as lizards and snakes.

The male usually constructs a nest in order to attract the attention of a female. If the nest fails in this purpose, it may be completely dismantled and a new one built. There are numerous species of weavers in East Africa. Reichenow's, Golden, Masked, White-browed Sparrow and White-headed Buffalo Weavers are among the most frequently encountered.

come to drink. Hippopotamuses are resident in the pools and only emerge onto land after dark.

Elsewhere in the park, small herds of Zebra can be found in open areas while in areas of cover, Kirk's Dikdiks and Bushbucks reside but are difficult to see. Black-and-white Colobus Monkeys and Blue Monkeys can be found in wooded areas, especially around the rim of Ngardoto Crater. The former species is particularly noticeable because of its loud calls and attractive markings.

Birds
Momela Lakes usually play host to numbers of both Greater and Lesser Flamingos which

feed around the margins, wading as far as their long legs permit. Also much in evidence are Long-tailed Cormorants and Pink-backed and White Pelicans. All manner of other waterbirds can be seen around the lakes, the numbers and species depending partly on the time of year, as the lakes receive visitors from Europe and Asia which remain here during the northern hemisphere winter.

Great Egret, Squacco Heron, Yellow-billed Stork, African Jacana, Blacksmith Plover, Crowned Plover, Egyptian Goose and White-backed Duck are usually present year-round but seasonal visitors include Garganey, Wood Sandpiper and Marsh Sandpiper. Visitors from Europe and Asia are not just confined to waterbirds – European Swallow, Yellow Wagtail and European Bee-eater are among those seen in more open terrain and are an intriguing sight for human visitors from Europe familiar with them in very different settings.

Mt Meru

Mt Meru lies in the western sector of the park. To reach it, head west from Momela crossing the Ngare Nanyuki River. A four-wheel-drive vehicle is essential. You pass the viewpoint at Kitoto and arrive at Meru Crater at the foot of Mt Meru. The drive takes you through fabulous montane forest and the ascent of Mt Meru passes above the treeline into upland moorland vegetation. There are mountain huts in Meru Crater and on the ascent route.

Staying at Arusha National Park

Many people visit the national park as a day trip from Arusha which is a popular base from which to explore many of Tanzania's northern parks and reserves. The Momela Game Lodge lies close to the Ngurdoto Gate and there are campsites within the park.

42 TARANGIRE NATIONAL PARK

Location:	c. 115km SW of Arusha.
Access:	Network of tracks and circular routes around the park
Terrain:	Open grassland, rivers and swamps; parts are inaccessible during the rainy season
Specialities:	Baobab tree, Elephant, Fringe-eared Oryx
Accommodation:	Lodge and campsites

Getting there

To reach the park, follow the A 23 west from Arusha and continue south-west on the A 104 at Makuyuni, ignoring the turning to Ngorongoro. The entrance to the park is to the left, just past Kwa Kuchinja (*see* map on page 160).

About the park

Tarangire National Park is the most southern of the accessible parks of northern Tanzania. It covers more than 2500km² of land made up of a variety of habitats. Much of the park is open, grassy savannah dotted with splendid specimens of Baobab trees, but there are also areas of swamp in the south and permanent water in the form of the Tarangire River.

The Tarangire River is the focal point of the national park, especially during the dry season from July to October. Once the short rainy season starts in October, the animals disperse to find fresh grazing. They maintain this widespread distribution until after the end of the long rains in June, when they begin to converge on the watercourse again. In particularly dry seasons, the water may not reach the surface of the river bed. At such times, Elephants play a vital role in gouging out waterholes.

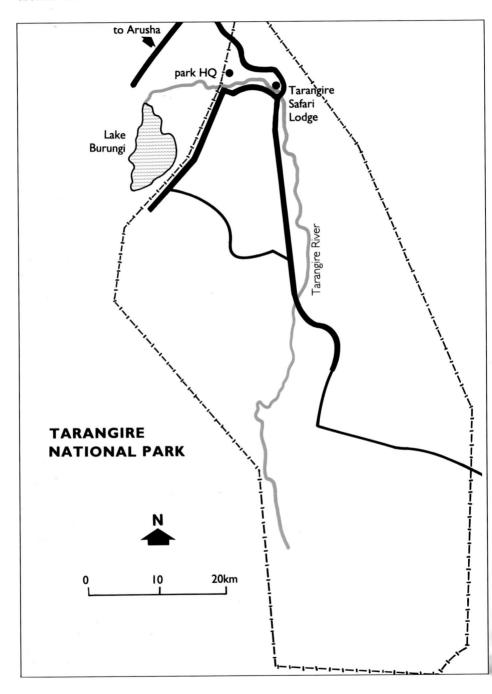

to Arusha

park HQ

Tarangire
Safari
Lodge

Lake
Burungi

Tarangire River

**TARANGIRE
NATIONAL PARK**

N

| 0 | 10 | 20km |

The time of year when the animals are most concentrated, and hence game watching is at its best in Tarangire, coincides with the period in the Serengeti when game watching is least productive. The vast herds have moved northwards to the Masai Mara.

Tarangire's wildlife
During the best game-watching months of July to September, much of the park's wildlife is concentrated in the vicinity of the Tarangire River watercourse and its tributaries. Resident mammals include species such as Warthog, Giraffe, Lesser Kudu, Kirk's Dikdik and Common Waterbuck and these are joined by more wide-ranging migrant species like Wildebeest, Zebra and Fringe-eared Oryx. The latter are elegant antelopes, with long, straight horns. They are usually seen in groups of 5–15 and are reasonably common in the national park.

Bird life is equally varied and abundant in Tarangire. Open grassland is home to bustards, Secretary Birds, Red-necked Spurfowl and Helmetted Guineafowl while low bushes and dead branches serve as perches for birds of prey, White-throated Bee-eaters and Lilac-breasted Rollers among many others. The watercourses are also important focal points for the birds especially during the dry season: look for waders, and in particular Water Dikkop and Blacksmith Plover, as well as Egyptian Goose, Crowned Crane, herons, storks and egrets.

Staying at Tarangire National Park
The Tarangire Safari Lodge offers tented accommodation and is situated in the north of the park near the headquarters. Elsewhere in the park, there are campsites close to the Tarangire River.

Opposite: *map of Tarangire National Park.*

43 GOMBE NATIONAL PARK	
Location:	On E shores of Lake Tanganyika in W Tanzania; nearest town Kigoma
Access:	Reached by boat; trails through park
Terrain:	Hill forest
Specialities:	Chimpanzee
Accommodation:	Hostel

Getting there
Compared to most reserves in Kenya and northern Tanzania, Gombe is difficult to reach. There is no road transport into the reserve, which lies at the north-east end of Lake Tanganyika, and access is therefore by

Crowned Crane *Balearica regulorum* L 100

The Crowned Crane is one of East Africa's largest and most distinctive birds. Standing over 1.2m tall, it has a beautiful plumage: the neck and mantle are grey, the head has patches of black, white and red, there are white shoulder patches and orange-yellow plumes. However, the most distinctive feature, and the one for which the species is named, is the crown of yellow spike-like plumes on the head.

Crowned Cranes are generally seen in pairs, males and females being similar in appearance. Their preferred habitat is marshy ground where they often wade into quite deep water. They make a loud, honking call reminiscent of geese.

Chimpanzee *Pan troglodytes*
L 64–94 (head and body)

The Chimpanzee is generally considered to be man's closest living relative. Most of the body is covered in thick, black hair except for the face, ears, palms and soles of the feet. They have expressive eyes and communicate with each other by a complex language of facial signs, sounds and postures. They live in family groups and during the daytime spend much of their time foraging for nuts, seeds and leaves. Occasionally they hunt as a group for animals such as monkeys but this is not a commonly observed event.

Chimps have powerful arms and legs which allow them to move with ease among the branches of trees. Although they were once fairly widespread in central Africa and western Tanzania, they are now local and generally wary of man, and with good reason. At Gombe National Park, where some of them have become habituated to man, they can be seen at close range. Habitat loss and hunting are the main threats to the species.

boat. The point of departure is Kigoma which lies to the south and, depending on the type of boat you travel in, the journey can take between one and five hours. Kigoma can be reached by air, train or road.

About the park
The national park is centred around Gombe Stream and was established primarily to protect its Chimpanzees. It comprises an area of only 50km², running along the shores of Lake Tanganyika and rising up the forested slopes away from the lake.

The Chimps at Gombe have become famous largely through the studies and efforts of one person, Dr Jane Goodall. Her work started in the early 1960s when she worked alone in this remote corner of Tanzania. At first, the chimps were distinctly wary of her but gradually over the months and years that followed, they became accustomed to her presence and allowed her to observe and record their behaviour at close range without modifying it.

Dr Goodall was able to record the struggles within her study group for hierarchical position, watch incidents of group hunting activity when they regularly caught monkeys, and perhaps most significantly, observe Chimps making and modifying tools. In particular, they were seen to fashion stems and grasses in order to 'fish' for termites in termite mounds (*see* box).

Over the years, many other people have assisted Jane Goodall in her research and consequently most of the Chimps around the research station are habituated to man. This is not to say that they are not wild and they should most definitely be treated as such. Groups of Chimps that live elsewhere in the park are less tolerant of man and may require considerable tracking with the aid of a ranger guide.

Gombe's other wildlife

Apart from man and Chimpanzees, other primates found in the Gombe National Park include Red Colobus Monkey, Baboon and Blue Monkey. Bushbuck, Buffalo and Defassa Waterbuck also occur.

Forest birds can also be difficult to observe among the dense foliage. Look out for Red-headed Malimbe, Double-toothed Barbet and Equatorial Akalat. The latter are shy, robin-like birds that feed close to the ground. Pigeons, also known as Scaly-grey Pigeons, keep to tree cover and Palmnut Vultures occasionally soar overhead.

Mahale Mountains National Park

Also lying on the eastern shores of Lake Tanganyika is the Mahale Mountains National Park. Like Gombe National Park, it too was established to protect the Chimpanzees that roam in its forests. However, it requires even more effort and planning to reach.

This National Park covers 1300km² and rises from the eastern shores of Lake Tanganyika at about 700m (2300 feet) to nearly 2500m (8200 feet) on the slopes of the eastern wall of the Great Rift Valley. A gradation of woodland with altitude can be seen within the boundaries of the park. Access is by boat from Kigoma to the north. Ensure you find out about current transport possibilities before turning up at the town.

44 SELOUS GAME RESERVE	
Location:	S Tanzania, nearest town Iringa
Access:	Walking and boat safaris; four-wheel-drive vehicles
Terrain:	Savannah, watercourses, swamps
Specialities:	Elephant, Sable Antelope
Accommodation:	Tented camps and campsites

Getting there

Selous Game Reserve is one of the more remote of Tanzania's reserves and, because of its large size, only a small part of it is actually accessible. It is possible to take a train from Dar-es-Salaam or even drive during the dry season, reaching the park from Mikumi. However, most visitors reach Selous by charter flights from the capital, the tented camps having landing strips.

Named after the explorer and hunter Frederick Selous and covering some 51,000km², Selous Game Reserve is the largest reserve in Africa. By contemporary East African standards, it is wild and inaccessible and consequently seldom features on the itineraries of more casual visitors to Tanzania. The lack of visitors only adds to its appeal to the adventurous traveller who is rewarded with scenery and wildlife that would have been familiar to Selous himself.

163

Kirk's Dikdik *Madoqua kirki*
L 55–57 (head and body)
The dikdik is among the smallest of the antelopes with only the Suni and some species of duikers being smaller. They have warm brown coats, the legs being brighter in colour than the rest of the body. The eyes are large in proportion to the size of the head and there is a conspicuous black, glandular patch in front of the eye. Their snout is elongated and overall, the head has a most distinctive appearance.

Dikdiks are invariably seen in pairs since they bond and remain within a distinct territory. They are generally secretive, preferring to keep to the cover of bushes where they are well camauflaged as shown in the lower picture. In the early mornings, they occasionally emerge to browse on low bushes. Guenther's Dikdik, a similar species, occurs in the north of the region; Kirk's Dikdik is more widespread.

About the reserve

Named after the explorer and hunter Frederick Selous, the game reserve is the largest in Africa and covers more than 51,000km^2. Visitors can experience a real taste of the original African bush here.

Like Tsavo in Kenya, Selous is in part protected by its sheer size. It is also extremely remote, but its size and remoteness have been both a blessing and a curse to the wildlife. Being so far from population centres, man has had little effect on the vegetation and much of the wildlife. However, its very isolation has meant that ivory poaching has raged almost unchecked. In the last decade, Selous has lost almost half of its Elephants.

Selous' wildlife

The dry season from July to September offers the best opportunities for game watching when the animals converge on the reserve's watercourses: the Kilombero, Great Ruaha and Luwegu Rivers. Despite poaching, Elephants are still common and as many as 50,000 may be present. Other mammals include Brindled Gnu, Sable Antelope, Roan Antelope and Greater and Lesser Kudus. Lions are common and Nile Crocodiles and Hippopotamuses frequent the rivers.

Woodland prevails in many parts of the park and provides excellent opportunities for the visiting birdwatcher. Look for species such as Grey-headed and Sulphur-breasted Bush Shrikes, Golden-rumped Tinkerbird, Cardinal and Bearded Woodpeckers, Pearl-spotted Owlet and Green Wood Hoopoe.

Staying in Selous

Mbuyu Safari Camp and Rifiji River Camp offer tents; Selous Safari Camp and Steigler's Gorge Lodge have chalets and bandas. Walking and boat safaris, and game drives can be arranged at the camps.

45 RUAHA NATIONAL PARK

Location:	S Tanzania; nearest town Iringa
Access:	Tracks, many of which are impassable in rainy season; usually closed during heavy rains from March to May
Terrain:	Savannah, woodland, rivers and mountains
Specialities:	Elephant, Greater Kudu
Accommodation:	Tented camps and campsites

Getting there

Like neighbouring Selous Game Reserve, Ruaha National Park is remote and comparatively difficult to reach. By far the easiest way to get there is to fly in, either to Iringa or to the park headquarters at Msembe.

About the park

Ruaha National Park covers more than 10,000km² and within Tanzania it is the second largest national park behind the Serengeti. It is wild and unspoilt and extremely varied in terrain: there are extensive mountain ranges cloaked in montane forest, open savannah and Miombo woodland.

The park is also strongly influenced by the Ruaha River that flows along its southeastern boundary. This is a focal point for wildlife during the dry season. It is also along this watercourse that the best game-watching tracks can be found. During the dry season the flow of the river diminishes dramatically, but its importance to wildlife increases.

White-browed Coucal (Centropus superciliosus), a widespread species.

Hadada Ibis *Hagedashia hagedash* L 75

The Hadada Ibis is a rather plump waterbird with a long, downcurved bill. It gets its name from the call, a loud 'ha-da-da', which is a familiar sound throughout East Africa. It is a wetland bird and its preferred habitat is wooded river courses, the birds generally roosting in the trees. They have a brown plumage with a metallic green sheen on the wings and mantle. There is a distinctive white streak on the head from the line of the bill. In flight, the Hadada like other ibises, carries its head and neck straight out and not tucked in like herons.

Miombo woodland is a dominant feature of much of the park. It is found in many parts of Tanzania and has a characteristic open, park-like appearance, composed mainly of species of *Brachystegia*. It is the domain of birds and game mammals.

Like the other southern Tanzanian parks and reserves, it is best to visit Ruaha National Park during the dry months of July to September. This is not only because game watching is better then but also for the more practical reason that outside this period, getting around is difficult and many tracks become muddy and impassable.

Ruaha's wildlife

Large numbers of Elephants can still be found in the park, despite the effects of ivory poaching, and other large game mammals include Giraffes, Buffaloes and Hippopotamuses. Also look for Greater and Lesser Kudus, Warthogs, Common Waterbucks, and Sable and Roan Antelopes.

Bird life is most abundant and varied along the course of the river. Ducks, geese, herons, egrets and storks and African Fish Eagles are attendant in the trees bordering the river. A variety of waders and kingfishers can also be found in the area.

The Whistling Thorn (Acacia drepanolobium) has swollen structures along its stems in which ants live. When the wind blows across the openings in these structures, a whistling sound is produced.

46 MIKUMI NATIONAL PARK	
Location:	c. 290km SW of Dar-es-Salaam; N of Selous Game Reserve
Access:	Roads and tracks
Terrain:	Savannah woodland, grassland, river and swamps
Specialities:	Elephant, Lion, Baobab Tree
Accommodation:	Lodge, tented camp and campsites

Getting there

Mikumi National Park lies south-west of Dar-es-Salaam and is bisected by the main road to Zambia. There is an airstrip near the park headquarters allowing access by air.

About the park

Mikumi National Park covers an area of over 3000km². Its southern boundary is marked by the railway line from Dar-es-Salaam to Zambia and the main road from the capital cuts through the park.

The Mkata River and its floodplain provide the best opportunities for watching wildlife and are crossed by a network of tracks. Baobab trees are a characteristic feature of the landscape and Miombo woodland is widespread.

As in the neighbouring Selous Game Reserve, typical mammals to be found in the park include Elephant, Buffalo, Giraffe, Zebra, Impala and Hippopotamus. Taking advantage of the game mammals, predators including Lions, Leopards and Hunting Dogs are regularly encountered. Bird life is similar to that in Selous.

Opposite: the Impala (Aepeceros melampus), an antelope of acacia woods and dry savannah.

4. RWANDA AND ZAIRE

INTRODUCTION

Rwanda is one of Africa's smallest countries covering an area of just over 26,000km². To put this in perspective, this is roughly half the size of the Selous Game Reserve in Tanzania.

The country has one of the highest population densities in Africa and this has had a marked effect upon Rwanda's vegetation. Most of the land that could be farmed is cultivated, with subsistence farming and coffee production dominating the agriculture. The comparative inaccessibility of some of the hill and mountain regions has enabled montane rainforest to persist, although the ability of the people to terrace the hillsides makes one wonder for how much longer.

Rwanda has a mild climate which lacks extremes with fairly dry periods in July and August and again in January and February. The country is dominated by rolling hills and mountains, the highest point being over 4500m (14,760 feet) above sea level.

The country boasts two superb national parks, each very different in character. Akagera National Park is an area of rolling savannah and a series of lakes; it has superb game-watching opportunities including the chance of seeing Sitatunga. On the other hand, Volcanoes National Park is a forested, mountain region which is home to Rwanda's best known wildlife attraction, Mountain Gorillas. In addition, the Nyungwe Forest is a fabulous area for birds and primates. Regrettably, there has been fighting between the country's troops and those from Zaire and Uganda and this has been centred on Akagera. Recently, a lodge was blown up and the area is no longer a safe destination.

By contrast with Rwanda, Zaire is one of Africa's largest countries and is nearly 100 times larger. Although a Central African country and therefore outside the scope of this book, it shares with Rwanda the attraction of Gorilla watching in the Virunga National Park on its eastern border. Indeed, this park is contiguous with the Volcanoes National Park in Rwanda and the Gorilla Sanctuary in Uganda. It is frequently visited as an excursion by visitors to East Africa and therefore is worth detailing here.

47 AKAGERA NATIONAL PARK (PARK NATIONAL DE L'AKAGERA)	
Location:	E Rwanda, 125km E of Kigali
Access:	Boat trips, game drives and observation platforms. Due to military action, check on current status before visiting
Terrain:	Lakes, savannah
Specialities:	Sitatunga, wetland birds
Accommodation:	Hotel, guest house and campsites

Getting there

This park lies on the eastern border of Rwanda, with Tanzania forming its eastern boundary. From the capital Kigali, a road runs east to the park. It is about 125km to the southern part of the park and 150km to Gabiro mid-way along the park's length.

About the park and local accommodation

The main feature of Akagera National Park is the series of lakes that run down its eastern side. Together with the swamps and marshes that surround them, these wetlands are the focal point for wildlife and wildlife watchers.

River margin showing Papyrus in Akagera National Park.

Each lake has its own special features and, on many, there are organized boat trips or boats for hire. These offer superb opportunities for watching waterbirds including egrets, herons, waders and jacanas. In addition, Hippopotamuses can be seen at the Plage aux Hippos on Lake Mahindi and an observation tower beside the Papyrus swamps of Lake Rwanyakizinga allows visitors to see Sitatunga, although a measure of patience may be required to get good views.

The northern part of the park comprises rolling hills covered with grassy savannah and many game drives operate from Gabiro. Species seen usually include Topi, Impala, Waterbuck, Zebra and Buffalo. Night game drives are also permitted in the park when nocturnal species such as civets and genets may be seen.

Recent military incursions in the area are reportedly having a devastating effect upon the wildlife of the national park. Consequently, the area is no longer safe to visit and may not be for some time to come.

At Gabiro on the western boundary of the park is the Gabiro Guest House while in the southern part of the park is the Hotel Akagera. In addition, campsites, which have to be booked in advance, are available in the park. Because of the military action the accommodation and facilities will undoubtedly have changed if the park is re-opened.

48 VOLCANOES NATIONAL PARK (PARK NATIONAL DES VOLCANS)

Location:	NW Rwanda; nearest town Ruhengeri
Access:	Trekking on foot
Terrain:	Lowland forest, highland rainforest, Afro-alpine flora
Specialities:	Gorilla
Accommodation:	Hotels in Ruhengeri; chalets and campsites at park headquarters

Getting there
The park headquarters is at the north-east of the village of Kinigi which is roughly 10km from Ruhengeri where most people stay. Unless you are camping at the park headquarters, you will have to make an early start as you must check in before 8.00am to obtain a voucher for the trek.

About the park
Volcanoes National Park covers an area of 125km² with its north-western boundary marked by the borders with Zaire and Uganda. Indeed, the park is contiguous with the Virunga National Park in Zaire.

Because the park embraces a considerable

altitudinal range, several of the volcanic peaks being over 3500m (11,480 feet), there is a wide range of vegetation types found within its border. Dense forest cloaks the lower slopes, but most of the land outside the park has been cleared for agriculture. Above 2300m (7545 feet), the vegetation changes, the habitat being dominated first by Bamboo and then by *Hagenia* and giant *Hypericum* trees. Epiphytic plants festoon the trees and species of orchids, lichens, mosses and ferns are abundant. Above about 3300m (10,830 feet), open moorland, reminiscent of the Aberdares or Mt Kenya in Kenya, predominates with Afro-alpine specialities such as giant lobelias and giant senecios being found.

Gorilla watching

In the Volcanoes National Park, there are four groups of Gorillas that have been habituated to man and which visitors can see. Treks to see three of these groups have to be booked well in advance, either through the tourist office in Kigali (Office Rwandais du Tourisme et des Parcs Nationaux, B.P.905, Kigali, Rwanda; Tel: 76512, 76514, 76515) or through one of the major tour operators which often block-book trips. The fourth group, which occasionally ranges over the border into Zaire, can only be booked a day in advance at the park headquarters.

Gorilla watching is not cheap. In addition to the large park entrance fee, visitors have to pay a further fee to visit the Gorillas, which is approximately $180. This fee includes the cost of the guide but not the cost of porters. Children under fifteen and people with colds or flu are not allowed on treks as Gorillas are susceptible to human ailments. A maximum of six people are allowed in each party.

Once visitors have checked in at the park headquarters, they then have to drive up to 15km to one of several designated departure

Gorilla *Gorilla gorilla*
L 140–180 (when standing erect)

Male gorillas may weigh as much as 175kg and yet despite their size they are generally placid creatures. They live in family groups of up to twenty animals and spend their days foraging for food, which consists mainly of leaves and shoots. At night, they sleep in nests constructed from the surrounding vegetation. Each Gorilla group is dominated by a male which is usually a silverback, thus named as the hairs on the back become silvery-grey with age. Females and young make up the rest of the group.

The Gorillas of Rwanda received worldwide publicity through the work of Dian Fossey, who was sadly murdered in Volcanoes National Park in 1985. Her book *Gorillas in the Mist* has been made into a moving film telling her story.

points where they meet their obligatory guide no later than 9.00am. The search for Gorillas continues on foot to the point where the group was seen the previous day and from there they are tracked. It may take three or four hours to find the great apes.

Visitors are allowed an hour with the Gorillas. Eye-contact is discouraged as Gorillas, like humans, may interpret a stare as a threat; flash photography is not permitted. The Gorillas are often in deep shade so fast film of 200ASA or more is advisable.

The best time of year to visit the Gorillas is from July to September or December to

February when there is least rainfall. However, the terrain is often misty and damp and appropriate clothing should be worn.

49 NYUNGWE FOREST (FORET NATURELLE DE NYUNGWE)	
Location:	SW Rwanda; near Butare and Cyangugu
Access:	Forest tracks
Terrain:	Rainforest
Specialities:	l'Hoest's Monkey
Accommodation:	None

Nyungwe Forest Reserve lies in south-west Rwanda with its southern boundary on the border with Burundi. The road from Butare to Cyangugu cuts through the reserve, the former town being the best base from which to explore the area.

Nyungwe Forest covers 975km² of thickly forested hill slopes. At least ten species of primate have been recorded here including l'Hoest's Monkey and the Black-and-white Colobus Monkey. The latter are generally considered to be a separate species from those found in the highlands of Kenya. Bird life too is prolific with many of the species more usually associated with central or west Africa.

50 VIRUNGA NATIONAL PARK (ZAIRE)	
Location:	E Zaire
Access:	Forest tracks
Terrain:	Forested hills
Specialities:	Gorilla, active volcanoes
Accommodation:	Cabins and campsites

Gorilla-watching treks start from Djomba Camp which is reached by walking from the park headquarters. The headquarters itself lies roughly 140km north of Goma.

Virunga National Park covers an area of more than 8500km² in eastern Zaire. The park is long and narrow with its eastern boundary bordering Rwanda in the south and Uganda to the north. It is divided into several sections, but one, the Djomba Gorilla Sanctuary, offers excellent opportunities for seeing these great apes. The sanctuary is in the Virunga Mountains, the same range which harbours Gorillas in Rwanda. Gorilla watchers are allowed to spend two hours with a family group as opposed to only the one hour which is allowed in Rwanda. Permits must be booked in advance, either through a tour company or through the National Parks office in Goma.

A typical scene in the rainforests of Nyungwe in Rwanda. Rainforests, characterized by high annual rainfall and lush vegetation, have disappeared from much of the region. Many of the birds in this 975km² forest are species that are more usually associated with west Africa.

SECTION III:
FIELD GUIDE TO COMMONER
ANIMALS AND PLANTS

The field-guide section of this book is intended to enable visitors to East Africa to identify most of the common larger mammals and birds of the region. Some of the more conspicuous reptiles, such as the Nile Crocodile, and plants are also covered although the space devoted to them is of necessity limited by comparison to the birds and mammals.

The emphasis on mammals and birds in this section and indeed throughout the rest of the book is a deliberate one. Within the scope of a book of this size, it would not be possible to cover all aspects of the wildlife in detail and to do them justice. By concentrating on the mammals and birds, it should be possible for the visitor to East Africa to identify most of the larger mammals and the birds encountered on safari using the field guide section and the box features which complement the main text of the book. These two groups are, afterall, among the major attractions that lure visitors to East Africa in the first place.

Although most of the larger mammals that are regularly encountered in Kenya and Tanzania are covered by the book, the same cannot be said for the birds. With a list that exceeds 1200 species for Kenya alone, there is only space to include the commoner

species encountered along with the larger and more conspicuous birds even if they have a range which is more limited.

The colour identification plates are clear and should be largely self-explanatory. With regard to the birds, the males are depicted in all cases. Many of the species have sexes where the males and females have similar plumages and the illustrations will therefore be appropriate for both sexes. Where this is not the case, mention has been made in the text to aid identification. Similarly, where immature birds have a plumage distinct from the adults, attention has been drawn to this in the text.

Many of the mammals have males and females that are similar in appearance and in these cases the illustration serves for both sexes. Where this is not the case, for example in some of the antelopes where males and females have different size horns, mention of this is made in the text. Only the male has been illustrated where there is a difference between the sexes.

The measurements that accompany the description of each species are given in centimetres unless otherwise stated. In the case of birds, the length refers to the distance from the tip of the bill to the tip of the tail. With some of the larger, more stately species, the height is given as it is a more appropriate measurement. With the mammals, measurement of height is given from the ground to the highest point on the animal and length is from nose to tail.

Opposite: the Tawny Eagle (Aquila rapax) is widespread in open country and is often attracted to kills.

173

Ostrich *Struthio camelus* **H 2.5m**
Unmistakable flightless bird. Males have black plumage with white tail and wing plumes. Females are sandy brown. Neck and thighs are bare, pink in southern (Masai) race but blue in northern (Somali) race. Can run at great speed. Usually in small parties. Widespread in open savannah parks. Easily seen in Nairobi NP.

Long-tailed Cormorant
Phalacrocorax africanus **L 60**
Common around lakes and marshes throughout region. Often seen perching on dead branches. All black plumage and proportionally longer tail distinguishes adult from white-necked race of Cormorant which has white throat and upper breast.

African Darter *Anhinga rufa* **L 40**
Long, slender neck with distinctive kink distinguishes African Darter or Anhinga from cormorants. Immature lacks chestnut throat of adult. Often seen perching on branches drying wings. Widespread on lakes and rivers throughout region.

White Pelican *Pelicanus onocrotalus* **L 160**
Usually seen in large groups fishing on lakes or roosting around shore. Black primary wing feathers conspicuous in flight. Immatures brownish. Similar Pink-backed Pelican is smaller and has greyish plumage with pinkish rump. Widespread throughout.

Black-headed Heron
Ardea melanocephala **L 100**
Black head and neck with contrasting white throat separates it from Grey Heron. Widespread and common around freshwater marshes and lakes as well as coast. Sometimes found in grassy areas away from water. In contrast, the Grey Heron is invariably associated with water.

Goliath Heron *Ardea goliath* **L 150**
Immense size and rufous crown, neck and upper breast are distinctive. Widespread but seldom common around marshes and lakes as well as on coast. Purple Heron is similar but much smaller and has conspicuous black crown. Frequents lakeside vegetation and marshes.

Little Egret *Egretta alba* **L 60**
All-white plumage, black bill and black legs with bright yellow feet are distinctive. Feeds actively around lake margins and marshes. Widespread and sometimes common where feeding is good. Cattle Egret has yellowish legs and bill. Often feeds alongside game animals.

Great Egret *Egretta alba* **L 90**
Large size, all-white plumage, yellow bill and all-black legs are distinctive. Feeds deliberately and slowly in marshes and shallow lakes throughout the region. Widespread but seldom common. Intermediate Egret is similar but much smaller with smaller bill.

Saddlebill Stork
Ephippiorhynchus senegalensis **L 170**
Immense size, black-and-white plumage and distinctively marked bill are unmistakable. Found around marshes, lakes and rivers throughout region but usually only seen singly or in small numbers. Abdims' (White-bellied) Stork is much smaller. All-black plumage with white breast and short bill.

Yellow-billed Stork *Ibis Ibis* **L 105**
Widespread and sometimes common around lakes and marshes as well as on coast. Whitish plumage, black wings, bare red face and yellow bill are distinctive. Similar White Stork is a winter visitor and occurs in flocks on grassland. White with black wings and red bill and legs.

female

Goliath Heron

male

Ostrich

Little Egret   Great Egret

Long-tailed
Cormorant

drying
wings

African Darter

Saddlebill Stork

White Pelican

Pink-backed Pelican

Black-headed
Heron

Yellow-billed Stork

Marabou *Leptoptilos crumeniferus* **L 150**
Large size and grotesque appearance are unmistakable. Head and upper neck are bare and fleshy. Adults possess inflatable neck pouch. Head and immense bill are often dirty. Large flocks gather around kills and rubbish dumps. Common and widespread.

Hammerkop *Scopus umbretta* **L 60**
Heron-like bird with thick crest giving head distinctive appearance. Feeds mainly on frogs and usually seen singly around lake margins. Builds huge twiggy nest in tree fork. Often found in Nairobi and Amboseli NPs. Openbill Stork is a larger all-dark bird, lacking crest and with open bill tips.

Sacred Ibis *Threskiornis aethiopicus* **L 75**
White plumage, black plumes and bare, black neck are distinctive. Immatures have feathered necks. Common and widespread around marshes and lakes. Hadada Ibis (named after its call) is all brown with green on wings (*see* page 165).

African Spoonbill *Platalea alba* **L 90**
White plumage, bare red face and characteristically shaped bill are distinctive. Feeds by sifting through surface water and mud. Locally common especially around larger lakes. Sometimes found on coast. Often rests on one leg with bill hidden among feathers.

Greater Flamingo *Phoenicopterus ruber* **L 140**
Unmistakable shape. Plumage is pinkish white with black and red wings. Bill is pink with black tip. Immatures are duller. Common and often very abundant on alkaline lakes of Rift Valley. Lesser Flamingo is smaller with deep red, black-tipped bill and pinker plumage.

African Pochard *Aythya erythropthalamus* **L 45**
Drake has chestnut flanks but may look all dark in strong light. Female paler with white face markings. White wing-bar in both sexes. Dives frequently. Common on lakes throughout. Male Maccoa Duck is similar to male African Pochard but has chestnut back. Tail held erect.

Red-billed Duck *Anas erythrorhynchos* **L 40**
Red bill, dark cap, contrasting with white cheeks and mottled grey-brown plumage are distinctive. Pale speculum. Common and widespread on lakes large and small. Yellow-billed Duck is similar but has bright yellow bill and green speculum with black-and-white margins.

Knob-billed Duck *Sarkidiornis melanotos* **L 55**
Conspicuous black-and-white plumage in both sexes. Metallic sheen only visible in certain lights. Male larger than female and possesses black, fleshy knob on top of bill. Rather local around lakes and larger rivers throughout. Sometimes perches in trees.

Egyptian Goose *Alopochen aegyptiaca* **L 60**
Found in small parties around margins of lakes and rivers. Sometimes perches in trees. Chestnut patch around eye and on belly are characteristic. White patch on wings is noticeable in flight. Call is a loud honking.

Spur-winged Goose
Plectropterus gambensis **L 85**
A large goose with mainly dark plumage. Belly and face white. Bill and legs red. Local throughout region. Most easily seen on Great Rift Valley lakes. White-faced Whistling Duck is much smaller with chestnut plumage, barred flanks and white face. Rather local.

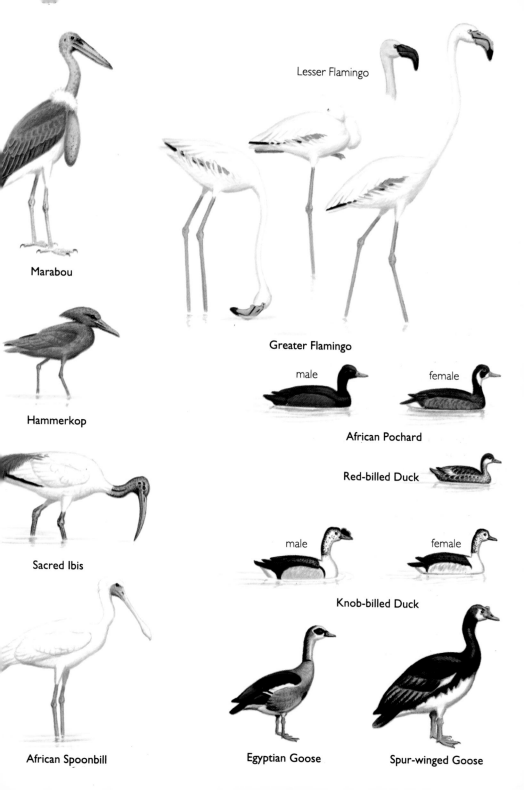

Marabou

Lesser Flamingo

Greater Flamingo

Hammerkop

African Pochard

male   female

Red-billed Duck

Sacred Ibis

Knob-billed Duck

male   female

African Spoonbill

Egyptian Goose

Spur-winged Goose

Secretary Bird *Sagittarius serpentarius* **L 100**
A distinctive, long-legged bird of prey. Generally seen walking through grass in search of snakes and lizards. Long central tail feathers and conspicuous crest raised when excited. Widespread throughout region in suitable habitats but nowhere common.

Verreaux's Eagle *Aquila verreauxii* **L 80**
Plumage all black except for white rump and white markings near wing tips. Flight silhouette is distinctive with wings narrower towards base. Widespread but rather local and usually in vicinity of cliffs and rocky crags. Regularly seen in Tsavo NP and occasionally in Nairobi NP.

Tawny Eagle *Aquila rapax* **L 70**
Plumage uniform brown although precise shade varies. In flight, tail looks short. Immatures have two pale wing bars and are paler than adults. Widespread in open country and often attracted to kills. Similar Steppe Eagle is a winter visitor. Adult is darker than Tawny.

Long-crested Hawk-eagle
Lophaetus occipitalis **L 55**
Long crest is conspicuous when perched. Plumage is mostly dark but white wing patches visible in flight. Silhouette shows tapering wings and relatively long tail. Sometimes seen perched beside roads but otherwise widespread in open country throughout Kenya and Tanzania.

Bateleur *Terathopius ecaudatus* **L 60**
Extraordinary flight silhouette is most distinctive. Appears almost tail-less with contrasting black body and white wings fringed with black. Soars effortlessly at great heights on stiffly held wings. Widespread and common. Immatures are uniform brown in colour.

African Fish Eagle *Haliaeetus vocifer* **L 75**
Elegant and unmistakable with white head, chest and tail and chestnut belly. Immatures are duller. Evocative, gull-like call carries a considerable distance. Usually found near water where it catches fish with powerful talons. Widespread and common in suitable sites.

Augur Buzzard *Buteo rufofuscus* **L 55**
Easily recognized by reddish tail, slaty-grey and white plumage, white undersides to wings visible in flight and barred wings at rest. Often perches beside roads. Widespread and common in highlands, preferring plains and lightly wooded areas. Often seen in Nairobi.

Pale Chanting Goshawk
Melierax poliopterus **L 50**
Grey plumage, yellow base to bill and orange legs are distinctive. Perches in acacias in dry bush and savannah country. White rump visible in flight. Common and widespread in east of region. Dark Chanting Goshawk has barred rump and red base to bill. West of region.

Pygmy Falcon *Poliohierax semitorquatus* **L 20**
Often seen perched on top of bushes where it resembles a large shrike. Mantle is grey in male and chestnut in female. Prefers arid scrub country and often seen near nests of Buffalo Weavers in which they nest. Rather local distribution and nowhere common.

Black Kite *Milvus migrans* **L 55**
Brownish plumage and forked tail are distinctive. African race has yellow bill while European race, a common winter visitor, has black bill. Common around habitation where they scavenge refuse. Large flocks seen within Nairobi. Call is a high-pitched whinnying.

Secretary Bird

Bataleur

African Fish Eagle

Verreaux's Eagle

Augur Buzzard

Tawny Eagle

Pale Chanting Goshawk

Long-crested
Hawk-eagle

Pygmy Falcon

Black Kite

Ruppell's Vulture *Gyps ruppellii* **L 85**
Common in open country. Usually seen soaring or feeding with other vultures at kills. Spotted appearance to back, wings and breast is characteristic. Three white wing-bars are visible in flight. Seen in most national parks and reserves. White-backed Vulture has unspotted plumage, white rump and white leading edge to wing in flight.

Lappet-faced Vulture *Torgos tracheliotus* **L 100**
Large size, massive bill and reddish-purple head and neck are distinctive. In flight, white bar near leading edge of wing is visible. Widespread but not numerous. Takes precedence over other vultures at kills. Hooded Vulture is much smaller with all-brown plumage and reddish bare face.

Crested Francolin *Francolinus sephaena* **L 25**
A chicken-like bird which inhabits arid scrub country. Often seen along dry river courses. Loud calls uttered at dawn and dusk. Sometimes walks with tail cocked up. Legs are bright red. Widespread and common in suitable habitats.

Yellow-necked Spurfowl
Francolinus leucoscepus **L 35**
Prefers dry bush country and often seen in small parties. Bright yellow bare throat and yellow legs are distinctive. Widespread and common in suitable habitats. Red-necked Spurfowl has red throat and legs. Prefers wooded habitat and scrub.

Helmeted Guineafowl *Numida meleagris* **L 55**
Bare blue throat and face and prominent red cap and helmet are distinctive. Often seen in large groups. Common in dry bush country and grassland. Vulturine Guineafowl has bare head and blue, white and black striped feathers on throat and mantle. Local in semi-deserts.

Black Crake *Limnocorax flavirostra* **L 20**
Black plumage, yellow-green bill and red legs are diagnostic. Locally common among emergent vegetation around lake margins. Often feeds in the open. Widespread in suitable habitats. Moorhen is larger with white under tail, greenish legs and red bill with yellow tip.

Crowned Crane *Balearica regulorum* **L 100**
Size and appearance make this species unmistakable. The sexes are similar and immatures are brown. Utters a loud honking call in flight. Seen usually in pairs or small groups. Widespread and locally common around marshes and swamps. Sometimes on grassland away from water.

Kori Bustard *Ardeotis kori* **L 100**
Immense size and coarse, grey neck feathers are characteristic. Male inflates neck when displaying. Widespread in Kenya and Tanzania in dry grassland and semi-desert. Easy to see in Amboseli NP. Buff-crested Bustard is much smaller with black belly and neck, and buff crest.

White-bellied Bustard
Eupodotis senegalensis **L 60**
The white belly and bluish-grey neck are characteristic. Males have black moustachial stripe. Found in open grassland and semi-desert. Local throughout the region. Black-bellied Bustard has black belly and throat in male. Less pronounced in female.

African Jacana *Actophilornis africanus* **L 25**
Easily recognized by chestnut plumage, white throat, black cap, blue bill and shield. Uses long toes to walk over surface vegetation on water. Widespread and common on suitable lakes and ponds. Lesser Jacana is smaller with brown upperparts and pale underneath.

Ruppell's Vulture

White-backed
Vulture in flight

Crowned Crane

Lappet-faced Vulture

Kori Bustard

Yellow-necked
Spurfowl

Crested Francolin

White-bellied
Bustard

Helmeted Guineafowl

Black
Crake

African Jacana

juv.

adult

Spotted Stone Curlew *Burhinus capensis* **L 40**
Mainly nocturnal but often seen at dusk or resting under shade in day. Sometimes caught in car headlights. Spotted plumage is characteristic. Widespread but local in dry areas throughout. Water Dikkop is found near water. Plumage greyish without spots.

Kittlitz's Plover *Charadrius pecuarius* **L 15**
Found on mudflats and beaches both on the coast and around lake margins. Runs with characteristic plover gait close to water's edge. Conspicuous white collar. Widespread and common in suitable habitats. White-fronted Sand Plover is paler with white forehead.

Three-banded Plover *Charadrius tricollaris* **L 18**
A striking species with two black bands on chest and red eye-ring, base to bill and legs. Widespread but restricted to margins of freshwater lakes, rivers and reservoirs. Immatures are somewhat paler than adults. Locally common throughout the region.

Crowned Plover *Vanellus coronatus* **L 28**
Mostly brown plumage with white belly and black crown with white ring. Widespread but local on grassy plains and semi-deserts. Black-winged Plover also has white belly but plumage is greyish brown and head lacks crown markings. A widespread but local, upland species.

Blacksmith Plover *Vanellus armatus* **L 27**
A distinctive black, white and grey bird. Prefers open country. Usually found close to lakes and rivers but occasionally away from water. Spur-winged Plover has brown back and mantle, black cap, throat and chest, and white belly and side of neck. Found around lakes and marshes, but also on the coast.

Long-toed Lapwing *Vanellus crassirostris* **L 30**
A distinctive species with white front, face and belly, black cap and chest and brown back. Found on lakes rich in aquatic vegetation across which it walks like a jacana. Easily seen at Amboseli NP. Wattled Plover has mostly brown plumage with red and yellow wattle.

Black-winged Stilt
Himantopus himantopus **L 36**
Unmistakable with black back and white head, neck and belly. Immatures are less strikingly marked. Needle-like bill is black. Wades in deep water on very long, red legs. In flight, wings are black and legs trail behind body. Common around Rift Valley lakes, more so in winter.

Crab Plover *Dromas ardeola* **L 35**
A non-breeding visitor to the coast where it frequents estuaries, mudflats and sand bars. Striking black-and-white plumage and heavy bill make it unmistakable but could possibly be confused with Avocet from a distance. Feeds in a deliberate manner while searching for crabs

Marsh Sandpiper *Tringa stagnatilis* **L 22**
An elegant winter visitor to East Africa which is sometimes common along the shores of larger lakes. Long thin bill and legs are characteristic. Green Sandpiper has proportionately shorter legs and bill and bobbing action to tail. Wood Sandpiper has yellowish legs.

Avocet *Recurvirostra avosetta* **L 40**
A common winter visitor to lakes in the region and is resident in smaller numbers. Striking black-and-white plumage and upturned bill is distinctive. Feeds actively by scything through water from side to side. Long blue legs trail in flight. Easily seen on most Rift Valley lakes.

Spotted Stone
Curlew

Long-toed Lapwing

Kittlitz's Plover

Three-banded
Plover

Black-winged
Stilt

Crowned Plover

Crab Plover

Blacksmith
Plover

Marsh
Sandpiper

Avocet

Temminck's Courser *Cursorius temminckii* L 20
Large-headed plover-like bird found on open plains and grassland often away from water. Widespread but restricted to suitable habitats. Pale supercilium and black belly patch are characteristic. Cream-coloured Courser is pale buff without dark patch on belly.

Pratincole *Glareola pratincola* L 25
Unusual wader which resembles a tern in flight. Short legs and bill, and creamy throat patch are characteristic. Widespread and found around the drying margins of lakes. Madagascar Pratincole is smaller with less forked tail. Non-breeding visitor to coastal areas such as Malindi.

Grey-headed Gull *Larus cirrocephalus* L 40
An attractive gull with grey head and red bill and legs. Immatures are mottled greyish brown. Most frequently seen on inland waters and easy to see on most Rift Valley lakes. Sooty Gull is a coastal species. Dark hood and yellow bill tipped with black and red.

White-winged Black Tern
Chlidonias leucoptera L 25
Common winter visitor and migrant through region. Found on inland waters and easy to see on most Rift Valley lakes. Usually seen in small flocks hawking for insects. Distinctive breeding plumage. Non-breeding plumage similar to Whiskered Tern. Look for pale rump.

Whiskered Tern *Chlidonias hybrida* L 25
Distinctive breeding plumage with grey body, black cap and white stripe on cheek. In winter, paler with dark streak through eye. Local resident on inland waters but numbers augmented in winter by migrants. Easy to see on many Rift Valley lakes such as Nakuru.

Chestnut-bellied Sandgrouse
Pterocles exustus L 30
Widespread and common in semi-desert areas sometimes forming flocks. Visits watering holes to drink at dawn. Long tail is noticeable in flight. Male is unstreaked with dark breast band. Female is streaked. Black-faced Sandgrouse has black on face in male and short tail.

Red-eyed Dove *Streptopelia semitorquata* L 30
Common and widespread in gardens and forest edge. Red eye-ring, black half collar and reddish underparts are characteristic. 'Cooing' call is a familiar sound. Easy to see in Nairobi. Dusky Turtle Dove lacks collar and has chestnut patch on the wing.

Ring-necked Dove *Streptopelia capicola* L 25
Smaller version of the Red-eyed Dove which has white belly and lacks reddish flush on underparts. Common and widespread in a wide range of habitats. Call is a repetitive *coo coco*. African Mourning Dove is similar but paler with pale eye. Local in open woodland.

Laughing Dove *Streptopelia senegalensis* L 25
Widespread and common throughout region. Found in a variety of habitats from gardens to open woodland. Attractively marked with reddish upperparts, blue-grey on wings and white lower belly. White on tail noticeable in flight. Distinctive five note call.

Namaqua Dove *Oena capensis* L 20
Widespread and common throughout but restricted to areas of semi-desert and dry bush. Long tail is particularly noticeable in flight as are chestnut patches on wings. Male has black face and throat. Sometimes seen feeding beside roads in arid regions. Generally silent.

Temminck's Courser

Chestnut-bellied Sandgrouse

Pratincole

Red-eyed Dove

Grey-headed Gull

Ring-necked Dove

White-winged Black Tern

Laughing Dove

Whiskered Tern

Namaqua Dove

Hartlaub's Turaco *Tauraco hartlaubi* **L 40**
Common and widespread in highland forests of
Kenya and Tanzania. Mostly green plumage with
dark cap and white patch in front of eye. Can be
difficult to spot as colouring helps it merge with
vegetation. Loud calls attract attention. Easy to
see in Nairobi City Park.

White-bellied Go-away-bird
Corythaixoides leucogaster **L 50**
Distinctive grey, black and white bird. Long tail,
white belly and noticeable crest are diagnostic.
Locally common in dry bush country in Kenya
and northern Tanzania. Loud 'go-away' call.
Bare-faced Go-away-bird is grey with white breast
and black face. Locally common.

Brown Parrot *Poicephalus meyeri* **L 25**
Widespread but local throughout region. Found
mainly in open forest and bush. Typical parrot-
like calls attract attention. Often seen in small
groups. Greenish underparts and yellow on crown
and wings. Brown-headed Parrot is coastal and
lacks yellow on crown.

Lilac-breasted Roller *Coracias caudata* **L 40**
Conspicuous bird of open plains and bush.
Perches on posts and dead branches. Long tail
streamers noticeable in flight. Abyssinian Roller
occurs in northern Kenya, lacks lilac breast and
has longer tail. European Roller is winter visitor
and lacks tail streamers.

Pied Kingfisher *Ceryle rudis* **L 25**
Distinctive black-and-white-bird. Male has two
black breast bands, female only one. Widespread
and reasonably common along rivers and around
lake margins. Sometimes seen in pairs. Perches on
branches and wires overhanging water but will
sometimes hover.

Malachite Kingfisher *Alcedo cristata* **L 14**
Distinctive with deep blue back, orange underparts, blue-barred crown and crest, and white
cheek patch. Widespread but restricted to freshwater lakes and larger ponds. Perches on reeds
and branches overhanging water. Pygmy Kingfisher is smaller and lacks crest.

Woodland Kingfisher *Halcyon senegalensis* **L 20**
Conspicuous with greyish head and underparts
and blue back, tail and wings. Upper mandible of
bill is red, lower black. Common and widespread.
Feeds away from water in forest glades and open
savannah. Striped Kingfisher has greyish plumage
and has streaked underparts.

Carmine Bee-eater *Merops nubicus* **L 36**
Carmine-red plumage and dark head are diagnostic. Long tail streamers conspicuous in flight.
Locally common in dry country. Breeds in
northern part of Kenya and north-east Tanzania.
Common non-breeding visitor to Kenyan coast
between December and March. Forms large
communal roosts.

European Bee-eater *Merops apiaster* **L 28**
Common winter visitor and passage migrant to
savannah areas. Unmistakable plumage. Perches
in the open. Catches insects in flight. White-
fronted Bee-eater is resident in Rift Valley. Green
back, wings and tail. Reddish head, neck and
breast and black-and-white through eyes.

Little Bee-eater *Merops pusillus* **L 15**
Mainly green plumage, yellow throat and dark
upper breast are characteristic. Common and
widespread in a variety of habitats. Perches
conspicuously, sometimes in small groups. The
Cinnamon-chested Bee-eater is a larger forest
species with rich cinnamon chest.

Hartlaub's Turaco

Malachite Kingfisher

White-bellied
Go-away-bird

Woodland Kingfisher

Brown Parrot

Carmine Bee-eater

Lilac-breasted
Roller

European Bee-eater

Pied Kingfisher

Little Bee-eater

Silvery-cheeked Hornbill *Bycanistes brevis* **L 70**
Recognized by large size and mainly black plumage including wings. Casque is pale and smaller in female than in male. Widespread but local in forests from coast to highlands. Trumpeter Hornbill is slightly smaller and has white breast and belly and white on wings.

Red-billed Hornbill
Tockus erythrorhynchus **L 45**
Widespread and common in dry country throughout region. Often visits game lodges for food. Spotted white on wing coverts and prominent white supercilium. Yellow-billed Hornbill is rather local and has larger white spots on wing and downcurved yellow bill.

Ground Hornbill *Bucorvus leadbeateri* **L 105**
Widespread but local in open country such as Masai Mara NP. Ground-dwelling, walking with a stately plod. Often seen in small groups. White on wings visible only in flight (comparatively rare). Abyssinian Ground Hornbill has more prominent casque and occurs in northern Kenya.

Verreaux's Eagle Owl *Bubo lacteus* **L 65**
Large owl which frequents acacia woodland, generally in the vicinity of water. Sometimes seen roosting among dense foliage during the daytime. Unspotted breast and pale face, bordered with black are diagnostic. Widespread and locally common but easily overlooked.

Speckled Mousebird *Colius striatus* **L 30**
Speckled brown plumage, long tail and pale cheeks are diagnostic. Widespread and locally common in woodlands, gardens and scrub. Often seen in small groups. Blue-naped Mousebird is similar shape but has greyish plumage, blue nape and bare red face. Usually found in more open bush country.

Cardinal Woodpecker
Dendropicos fuscescens **L 13**
Recognized by small size, streaked breast, barred back and red crown in male. Widespread and common throughout range in wooded areas and scrub. Little Spotted Woodpecker has green back, spotted underparts and red crown in male. Widely distributed in wooded habitats.

Bearded Woodpecker *Thripias namaquus* **L 23**
Attractively marked species with mostly dark plumage and black-and-white stripes on head. Crown is red in male and black in female. Locally common in forests and open woodland throughout range. 'Yaffling' call reminiscent of European Green Woodpecker.

Narina's Trogon *Apaloderma narina* **L 30**
Locally common in forests from coast to highlands. Green plumage, red breast and belly, and white outer-tail feathers are diagnostic. Rather difficult to locate since it often sits motionless among dappled foliage. Comparatively easy to see in Nairobi City Park.

Red-and-yellow Barbet
Trachyphonus erythrocephalus **L 23**
Distinctively marked with red and yellow plumage, spotted back, wings and tail. Locally common in areas of dry bush and scrub in Kenya and northern Tanzania. Sometimes seen in small parties. Levaillant's Barbet is local in Tanzania. The dark crown and back are unspotted.

d'Arnaud's Barbet *Trachyphonus darnaudii* **L 17**
Locally common in areas of dry savannah scrub and bush country. Spotted back and tail, speckled yellow throat, white breast and red vent are distinctive. Amount of black on throat and crown varies throughout range. Sometimes tame at game lodges, especially in Tsavo NP.

188

Silvery-cheeked Hornbill

Red-billed Hornbill

Ground Hornbill

Narina's Trogon

Cardinal Woodpecker

Red-and-yellow Barbet

Verreaux's Eagle Owl

Bearded Woodpecker

Speckled Mousebird

d'Arnaud's Barbet

Nyanza Swift *Apus niansae* **L 15**
All dark swift with forked tail. Flocks seen almost anywhere in the highlands, descending lower at the approach of thunderstorms. Swifts with white rumps also occur: White-rumped Swift has deeply forked tail, Horus Swift slightly forked tail and Little Swift unforked tail. Alpine Swift is much larger with white underparts and dark chest band.

African Palm Swift *Cypsiurus parvus* **L 12**
Distinctive appearance in flight with long wings and long, deeply forked tail. Plumage is brownish. Invariably found in the vicinity of palm trees and so most easily seen along the coast.

Rufous-naped Lark *Mirafra africana* **L 16**
Widespread and sometimes common in grassy areas and open plains. Rufous nape indistinct in many races. Rounded, rufous wings conspicuous in flight. Song is a five-note whistle delivered from post. Pink-breasted Lark has a longer tail and breast blotched with pink. Widespread.

Yellow-throated Longclaw
Macronyx croceus **L 20**
Locally common in grassland with scrub. A stocky pipit with unmistakable colouring. Golden Pipit is superficially similar but smaller with yellow on wings. Yellow throat is not as clearly bordered with black. Rosy-breasted Longclaw has yellow replaced by reddish-pink.

Common Bulbul *Pyconotus barbatus* **L 18**
Common and widespread throughout region in open woodland but more especially in gardens. Easy to see in Nairobi. Dark hood and yellow vent are characteristic. Yellow-whiskered Greenbul is common in parts of Kenyan highlands. Sombre olive plumage with conspicuous yellow cheek stripe.

South African Black Flycatcher
Melaenornis pammelaina **L 20**
Rather local in open acacia woodland. All black glossy plumage, dark eye and square-ended tail are distinctive. White-eyed Slaty Flycatcher has greyish plumage and dark eye surrounded by conspicuous white eye-ring. Local in highland forests.

Paradise Flycatcher *Terpsiphone viridis*
male **L 35**, female **L 20**
Common and widespread in open woodlands and gardens. Male unmistakable with incredibly long red tail, red back and black head and underparts. Female similar but with shorter tail. White phase occurs locally. Red-bellied Paradise Flycatcher has black hood and mainly red plumage.

Olive Thrush *Turdus olivaceous* **L 23**
Locally common in forests, open woodlands and gardens. Easily seen in the Kenyan highlands and even in Nairobi. Slaty-brown back, orange belly, streaked throat and reddish bill are characteristic. Loud scolding alarm call. African Thrush has grey plumage and belly suffused buff.

White-browed Robin Chat
Cossypha heuglini **L 20**
Common and widespread in gardens and woodland edge. Red underparts, dark brown upperparts and conspicuous white eye-stripe. Tail mostly rufous. Ruppell's Robin Chat is similar and found in highland forests of Kenya. Tail has black central feathers.

Anteater Chat *Myrmecochichla aethiops* **L 20**
Found in open country. Common in the Kenyan highlands. Often seen perched beside roads. Alert posture and all-black plumage are characteristic. In flight, white in wings is noticeable. Male Schalow's (Mourning) Wheatear has mainly dark plumage, white belly and buff rump.

South African
Black Flycatcher

African
Palm Swift

Nyanza Swift

female

male

Paradise
Flycatcher

Rufous-naped Lark

Yellow-throated
Longclaw

Olive Thrush

White-browed
Robin Chat

Common
Bulbul

Anteater
Chat

Grey-backed Cameroptera
Cameroptera brevicaudata L 10
Common species of forest and dense scrub but skulking and often overlooked. Dumpy appearance, greyish plumage, green wings and relatively short, rounded tail are characteristic. Brown Woodland Warbler is widespread. Brownish plumage with wing and tail feathers edged green.

Winding Cisticola *Cisticola galactotes* L 13
Common around marshes and swamps, frequenting lush vegetation. Trilling song, white underparts and rufous tail tipped black-and-white are characteristic. Singing Cisticola has greyish plumage, dirty white underparts and rufous crown. Found in grassy places.

Tawny-flanked Prinia *Prinia subflava* L 13
Common and widespread in overgrown grassy places, often near water. Greyish-brown plumage, paler underneath with tawny flanks. Graduated tail often flicked or raised. Redwing Warbler is local in grassy wooded areas. Greyish plumage, red wings and graduated tail.

Striped Swallow *Hirundo abyssinica* L 18
Rufous cap and rump, deeply forked tail, deep-blue upperparts and striped underparts. Widespread in most habitats except woodland. Angola Swallow has blue-black upperparts, red forehead and throat, and less forked tail. European Swallow is common in winter. Similar to Angola but has dark chest band and deeply forked tail.

Fork-tailed Drongo *Dicrurus adsimilis* L 25
Distinctive all-black bird with red eye and forked tail resembling fish tail. Common and widespread throughout region. Found in open woodlands and gardens. Uses regular perch from which to catch insects.

Fiscal Shrike *Lanius collaris* L 23
Mainly black upperparts and white underparts, but conspicuous white 'V' on mantle and pale rump. Widespread and common in open woodland and around habitation. Easily seen in Nairobi. Long-tailed Fiscal is locally common. Mostly black plumage with white 'V' on mantle.

White-crowned Shrike
Eurocephalus ruppelli L 23
White crown, rump and underparts. Local and restricted to arid bush country. Perches on branches and usually seen in small groups. Gliding flight. Straight-crested Helmet Shrike inhabits open woodland. Black, white and grey plumage with yellow eye wattle and short crest are distinctive features.

Black-headed Oriole *Oriolus larvatus* L 23
Distinctive with mainly yellow plumage and black hood and throat. Common and widespread in open woodland and forest. Song is a series of liquid notes. Male African Golden Oriole is yellow with black through eye and black tail edged with yellow. Female greenish yellow.

Pied Crow *Corvus albus* L 45
Large, mainly black bird with prominent white collar and breast. Widespread and sometimes common in open country but also in and around habitation. White-naped Raven is mainly black with white half collar on back of neck and thick bill. Scavenges around remote habitation.

Indian House Crow *Corvus splendens* L 32
Introduced species which is extremely common along the coast, especially between Mombasa and Malindi. All black but neck suffused with grey. Cape Rook has all-black plumage and is locally common on grassy plains.

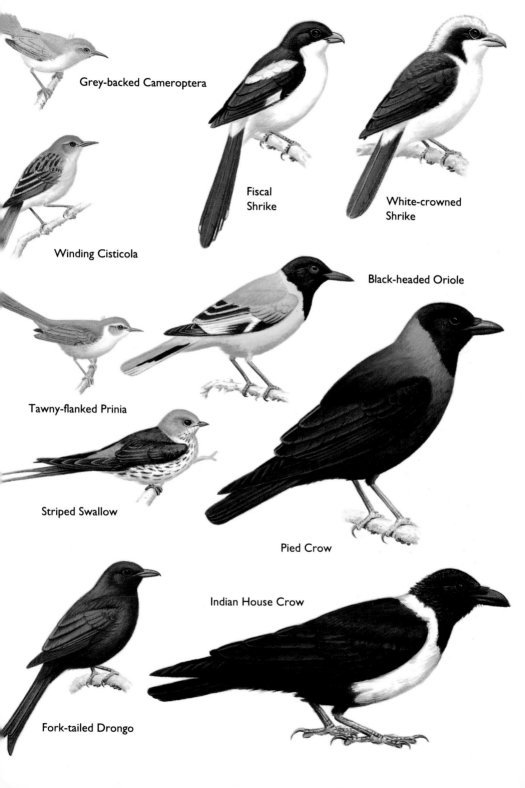

Grey-backed Cameroptera

Fiscal
Shrike

White-crowned
Shrike

Winding Cisticola

Black-headed Oriole

Tawny-flanked Prinia

Striped Swallow

Pied Crow

Indian House Crow

Fork-tailed Drongo

Blue-eared Glossy Starling
Lamprotornis chalybaeus **L 23**
Widespread and common in a variety of habitats from open woodland to parks and gardens. Metallic green plumage with head and chest bluish. Yellow eye. Often feeds on ground. Ruppell's Long-tailed Starling is metallic green with much longer tail. Local in bush country.

Superb Starling *Spreo superbus* **L 18**
Widespread and common in open woodland, parks and gardens. Easy to see in Nairobi. Blue-green upperparts and throat, white breast band, red belly and white vent are characteristic. Pale eye. Hildebrandt's Starling is similar but lacks white vent and breast band.

Red-billed Oxpecker
Buphagus erythrorhynchus **L 18**
Invariably found in small groups riding on both game and domesticated animals from which it picks parasites. Easy to see in national parks where Rhinoceros, Giraffe, Buffalo and Elephant occur. Red bill and yellow eye wattle. Yellow-billed Oxpecker has yellow bill and lacks eye wattle. Much less common.

Yellow White-eye *Zosterops senegalensis* **L 10**
Widespread in a variety of habitats from scrub to open woodland and gardens. Greenish yellow plumage with conspicuous white eye-ring. The race known as Kikuyu White-eye (sometimes considered a separate species), with a larger white eye ring, is common in Nairobi and the Kenyan highlands.

Variable Sunbird *Nectarinia venusta* **L 9**
Male has metallic blue-green plumage with yellow belly which varies in shade in different regions. Female has brownish upperparts and yellowish underparts. Occurs in open woodland, parks and gardens. Easy to see in Nairobi. Feeds on nectar, especially from flowers of *Leonotis*.

Malachite Sunbird *Nectarinia famosa*
male **L 22**, female **L 13**
Male has beautiful green plumage, yellow pectoral tufts and long central tail feathers. Female is brownish with short tail. Found in highland bush country where they feed on flowers of Red Hot Poker and *Leonotis*. Tacazze Sunbird is similar but with a metallic violet-bronze plumage and black belly.

Bronze Sunbird *Nectarinia kilimensis*
male **L 24**, female **L 14**
Male is metallic green and bronze with long central tail feathers. Female has short tail and is olive brown, paler and streaked below. A highland species which frequents open woodland and gardens. Common and easy to see in Nairobi.

Vitelline Masked Weaver *Ploceus velatus* **L 14**
Widespread and locally common in dry bush country. Male has mainly yellow plumage with black mask. Orange on crown extends in front of eye. Female is yellowish. Builds suspended nest. Masked Weaver is similar but black on crown extends behind eye. Colonial nester.

Golden Palm Weaver *Ploceus bojeri* **L 15**
Common resident along Kenyan coast where it nests colonially in palm trees. Yellow plumage with bright orange head and breast. Taveta Golden Weaver is similar but has orange only on crown and breast. Rather local but the commonest weaver in Amboseli NP.

Reichenow's Weaver
Ploceus baglafecht reichenowi **L 15**
Attractive species. Male has black mantle and nape, black mask and pale eye. Female has black mask and crown. Yellow underparts in both sexes. Locally common in Kenyan and Tanzanian highlands. Speke's Weaver has black mask and throat, yellow underparts and a mottled yellow and brown mantle.

Blue-eared Glossy Starling

Malachite Sunbird

Superb Starling

Bronze Sunbird

Red-billed Oxpecker

Vitelline Masked Weaver

Yellow White-eye

Golden Palm Weaver

Reichenow's Weaver

male

female

Variable Sunbird

Jackson's Widowbird *Euplectes jacksoni*
male **L 34**, female **L 14**
Male breeding plumage unmistakable with long, downcurved tail, all-black plumage and rufous on wings. During breeding season displays by leaping in the air. Female and non-breeding males are brown and streaked. Locally common in grassland.

Red Bishop *Euplectes orix* **L 11**
Male has red plumage with black face and breast. Female is dull brown and streaked. Rather local. Found in areas of grassland and sometimes cultivation. During breeding season male performs display flight. Zanzibar Red Bishop has black underparts. Common on Kenyan coast.

Bronze Mannikin *Lonchura cucullata* **L 9**
Common and widespread in a wide variety of habitats from grassland to cultivated land and open woodland. Brown back, black hood and white underparts. Dumpy appearance with short tail. Black-and-white Mannikin has black upperparts and white underparts. It is found in open woodlands.

Red-cheeked Cordon-bleu
Uraeginthus bengalus **L 12**
Brown back and crown, blue tail and underparts, and red ear coverts are characteristic. Female lacks red on cheeks. Common and widespread in grassland and abandoned cultivated areas. Blue-capped Cordon-bleu has a blue plumage except for brown back, and lacks red cheek patch. Local in dry areas.

Common Waxbill *Estrilda astrild* **L 10**
Locally abundant, flocks gathering on grasslands and abandoned cultivated areas. Brownish plumage, red eye-stripe and belly, and bright red bill. Crimson-rumped Waxbill has black bill and crimson rump. Black-faced Waxbill has dark bill, black mask and crimson rump.

Pin-tailed Whydah *Vidua macroura*
male **L 30**, female **L 12**
Breeding male is unmistakable with long black tail, black-and-white upperparts and red bill. Outside breeding season, resembles female with streaky brown plumage. Red bill is always a good character. Male Paradise Whydah has long, broad tail and orange collar and breast.

Purple Indigobird *Hypochera chalybeata* **L 11**
Dumpy little bird. In breeding plumage male is blackish-purple with a pale bill and red legs. In non-breeding plumage resembles streaked brown female. Common and widespread. Found in a wide variety of habitats from grassland and cultivated areas to open woodland.

Yellow-rumped Seedeater
Serinus atrogularis **L 10**
Locally common in a wide variety of open habitats. Plumage is streaked greyish-brown with a conspicuous yellow rump in flight. Yellow-fronted Canary is locally common in open woodland. Mainly yellow plumage with black streaks on head and yellow forehead.

Streaky Seedeater *Serinus striolatus* **L 15**
Common and widespread in highland regions and easily seen around Nairobi. Streaked brown plumage including rump with pale throat and eye-stripe are diagnostic. Brimstone Canary has similar build but bright yellow-green plumage and pale greenish bill. Widespread in open country.

Golden-breasted Bunting
Emberiza flaviventris **L 15**
Widespread and sometimes common in open woodland and forest edge. Recognized by orange breast, rufous back and black-and-white markings on head. Feeds on the ground. Somali Golden-breasted Bunting is similar but has more white on underparts and on mantle.

Jackson's Widowbird

Pin-tailed Whydah

Red Bishop

Purple Indigobird

Yellow-rumped
Seedeater

Bronze Mannikin

Red-cheeked
Cordon-bleu

Streaky Seedeater

Common Waxbill

Golden-breasted
Bunting

Greater Galago *Galago crassicaudatus* **L 75**
Also called 'Bushbaby'. Entirely nocturnal and invariably in trees. Sometimes seen in small groups but usually solitary. Call is a plaintive squeal which attracts attention around campsites. Large eyes are sometimes picked up by torchlight. Tail is long and bushy. Widespread in woodland throughout region.

Lesser Bushbaby *Galago senegalensis* **L 35**
Thin tail and large ears and eyes are characteristic. Entirely nocturnal and almost always found in trees. Feeds on insects and gum in acacia trees. Widespread and frequently seen by torchlight when camping in woodland. Rustling branches and leaves attract attention.

Black-faced Vervet Monkey
Cercopithecus aethiops **L 100**
Lives in groups of 10–30 animals in areas of open woodland and savannah scrub. Black face, bordered with white is characteristic. Black-tipped tail held above body when walking. Often accustomed to man's presence, especially around campsites. Will even steal from tents or rucksacks, some individuals tackling zips. Widespread and common. Found in many national parks and reserves.

Sykes' (Blue) Monkey
Cercopithecus mitis **L 125**
An attractive species which lives in open woodlands and forests. Colour and pattern varies considerably throughout range. Sykes' Monkeys occur in west and are orange-brown with a white ring around neck. Blue Monkeys are blue-grey with white cheeks. Found in eastern, coastal districts. Sykes' Monkeys are easily seen in Nairobi City Park. Widespread and common.

Striped Ground Squirrel
Xerus erythropus **L 50**
Lives entirely on the ground. Large, sociable colonies inhabit networks of burrows and tunnels. Often seen sitting outside entrance resting on hind legs in alert posture. Sometimes uses tail to shade sun. Common throughout the region. Unstriped Ground Squirrel lacks stripe along the flanks.

African Hare *Lepus capensis* **L 50**
Generally rather shy. Spends most of the day crouched in cover but sometimes seen at dawn and dusk or when disturbed. Does not live in burrows. Large ears and long hind legs are characteristic but the Scrub Hare is larger with proportionately bigger ears. Widespread in grassland habitat, sometimes among open woodland.

Olive Baboon *Papio anubis* **L 125**
Lives in large troops of 20–80 animals in all types of savannah and open woodland. Often seen crossing roads. Can become a nuisance at some designated campsites. Spends night in trees and feeds during the day with sentries on look-out. Mothers carry young on their backs. Widespread and common throughout most of region. Yellow Baboon is similar but yellowish.

Black-and-white Colobus
Colobus abyssinicus **L 175**
An attractive monkey with distinctive black-and-white markings. They live in groups of 10–40 animals in forested areas and feed on leaves. Despite their bulk, thick bushy tail and lack of an opposing thumb on the hand, they are extremely agile in the tree tops. Often very vocal at dawn. Widespread and locally common in the Kenyan highlands, especially in the Aberdares.

Greater Galago

Striped Ground Squirrel

African Hare

Lesser Bushbaby

Olive Baboon

Black-faced
Vervet Monkey

Black-and-white
Colobus

Sykes' (Blue) Monkey

Golden Jackal *Canis aureus* **H 45**
Mainly nocturnal and so usually seen at dawn and dusk. Sometimes scavenges at kills. Golden-yellow colour predominates but some have darker backs. Generally a solitary animal but sometimes seen in pairs. Utters loud, yelping calls. Widespread but easiest to see in Ngorongoro and the Serengeti where not persecuted.

Black-backed Jackal *Canis mesomelas* **H 45**
Generally solitary; both nocturnal and diurnal in habits. Scavenges at kills but also catches small birds and mammals. Yelping and howling calls. Widespread throughout the region in both woodland and grassland. Side-striped Jackal is similar but has white-tipped tail (black-tipped in Black-backed Jackal) and prominent white side-stripe; widespread but generally a more nocturnal animal.

Large-spotted Genet *Genetta tigrina* **L 100**
Elegant, cat-like mammal with beautifully spotted coat. Nocturnal so usually seen at dawn and dusk. In some areas, visits prescribed campsites for scraps of food. Climbs well. Widespread in wooded regions. Small-spotted Genet is similar but has white-tipped tail (black-tipped in Large-spotted). Coat markings are variable in both species.

Spotted Hyena *Crocuta crocuta* **H 75**
Generally most active after dark, but often seen in daytime. Lives in packs which both hunt live quarry and scavenge at Lion kills. Blood-curdling laughing call is a familiar sound at night for anyone camping in the bush. Often caked in blood and mud. Widespread and common except in proximity to man. Striped Hyena has irregular stripes on shaggy coat.

Bat-eared Fox *Otocyon megalotis* **H 30**
Outsize ears and bushy tail are diagnostic. Ears help to locate prey such as insects and lizards. Mainly nocturnal but may bask at den entrance during daytime. Utters a whining call. Inhabits open grassland and best seen in Serengeti and Masai Mara.

African Hunting Dog *Lycaon pictus* **H 75**
Hunts in packs of twelve or more enabling prey as large as Wildebeest to be tackled. Dog-like appearance and blotchy coat are diagnostic. Utters loud, howling calls. Generally diurnal. Inhabits open, grassy plains but persecuted and now rather local. Easiest to see in Serengeti and Masai Mara.

White-tailed Mongoose
Ichneumia albicauda **L 100**
A large species with a white, bushy tail. Rarely, the tail may be black. Generally solitary and nocturnal. May visit lodges and campsites in some areas. Inhabits savannah and woodland, usually close to water. Widespread in the region.

Slender Mongoose *Galerella sanguinea* **L 60**
Solitary and diurnal. Extremely slim with long, black-tipped tail. Widespread and common in a variety of habitats from grassland to woodland. Large-grey or Egyptian Mongoose also has a slender, black-tipped tail but is much larger (L 100cm); widespread but usually found near water.

Dwarf Mongoose *Helogale parvula* **L 40**
A small species, living colonially in excavated termite mounds. Often sunbathes near entrance holes. Groups embark on feeding forays in daytime. Widespread and common throughout.

Golden Jackal

Bat-eared Fox

Black-backed Jackal

African Hunting Dog

Large-spotted
Genet

White-tailed Mongoose

Slender Mongoose

Spotted
Hyena

Dwarf Mongoose

Lion *Panthera leo* **H 100**
Largest African cat. Full grown male and female are unmistakable. Young and juveniles are generally rather spotted. Despite its size, blends in with surroundings extremely well. Prides spend much of the day resting. Usual prey includes Zebra and Wildebeest. More-or-less restricted to parks and reserves nowadays. Most easily seen in Masai Mara, Amboseli and Serengeti but often seen in Nairobi NP.

Leopard *Panthera pardus* **H 70**
Generally solitary and rather shy. Largely nocturnal but sometimes seen during daylight in areas such as national parks where it is not persecuted. Occasionally rests up trees. Prefers habitat with plenty of cover including caves and rocky slopes. Widespread but usually only seen by chance. Most regularly sighted in Masai Mara.

Cheetah *Acinonyx jubatus* **H 75**
Much more slender and graceful in appearance than Leopard. Prefers open grassland where prey such as gazelle and Impala are common. Capable of extraordinary bursts of speed when in pursuit. Usually found in small groups. Most easily seen in parks and reserves including Nairobi, Amboseli, Masai Mara and Serengeti. Usually hunts at dawn or dusk.

Black Rhinoceros *Diceros bicornis* **H 150**
Despite their massive bulk, can be difficult to spot in tall grassland. Disturbance and poaching mean they are often nocturnal and usually seen at dawn and dusk. Rare and endangered but regularly seen in Amboseli, Masai Mara and Nairobi NP (introduced). White Rhinoceros is similar but has square muzzle when seen head-on (Black Rhinoceros has hooked lip). Virtually extinct as a wild species in the region.

Rock Hyrax *Heterohyrax brucei* **L 50**
Colonies are found on rocky outcrops and cliffs. Often sunbathes but always alert to danger. Squeaks loudly when alarmed. It is a favourite quarry of Verreaux's Eagle. Widespread and often common. Found in most national parks and reserves where suitable rocky habitats occur. Tree Hyrax is similar but has a white, not yellowish, mark on the back. Lives in trees and utters piercing squeal at night.

Common or **Burchell's Zebra**
Equus burchelli **H 135**
Found in large herds, often in association with Wildebeest. Migrates seasonally to areas of recent rain and fresh grass growth. Pattern of stripes is rather variable. Males utter loud, braying whinny. Common in suitable areas of open savannah and grassland. Huge herds in Serengeti, Masai Mara and Amboseli. Easy to see in Nairobi NP. Grevy's Zebra is similar but larger, with narrower stripes and a white belly and rump. Prefers arid habitats and has a more northerly distribution than the Common Zebra. Easiest to see in Meru, Samburu and at Lake Turkana.

African Elephant *Loxodonta africana* **H 300**
Huge and unmistakable; the largest land mammal. Males grow longer tusks than females. Large 'tuskers' are an increasingly rare sight due to ivory poaching. Large herds generally comprise females and young. Pays frequent visits to water to drink and bathe. The loud trumpeting carries a long distance. Much reduced in numbers due to poaching and changes in land use. More or less restricted to areas of sanctuary such as national parks and reserves. Still seen in Amboseli, Masai Mara, Lake Manyara and Selous.

Lioness

Lion

Rock Hyrax

Leopard

Common or Burchell's Zebra

Cheetah

African Elephant

Black Rhinoceros

Hippopotamus
Hippopotamus amphibius **H 150**
Invariably found in or near water; rivers and lakes are preferred. Wanders overland after dark to graze on grass. Usually found in groups. Shape and immense size make identification easy although spends most of day partially submerged with just nostrils and eyes above water. Easy to see in the Mara River and in Athi River in Nairobi NP.

Warthog *Phacochoerus aethiopicus* **H 70**
Pig-like animal with sparse covering of bristles. Skin colour varies due to habit of wallowing in mud. At close range, warts are visible on the face. Often runs with tail held erect. Digs for underground roots but will graze grass by kneeling on front legs. Often seen in family groups. Common throughout the region and easily seen in most national parks, especially in the vicinity of water and mud.

Giraffe *Giraffa camelopardalis* **H 550**
Size and shape make it unmistakable. However, often feeds in dense acacia scrub with which it blends in well. Thick lips and tongue allow them to eat from even the spiniest bushes. Usually found in herds of 5–20 animals. Males fight by twining necks. Found in most of the national parks and reserves in Kenya and Tanzania including Nairobi NP. Reticulated Giraffe is similar in size and shape but dark markings are sharply outlined and resemble crazy paving. Inhabits drier country than Giraffe. Most easily seen in Meru and Samburu. Considered by some authorities to be a distinct species but by others to be just a race of the common Giraffe.

Lesser Kudu *Tragelaphus strepsiceros* **H 150**
Shy and elegant antelope. Back characteristically has small hump. Two conspicuous white marks on throat. Only males have spiralled horns. Found in dense scrub where often difficult to see. Often encountered in Tsavo NP and Meru. Greater Kudu is similar but larger and lacks white marks on throat. Rare in Kenya but seen in Selous.

Fringe-eared Oryx *Oryx gazella* **H 125**
Found in thorn scrub and grassland usually where water is present. Usually seen in herds of 10–30 animals. Long, straight horns are seen in both sexes. Found in Tsavo NP and Amboseli NP in Kenya and in northern Tanzania. Beisa Oryx is similar but lacks black ear tufts of Fringe-eared Oryx. Prefers arid country. Seen in Samburu and Meru.

Sable Antelope *Hippotragus niger* **H 130**
Found in herds of 10–30 animals. Prefers woodland with grass for grazing and consequently can be difficult to see well. Dark flanks contrasting with white belly, longer horns and lack of ear tufts distinguishes Sable from Roan. Facial markings are also characteristic. Herds often visit water to drink. Widespread but nowhere numerous.

Roan Antelope *Hippotragus equinus* **H 150**
A shy antelope, usually found in grassy areas with patches of woodland and scrub. Never strays far from water and will move to find a new source in times of drought. Generally found in herds of 10–30 animals. Horns present in both sexes. Shorter and less curved than Sable Antelope. Black-and-white face markings, mane and tufted ears are characteristic. Rather rare in wooded hills in southern Kenya.

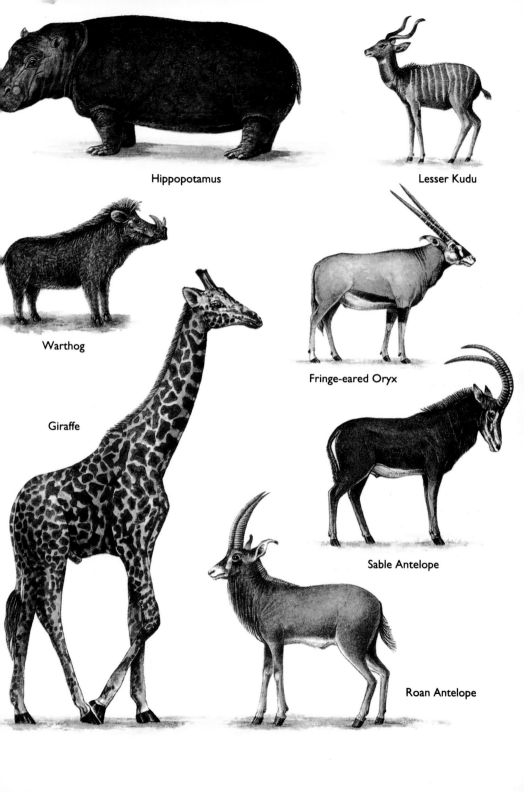

Hippopotamus

Lesser Kudu

Warthog

Fringe-eared Oryx

Giraffe

Sable Antelope

Roan Antelope

Eland *Taurotragus oryx* **H 150**
Massive build, short twisted horns in both sexes and throat dewlap are characteristic. Found on grassland and savannah and not dependent on water. Usually seen in herds of 10–50 animals and often mixes with other species. Can leap surprisingly well. Browses leaves from bushes. Widespread but nowhere common.

Bushbuck *Tragelaphus scriptus* **H 75**
An elegant and shy antelope which lives in dense cover, seldom far from water. Generally solitary. Nocturnal browser of leaves and often seen at dawn and dusk emerging from undergrowth. The two white spots on the neck and the black harness are characteristic. Males grow horns which become twisted with age. Widespread and common but often overlooked.

Bohor Reedbuck *Redunca redunca* **H 75**
Stocky but elegant antelope which prefers marshy ground with plenty of cover. Seen singly or in small groups of 4–8 animals. Males have characteristic forward-curving horns. Both sexes have black spot on jaw and white patch under tail. Widespread and seen in suitable habitat around Rift Valley lakes.

Common Waterbuck
Kobus ellipsiprymnus **H 120**
Usually seen in groups of 5–25 animals comprising females with young and a dominant male. A stocky antelope which is similar to Defassa Waterbuck but has conspicuous white ring on rump instead of white patch. Feeds on grassland but seldom far from water. Widespread and quite common east of the Great Rift Valley.

Defassa Waterbuck *Kobus defassa* **H 120**
A stocky antelope which is usually seen in groups of 10–30 animals comprising females and young with a dominant male. Only the males have elegantly curved horns. Found on grassland and in open woodland but seldom far from water. When alarmed, retreats into marshy vegetation. Widespread, mainly in west of region. Easy to see at Lake Nakuru.

Coke's Hartebeest *Alcelaphus buselaphus* **H 125**
Found in grassland and in open woodlands often far from water. Usually seen in groups of 5–30 animals often mixed with Zebras. Sentries stand on mounds or hummocks while herd is grazing. Distinctive horns present in both sexes. Locally common throughout range and can be seen in Nairobi NP.

Topi *Damaliscus lunatus* **H 130**
A distinctive and stocky antelope which lives in groups of 10–30 animals. Found on grasslands and plains, often mixing with Wildebeest and Zebra. Sentries stand on lookout while herd is grazing. Both sexes have horns although those of male are larger. Widespread in southern Kenya and northern Tanzania.

Wildebeest *Connochaetes taurinus* **H 130**
One of the most distinctive antelopes with characteristically doleful expression. Sometimes seen in herds numbering hundreds or thousands of animals. Migrates to find fresh grass after recent rainfall. Widespread throughout region in areas of grassland and plains. Movements between Serengeti and Masai Mara are spectacular. Easily seen in Nairobi NP.

Gerenuk *Litocranius walleri* **H 100**
Extremely distinctive antelope which lives in small groups in dry bush country often well away from water. Its long neck is its most noticeable feature. Often stands on hind legs to reach higher leaves on bushes. Only the males have horns. Widespread but restricted to dry country. Often seen in Amboseli and at Samburu.

Bushbuck

Eland

Bohor Reedbuck

Common Waterbuck

Defassa Waterbuck

Coke's Hartebeest

Topi

Wildebeest

Gerenuk

Thomson's Gazelle *Gazella thomsoni* **H 60**
Smaller than Grant's Gazelle with stocky build. Found in areas of grassland and plains and feeds on grass. Often seen in loose herds of 10–50 animals. During migration periods, herds may aggregate with thousands of animals in association. Dark side stripe pronounced in both sexes. Common in open habitats.

Impala *Aepyceros melampus* **H 90**
Elegant antelope usually seen in groups of 10–30 animals comprising either young males or females and young with a dominant male. Prefers open woodland and scrub but sometimes seen on plains well away from water. When alarmed, 'panic' and leap in all directions. Common and widespread throughout the region in most parks and reserves.

Grant's Gazelle *Gazella grantii* **H 90**
Inhabits open grassland, usually seen in groups of 10–30 animals. Often occurs well away from water and grazes in surprisingly arid country. Both sexes have horns but those of the male are enormous. The dark side stripe is darker in female than in male. Common in arid Tanzanian and Kenyan parks and reserves.

Common Duiker *Sylvicapra grimmia* **H 50**
Small and rather secretive antelope with variable coat colour from grey to fawn. Largely nocturnal but often seen at dawn and dusk. Found in a wide variety of habitats usually close to dense cover. Solitary or in pairs. Widespread in southern Kenya and Tanzania.

Klipspringer *Oreotragus oreotragus* **H 55**
Only found on rocky outcrops or on mountains. Usually solitary but sometimes seen in small groups. Walks on hoof tips, extremely sure-footed when running or leaping. Males have straight, short, horns. Shy but sometimes 'freezes' before fleeing. Widespread but local because of restricted suitable habitat.

Oribi *Ourebia ourebi* **H 55**
Found on grasslands, usually close to water. Solitary or seen in small groups. Black bushy tail and black spot below ear are distinctive. Males have short, straight horns. Utters whistling call when alarmed. Locally common in suitable habitats in southern Kenya and Tanzania.

Steinbok *Raphicerus campestris* **H 50**
A small, elegant antelope with huge ears. Males have short, straight horns. Underparts and rump noticeably white. Rather shy and alert. Generally solitary. Found on open grassy plains, often well away from water. Feeds during the day. Found in savannah parks in southern Kenya, such as Amboseli NP, and Tanzania.

African Buffalo *Syncerus caffer* **H 150**
Appearance and huge size are unmistakable. Horns present in both sexes, although larger in males. Found on grassy plains, usually near water. Generally seen in herds of 20–50 animals but sometimes much larger groups congregate. Cattle Egrets often attend the herds. Generally reckoned to be one of the most dangerous and unpredictable animals in East Africa. Common throughout most of region.

Kirk's Dikdik *Madoqua kirkii* **H 40**
A small, elegant antelope with characteristically elongated face. Tuft of hairs on head. Males have short, straight horns. The large eyes are surrounded by a pale eye ring. Black glandular spot in front of eye. Usually seen in pairs. Inhabits dense scrub and so often overlooked. Dappled coat provides superb camouflage even in comparatively light cover. Widely distributed.

Thomson's Gazelle

Impala

Grant's Gazelle

Common Duiker

Klipspringer

Oribi

Steinbok

African
Buffalo

Kirk's Dikdik

Nile Crocodile *Crocodylus niloticus* **L 500**
Widespread in lakes and along river courses. Sunbathes in the morning but then spends much of the day partly immersed in water. Feeds on fish but also catches mammals as large as Wildebeest that visit water to drink. Eggs laid in sandy river banks and guarded by females. Has disappeared from many rivers where humans are present.

Nile Monitor *Varanus niloticus* **L 200**
Largest African lizard. Climbs and swims well. Takes carrion but also catches fish and raids birds' nests for eggs and young. Some individuals will even tackle Crocodile nests when these are left unguarded. Widespread, especially near water. Large specimens are now unusual.

Puff Adder *Bitis arietans* **L 150**
Fat and sluggish but extremely venomous. Beautiful markings serve as superb camouflage when resting among fallen leaves. Widespread in hill forests but easily overlooked despite the fact that it often lies beside paths and tracks. Do not approach.

Red-headed Agama *Agama agama* **L 50**
Widespread and common in most habitats, especially among rocks. Only males have red head and blue body; females are duller. Males advertise territories by bobbing heads. They become indifferent to the presence of people around many tourist lodges.

Water Tortoise *Pelusios subniger* **L 25**
Widespread and common in a variety of aquatic habitats from ponds to rivers and lakes. Carnivorous, feeding on fish, tadpoles and insects. Usually wary, diving quickly if disturbed.

Common African Python *Python sebae* **L 500**
Beautifully marked snake which is widespread and common although difficult to see. Kills prey as large as small antelopes by constriction. Swims and climbs well. Female broods and guards eggs until they hatch.

Black Mamba *Dendroaspis polylepis* **L 400**
Widespread and common, generally in wooded habitat. Climbs well but often seen on ground. Venom potentially lethal to humans. May be territorial showing aggression to intruders. Colour variable but never jet black.

Spitting Cobra *Naja nigricollis* **L 250**
Common and widespread in savannah country but usually retreats from man. If threatened, can spit venom several feet by forcing it through tubular fangs. This causes acute pain if it enters eyes. Catches lizards, fish and birds.

House Gecko *Hemidactylus mabouia* **L 10**
Widespread and common throughout region. Usually associated with houses. Hides behind furniture and in cracks in walls during day. Emerges after dark to catch insects. Amazing ability to walk up walls and across ceilings. A familiar sight in many lodges.

Leopard Tortoise *Testudo pardalis* **L 25**
Widespread and common on grassy plains and savannahs. Often first located by the rustling sound that it makes as it moves through the vegetation. Named after the beautiful markings on its shell. Feeds on plant matter.

Nile Crocodile

Nile Monitor

Common African Python

Puff Adder

Black Mamba

Spitting Cobra

Red-headed Agama

House Gecko

Water Tortoise

Leopard Tortoise

Baobab Tree *Adansonia digitata* **H 10m**
Distinctive shape with swollen trunk and spreading branches give the appearance of an upside-down root system. Widespread from sea level to moderate altitudes. Not found in arid areas. Bark is smooth and grey. Fruits are pendulous.

Date Palm *Phoenix sp.* **H 8m**
Widespread and often cultivated beside streams and rivers. Generally found at lower, warmer altitudes, often near the coast. The tall stem produces a spray of leaves at the apex, under which the fruits are suspended.

Red Mangrove *Rhizophora mucronata* **H 3m**
Widespread and locally common along the East African coast. Grows with its arched roots immersed in mud and submerged at high tide. The root system helps create new land by allowing silt to settle. Leaves have a terminal point. Other mangrove species have different tolerances to sea water and grow at different places on the shore.

Candelabra Tree *Euphorbia kibwezensis* **H 7m**
Trunk is short and stout. From it arise an array of spiny branches which curve upwards and are flattened into wings. Yellowish flowers are produced in clusters. Found in arid country below 1500m (4920 feet). Locally common.

Doum Palm *Hyphaene coriacea* **H 10m**
Forms a very distinctive shape as a result of the slender stem regularly dividing into two. This supports a dense layer of leaves. The fruits are not worth eating although Elephants are extremely fond of them. Seen along water courses in Samburu and Buffalo Springs National Reserves.

Nandi Flame Tree
Spathodea campanulata **H 10m**
A widespread native species at medium altitudes in western Kenya but also widely planted as an ornamental tree. Flowers bright red with yellow centres. Leaves often in threes. Bark is rough and greyish.

Whistling Thorn *Acacia drepanolobium* **H 3m**
A typical acacia with bi-pinnate leaves and long thorns to deter browsing animals. Whitish flowers form dense inflorescences along branches. The swollen thorn bases harbour ant colonies. The openings to these catch the wind and produce the whistling sound. Common at medium altitudes and widespread in Nairobi NP.

Coconut Palm *Cocos nucifera* **H 10m**
Widespread and common along the coast of East Africa. Often found in plantations but also grows naturally. The seeds float in sea water and are carried by currents. They are often found washed up along the shore. Almost all parts of the plant are useful to humans, either for food or fibre.

Leonotis mollissima **H 1m**
Tall, woody shrub which is found at elevations above 2000m (6560 feet). Leaves are woolly. Flowers are bright orange and arranged in three spherical masses at the end of stems. Frequently visited by sunbirds for its nectar.

Baobab Tree

Whistling
Thorn

Doum Palm

Date Palm

Coconut Palm

Nandi Flame Tree

Red Mangrove

Candelabra
Tree

Leonotis mollissima

CHECKLIST OF BIRDS, MAMMALS AND REPTILES WHICH MAY BE SEEN IN EAST AFRICA

BIRDS

- [ ] Ostrich
- [ ] Little Grebe
- [ ] Great-crested Grebe
- [ ] White-necked Cormorant
- [ ] Long-tailed Cormorant
- [ ] African Darter
- [ ] White Pelican
- [ ] Pink-backed Pelican
- [ ] Grey Heron
- [ ] Black-necked Heron
- [ ] Goliath Heron
- [ ] Purple Heron
- [ ] Great Egret
- [ ] Intermediate Egret
- [ ] Little Egret
- [ ] Cattle Egret
- [ ] Squacco Heron
- [ ] Green Heron
- [ ] Night Heron
- [ ] Little Bittern
- [ ] Hammerkop
- [ ] White Stork
- [ ] Woolly-necked Stork
- [ ] Abdim's Stork
- [ ] Open-bill Stork
- [ ] Saddle-bill Stork
- [ ] Marabou Stork
- [ ] Yellow-necked Stork
- [ ] Sacred Ibis
- [ ] Hadada Ibis
- [ ] Glossy Ibis
- [ ] African Spoonbill
- [ ] Greater Flamingo
- [ ] Lesser Flamingo
- [ ] Maccoa Duck
- [ ] White-backed Duck
- [ ] African Pochard
- [ ] European Shoveler

- [ ] Yellow-billed Duck
- [ ] Garganey
- [ ] Cape Wigeon
- [ ] Hottentot Teal
- [ ] Red-billed Duck
- [ ] European Pintail
- [ ] White-faced Whistling Duck
- [ ] Fulvous Tree Duck
- [ ] African Pygmy Goose
- [ ] Knob-billed Goose
- [ ] Egyptian Goose
- [ ] Spur-winged Goose
- [ ] Secretary Bird
- [ ] Ruppell's Vulture
- [ ] White-backed Vulture
- [ ] Lappet-faced Vulture
- [ ] White-headed Vulture
- [ ] Egyptian Vulture
- [ ] Hooded Vulture
- [ ] Palmnut Vulture
- [ ] Peregrine
- [ ] Lanner Falcon
- [ ] European Hobby
- [ ] European Kestrel
- [ ] Greater Kestrel
- [ ] Lesser Kestrel
- [ ] Pygmy Falcon
- [ ] Black Kite
- [ ] Black-winged Kite
- [ ] Bat Hawk
- [ ] Verreaux's Eagle
- [ ] Steppe Eagle
- [ ] Tawny Eagle
- [ ] Wahlberg's Eagle
- [ ] African Hawk Eagle
- [ ] Martial Eagle
- [ ] Long-crested Hawk Eagle

- [ ] Crowned Hawk Eagle
- [ ] Lizard Buzzard
- [ ] Brown Harrier Eagle
- [ ] Black-chested Harrier Eagle
- [ ] Grasshopper Buzzard
- [ ] Bateleur
- [ ] African Fish Eagle
- [ ] Steppe Buzzard
- [ ] Augur Buzzard
- [ ] Little Sparrowhawk
- [ ] Gabar Goshawk
- [ ] Pale Chanting Goshawk
- [ ] Dark Chanting Goshawk
- [ ] Montagu's Harrier
- [ ] European Marsh Harrier
- [ ] African Marsh Harrier
- [ ] Harrier Hawk
- [ ] Osprey
- [ ] Coqui Francolin
- [ ] Crested Francolin
- [ ] Shelley's Francolin
- [ ] Yellow-necked Spurfowl
- [ ] Red-necked Spurfowl
- [ ] Harlequin Quail
- [ ] Helmeted Guineafowl
- [ ] Vulturine Guineafowl
- [ ] Black Crake
- [ ] Moorhen
- [ ] Crested Coot
- [ ] Crowned Crane
- [ ] Kori Bustard
- [ ] White-bellied Bustard
- [ ] Buff-crested Bustard
- [ ] Black-bellied Bustard

- [ ] Hartlaub's Bustard
- [ ] Spotted Stone Curlew
- [ ] Water Dikkop
- [ ] African Jacana
- [ ] Lesser Jacana
- [ ] Ringed Plover
- [ ] Little Ringed Plover
- [ ] Kittlitz's Plover
- [ ] White-fronted Sand Plover
- [ ] Greater Sand Plover
- [ ] Lesser Sand Plover
- [ ] Three-banded Plover
- [ ] Caspian Plover
- [ ] Grey Plover
- [ ] Crowned Plover
- [ ] Senegal Plover
- [ ] Blacksmith Plover
- [ ] Spur-winged Plover
- [ ] Wattled Plover
- [ ] Long-toed Lapwing
- [ ] Blackhead Plover
- [ ] Avocet
- [ ] Black-winged Stilt
- [ ] Painted Snipe
- [ ] European Snipe
- [ ] Great Snipe
- [ ] African Snipe
- [ ] Curlew Sandpiper
- [ ] Little Stint
- [ ] Ruff
- [ ] Common Sandpiper
- [ ] Green Sandpiper
- [ ] Wood Sandpiper
- [ ] Marsh Sandpiper
- [ ] Terek Sandpiper
- [ ] Broad-billed Sandpiper
- [ ] Redshank
- [ ] Spotted Redshank

- ☐ Greenshank
- ☐ Sanderling
- ☐ Turnstone
- ☐ Crab Plover
- ☐ Whimbrel
- ☐ Temminck's Courser
- ☐ Two-banded Courser
- ☐ Heuglin's Courser
- ☐ Pratincole
- ☐ Madagascar Pratincole
- ☐ Grey-headed Gull
- ☐ Sooty Gull
- ☐ Gull-billed Tern
- ☐ White-winged Black Tern
- ☐ Whiskered Tern
- ☐ White-cheeked Tern
- ☐ Roseate Tern
- ☐ Common Tern
- ☐ Crested Tern
- ☐ Lesser Crested Tern
- ☐ Caspian Tern
- ☐ Button Quail
- ☐ Chestnut-bellied Sandgrouse
- ☐ Black-faced Sandgrouse
- ☐ Yellow-throated Sandgrouse
- ☐ Speckled Pigeon
- ☐ Red-eyed Dove
- ☐ African Mourning Dove
- ☐ Ring-necked Dove
- ☐ Laughing Dove
- ☐ Namaqua Dove
- ☐ Tambourine Dove
- ☐ Emerald-spotted Wood Dove
- ☐ Green Pigeon
- ☐ Lemon Dove
- ☐ Cuckoo
- ☐ Red-chested Cuckoo

- ☐ Black Cuckoo
- ☐ Great Spotted Cuckoo
- ☐ Levaillant's Cuckoo
- ☐ Black-and-white Cuckoo
- ☐ Emerald Cuckoo
- ☐ Klaas' Cuckoo
- ☐ White-browed Coucal
- ☐ White-bellied Go-away-bird
- ☐ Hartlaub's Turaco
- ☐ Narina's Trogon
- ☐ Orange-bellied Parrot
- ☐ Brown Parrot
- ☐ Fischer's Lovebird
- ☐ European Roller
- ☐ Lilac-breasted Roller
- ☐ Rufous-crowned Roller
- ☐ Broad-billed Roller
- ☐ Racquet-tailed Roller
- ☐ Pied Kingfisher
- ☐ Giant Kingfisher
- ☐ Malachite Kingfisher
- ☐ Pygmy Kingfisher
- ☐ Grey-headed Kingfisher
- ☐ Brown-hooded Kingfisher
- ☐ Striped Kingfisher
- ☐ European Bee-eater
- ☐ Madagascar Bee-eater
- ☐ Blue-cheeked Bee-eater
- ☐ White-throated Bee-eater
- ☐ White-fronted Bee-eater
- ☐ Cinnamon-chested Bee-eater
- ☐ Little Bee-eater
- ☐ Somali Bee-eater
- ☐ Carmine Bee-eater

- ☐ Trumpeter Hornbill
- ☐ Grey Hornbill
- ☐ Red-billed Hornbill
- ☐ Yellow-billed Hornbill
- ☐ Von der Decken's Hornbill
- ☐ Hemprich's Hornbill
- ☐ Crowned Hornbill
- ☐ Silvery-cheeked Hornbill
- ☐ Ground Hornbill
- ☐ African Hoopoe
- ☐ Green Wood Hoopoe
- ☐ Abyssinian Scimitarbill
- ☐ African Marsh Owl
- ☐ White-faced Scop's Owl
- ☐ Pearl-spotted Owlet
- ☐ Spotted Eagle Owl
- ☐ Verreaux's Eagle Owl
- ☐ European Nightjar
- ☐ Abyssinian Nightjar
- ☐ Mozambique Nightjar
- ☐ Plain Nightjar
- ☐ Nubian Nightjar
- ☐ Speckled Mousebird
- ☐ Blue-naped Mousebird
- ☐ Spotted-flanked Barbet
- ☐ Red-fronted Barbet
- ☐ Red-fronted Tinkerbird
- ☐ Golden-rumped Tinkerbird
- ☐ Red-and-yellow Barbet
- ☐ D'Arnaud's Barbet
- ☐ Greater Honeyguide
- ☐ Lesser Honeyguide
- ☐ Scaly-throated Honeyguide
- ☐ Nubian Woodpecker
- ☐ Cardinal Woodpecker
- ☐ Bearded Woodpecker

- ☐ Grey Woodpecker
- ☐ Brown-eared Woodpecker
- ☐ Little-spotted Woodpecker
- ☐ Nyanza Swift
- ☐ Mottled Swift
- ☐ Little Swift
- ☐ Horus Swift
- ☐ Alpine Swift
- ☐ African Palm Swift
- ☐ Boehm's Spinetail
- ☐ Singing Bush Lark
- ☐ Flappet Lark
- ☐ Fawn-coloured Lark
- ☐ Pink-breasted Lark
- ☐ Fischer's Finch Lark
- ☐ Rufous-naped Lark
- ☐ Red-winged Bush Lark
- ☐ Red-capped Lark
- ☐ African Pied Wagtail
- ☐ Yellow Wagtail
- ☐ Mountain Wagtail
- ☐ Long-billed Pipit
- ☐ Richard's Pipit
- ☐ Golden Pipit
- ☐ Yellow-throated Longclaw
- ☐ Rosy-breasted Longclaw
- ☐ Northern Pied Babbler
- ☐ Rufous Chatterer
- ☐ Arrow-marked Babbler
- ☐ Northern Brownbul
- ☐ Common Bulbul
- ☐ Yellow-whiskered Greenbul
- ☐ Zanzibar Sombre Greenbul
- ☐ Spotted Flycatcher
- ☐ Dusky Flycatcher
- ☐ Grey Flycatcher

215

- ☐ White-eyed Slaty-flycatcher
- ☐ South African Black Flycatcher
- ☐ Silverbird
- ☐ Chin-spot Flycatcher
- ☐ Blue Flycatcher
- ☐ Black-throated Wattle-eye
- ☐ Paradise Flycatcher
- ☐ Olive Thrush
- ☐ Bare-eyed Thrush
- ☐ Rock Thrush
- ☐ Common Wheatear
- ☐ Isabelline Wheatear
- ☐ Pied Wheatear
- ☐ Schalow's (Mourning) Wheatear
- ☐ Capped Wheatear
- ☐ Cliff Chat
- ☐ Mountain Chat
- ☐ Anteater Chat
- ☐ Banded Tit Warbler
- ☐ Whinchat
- ☐ White-browed Robin Chat
- ☐ Ruppell's Robin Chat
- ☐ Red-capped Robin Chat
- ☐ Spotted Morning Warbler
- ☐ Red-backed Scrub Robin
- ☐ Eastern Bearded Scrub Robin
- ☐ White-throated Robin
- ☐ Nightingale
- ☐ Thrush Nightingale
- ☐ Whitethroat
- ☐ Garden Warbler
- ☐ Blackcap
- ☐ Barred Warbler
- ☐ Great Reed Warbler

- ☐ Sedge Warbler
- ☐ Greater Swamp Warbler
- ☐ Olivaceous Warbler
- ☐ Willow Warbler
- ☐ Brown Woodland Warbler
- ☐ Black-breasted Apalis
- ☐ Red-faced Apalis
- ☐ Crombec
- ☐ Red-faced Crombec
- ☐ Yellow-bellied Eremomela
- ☐ Grey-backed Cameroptera
- ☐ Rattling Cisticola
- ☐ Winding Cisticola
- ☐ Singing Cisticola
- ☐ Stout Cisticola
- ☐ Tinkling Cisticola
- ☐ Zitting Cisticola
- ☐ Tawny-flanked Prinia
- ☐ European Swallow
- ☐ Angola Swallow
- ☐ Ethiopian Swallow
- ☐ Wire-tailed Swallow
- ☐ Red-rumped Swallow
- ☐ Mosque Swallow
- ☐ Striped Swallow
- ☐ Grey-rumped Swallow
- ☐ Brown-throated Sand Martin
- ☐ European Sand Martin
- ☐ Banded Martin
- ☐ African Rock Martin
- ☐ House Martin
- ☐ Black Roughwing Swallow
- ☐ White-headed Roughwing Swallow
- ☐ Black Cuckoo Shrike
- ☐ Fork-tailed Drongo
- ☐ White-crowned Shrike

- ☐ Straight-crested Helmet Shrike
- ☐ Northern Brubru
- ☐ Grey-backed Fiscal
- ☐ Lesser Grey Shrike
- ☐ Fiscal Shrike
- ☐ Taita Fiscal
- ☐ Long-tailed Fiscal
- ☐ Red-backed Shrike
- ☐ Isabelline Shrike
- ☐ Slate-coloured Boubou
- ☐ Tropical Boubou
- ☐ Black-backed Puff-back
- ☐ Black-headed Bush Shrike
- ☐ Brown-headed Bush Shrike
- ☐ Sulphur-breasted Bush Shrike
- ☐ Grey-headed Bush Shrike
- ☐ Rosy-patched Shrike
- ☐ Grey Tit
- ☐ White-breasted Tit
- ☐ African Penduline Tit
- ☐ European Golden Oriole
- ☐ African Golden Oriole
- ☐ Black-headed Oriole
- ☐ Pied Crow
- ☐ White-naped Raven
- ☐ Fan-tailed Raven
- ☐ Indian House Crow
- ☐ Cape Rook
- ☐ Wattled Starling
- ☐ Violet-backed Starling
- ☐ Blue-eared Glossy Starling
- ☐ Black-breasted Starling
- ☐ Ruppell's Long-tailed Starling
- ☐ Red-winged Starling

- ☐ Fischer's Starling
- ☐ Hildebrandt's Starling
- ☐ Superb Starling
- ☐ Red-billed Oxpecker
- ☐ Yellow-billed Oxpecker
- ☐ Yellow White-eye
- ☐ Bronze Sunbird
- ☐ Beautiful Sunbird
- ☐ Mariqua Sunbird
- ☐ Variable Sunbird
- ☐ Amethyst Sunbird
- ☐ Scarlet-chested Sunbird
- ☐ Malachite Sunbird
- ☐ Scarlet-chested Malachite Sunbird
- ☐ Little Purple-banded Sunbird
- ☐ Hunter's Sunbird
- ☐ Olive Sunbird
- ☐ Collared Sunbird
- ☐ Kenya Violet-backed Sunbird
- ☐ Buffalo Weaver
- ☐ White-headed Buffalo Weaver
- ☐ White-browed Sparrow Weaver
- ☐ Grey-headed Social Weaver
- ☐ Kenya Rufous Sparrow
- ☐ Swahili Sparrow
- ☐ Parrot-billed Sparrow
- ☐ Chestnut Sparrow
- ☐ Yellow-spotted Petronia
- ☐ Speckle-fronted Weaver
- ☐ Speke's Weaver
- ☐ Masked Weaver
- ☐ Vitelline Masked Weaver

- ☐ Chestnut Weaver
- ☐ Taveta Golden
  Weaver
- ☐ Golden Palm Weaver
- ☐ Golden Weaver
- ☐ Black-necked Weaver
- ☐ Spectacled Weaver
- ☐ Holub's Golden
  Weaver
- ☐ Brown-capped
  Weaver
- ☐ Reichenow's Weaver
- ☐ Red-headed Weaver
- ☐ Red-billed Quelea
- ☐ Yellow Bishop
- ☐ Red Bishop
- ☐ Fan-tailed Widowbird
- ☐ Bronze Mannakin
- ☐ Silverbill
- ☐ Cut-throat
- ☐ African Firefinch
- ☐ Red-billed Firefinch
- ☐ Senegal Firefinch
- ☐ Waxbill
- ☐ Crimson-rumped
  Waxbill
- ☐ Black-faced Waxbill
- ☐ Red-cheeked Cordon-
  bleu
- ☐ Blue-capped Cordon-
  bleu
- ☐ Purple Grenadier
- ☐ Purple Indigobird
- ☐ Pin-tailed Whydah
- ☐ Steel-blue Whydah
- ☐ Paradise Whydah
- ☐ Yellow-fronted Canary
- ☐ White-bellied Canary
- ☐ Brimstone Canary
- ☐ Yellow-crowned
  Canary
- ☐ Yellow-rumped Seed-
  eater

- ☐ Streaky Seed-eater
- ☐ Golden-breasted
  Bunting
- ☐ Cinnamon-breasted
  Bunting
- ☐ ....
- ☐ ....
- ☐ ....
- ☐ ....
- ☐ ....
- ☐ ....
- ☐ ....

MAMMALS
- ☐ African Buffalo
- ☐ Eland
- ☐ Greater Kudu
- ☐ Lesser Kudu
- ☐ Bongo
- ☐ Sitatunga
- ☐ Bushbuck
- ☐ Roan Antelope
- ☐ Sable Antelope
- ☐ Oryx
- ☐ Wildebeest
- ☐ Coke's Hartebeest
- ☐ Topi
- ☐ Common Waterbuck
- ☐ Defassa Waterbuck
- ☐ Bohor Reedbuck
- ☐ Impala
- ☐ Gerenuk
- ☐ Grant's Gazelle
- ☐ Thomson's Gazelle
- ☐ Klipspringer
- ☐ Steinbok
- ☐ Kirk's Dikdik
- ☐ Suni
- ☐ Common Duiker
- ☐ Giant Forest Hog
- ☐ Warthog
- ☐ Bushpig

- ☐ Hippopotamus
- ☐ Common Giraffe
- ☐ Reticulated Giraffe
- ☐ Common Zebra
- ☐ Grevy's Zebra
- ☐ White Rhinoceros
- ☐ Black Rhinoceros
- ☐ African Elephant
- ☐ Spotted Hyena
- ☐ Striped Hyena
- ☐ African Hunting Dog
- ☐ Black-backed Jackal
- ☐ Side-striped Jackal
- ☐ Golden Jackal
- ☐ Bat-eared Fox
- ☐ Lion
- ☐ Leopard
- ☐ Cheetah
- ☐ Serval
- ☐ Caracal
- ☐ African Wild Cat
- ☐ African Civet
- ☐ Large-spotted Genet
- ☐ White-tailed
  Mongoose
- ☐ Slender Mongoose
- ☐ Banded Mongoose
- ☐ Dwarf Mongoose
- ☐ Clawless Otter
- ☐ Mountain Gorilla
- ☐ Chimpanzee
- ☐ Olive Baboon
- ☐ Yellow Baboon
- ☐ Syke's Monkey
- ☐ L'Hoest's Monkey
- ☐ De Brazza's Monkey
- ☐ Vervet Monkey
- ☐ Patas Monkey
- ☐ Black-and-white
  Colobus
- ☐ Red Colobus
- ☐ Tana River Mangabey
- ☐ Potto

- ☐ Greater Galago
- ☐ Lesser Bushbaby
- ☐ Aardvark
- ☐ Pangolin
- ☐ Porcupine
- ☐ Striped Ground
  Squirrel
- ☐ African Hare
- ☐ Rock Hyrax
- ☐ Tree Hyrax
- ☐ ....
- ☐ ....
- ☐ ....
- ☐ ....
- ☐ ....

REPTILES
- ☐ Royal Python
- ☐ Black Mamba
- ☐ Green Mamba
- ☐ Egg-eating Snake
- ☐ Boomslang
- ☐ Egyptian Cobra
- ☐ Spitting Cobra
- ☐ Puff Adder
- ☐ Gaboon Viper
- ☐ House Gecko
- ☐ Jackson's Chameleon
- ☐ Two-striped Skink
- ☐ Red-headed Agama
- ☐ Nile Monitor
- ☐ Savannah Monitor
- ☐ Nile Crocodile
- ☐ Green Turtle
- ☐ Soft-shelled Turtle
- ☐ Black Water Tortoise
- ☐ Leopard Tortoise
- ☐ ....
- ☐ ....
- ☐ ....
- ☐ ....
- ☐ ....

217

USEFUL ADDRESSES

Kenya Wildlife Conservation
& Management
Department
Ministry of Tourism &
Wildlife
PO Box 40241
Nairobi, Kenya

Office Rwandais du
Tourisme et des Parcs
Nationaux
BP 905
Kigali, Rwanda

Tanzania National Parks
(TANAPA)
PO Box 1994
Dar-es-Salaam, Tanzania

Tour operators – Kenya

Abercrombie & Kent Ltd
PO Box 59749, Nairobi

Across Africa Safaris Ltd
PO Box 49420, Nairobi

Bushbuck Adventures Ltd
PO Box 67449, Nairobi

Flamingo Tours Ltd
PO Box 44899, Nairobi

Let's Go Travel
PO Box 60342, Nairobi

United Touring Company
Ltd
PO Box 42196, Nairobi

Tour operators – Tanzania

Abercrombie & Kent Ltd
Box 427, Arusha

Bobby Tours
Box 716, Arusha

Simba Safaris
Box 1207, Arusha

State Travel Service
Box 5023, Dar-es-Salaam

BIBLIOGRAPHY

Blixen, K (Isak Dinesen), *Out of Africa* (Modern Library, 1981).
Camerapix, *Spectrum Guide to African Wildlife Safaris* (Moorland Publishing, 1989).
Dorst, J & Dandelot, P, *A Field Guide to the Larger Mammals of Africa* (Collins, 1976).

Grzimek, B, *Serengeti Shall Not Die* (Fontana, 1960).
Insight Guide, *East African Wildlife* (APA Insight Guides, 1989).
Nolting, MW, *Africa's Top Wildlife Countries* (Nolting, 1990).
Shelley, S, *Safari Guide to the Mammals of East and Central Africa* (Macmillan 1989).

Williams, JG & Arlott, N, *A Field Guide to the Birds of East Africa* (Collins 1980).
Williams, JG, *A Field Guide to the National Parks of East Africa* (Collins, 1967).

INDEX

Page numbers in *italic* refer to illustrations. Relevant text may also appear on pages indicated in italic.

PHOTOGRAPHIC ACKNOWLEDGEMENTS

All photographs by Paul Sterry of Nature Photographers, except for the following:

Brinsley Burbidge 11,115; Andrew Cleave 8, 10 (lower), 26, 35, 37 (right), 52 (lower), 53, 56, 60, 66, 73, 118, 120, 123, 128, 129, 133; R S Daniell 121, 140 (lower), 158 (right); Michael Gore 9, 82; James Hancock 23; David Hutton 67, 93; E A Janes 22; John Karmali 65 (right), 109; Hugo van Lawick 142, 150, 156, 162, 163; Hugh Miles 37 (left), 65 (left); W S Paton, 112; Roger Tidman 41, 42, 110 (right), 132, 169, 170, 171; Christopher Grey-Wilson 16 all of Nature Photographers.